US Foreign Policy
in the Twenty-First Century

Dilemmas in World Politics

Dilemmas in World Politics offers teachers and students in international relations a series of quality books on critical issues, trends, and regions in international politics. Each text examines a "real world" dilemma and is structured to cover the historical, theoretical, practical, and projected dimensions of its subject.

US Foreign Policy in the Twenty-First Century

---◀◉▶---

Gulliver's Travails

J. MARTIN ROCHESTER
University of Missouri, St. Louis

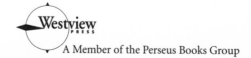
Westview PRESS

A Member of the Perseus Books Group

Library of Congress Cataloging-in-Publication Data

Rochester, J. Martin.
    US foreign policy in the twenty-first century : Gulliver's travails / J. Martin Rochester.
        p.   cm. — (Dilemmas in world politics)
    Includes bibliographical references and index.
    ISBN-13: 978-0-8133-4369-3
    ISBN-10: 0-8133-4369-0
    1. United States—Foreign relations—21st century. 2. United States—Foreign relations—1989– 3. United States—Foreign relations—Philosophy. 4. United States—Foreign relations—Decision making—Case studies. 5. Problem solving—United States—Case studies. I. Title.
E895.R63 2008
327.73009'05—dc22   2007033385

10 9 8 7 6 5 4 3 2 1

*To Ruth, whose "hard power" and, more importantly,
"soft power" have held our household together
throughout the Cold War and post–Cold War eras.*

Contents

List of Illustrations

Cartoons

Figures

Photos

Preface

This is a book about U.S. foreign policy. It is easy for a book on American foreign policy to be overtaken by events. As I write, the Iraq War may prove to be either a long-term quagmire that could last into the next decade or a short-lived conflict that, under the pressure of congressional and electoral impatience with an unpopular war, could end rather quickly. However, a premise of this book is that the problems that gave rise to the intervention and the issues raised by the war are symptomatic of much larger, systemic phenomena that are likely to continue to preoccupy American foreign policymakers for much of the early twenty-first century. The war on terror, the proliferation of weapons of mass destruction, the waging of asymmetrical warfare, humanitarian intervention, oil and energy politics, and a litany of other concerns figure to dominate the foreign policy agenda for the foreseeable future. Such matters pose complex "dilemmas" for which there are no simple answers.

I do not attempt to furnish answers here but to frame the questions in what I hope is a constructive fashion. I aim to engage students in an examination of American foreign policy past, present, and future, involving the reader in critical thinking about how foreign policy is made, what factors affect foreign policy decisions and behavior, and how one might go about not only describing and explaining foreign policy but also evaluating it and prescribing possible solutions. I am particularly interested in exploring the difficult foreign policy choices that confront the United States today in a post–Cold War environment that is arguably more complicated, if not more dangerous, than the Cold War system that lasted for a half century after World War II.

A central puzzle revolves around the "Gulliver" metaphor found in this book's subtitle. The U.S. position in the world today reminds one of *Gulliver's Travels*, Jonathan Swift's classic eighteenth-century tale of a giant man subdued by a group of tiny people in a strange world. Perhaps never before in history has there been a greater disconnect between potential and performance—never before has an actor seemingly achieved so little with so much going for it, and had its hands tied with so many ostensible advantages. Among the dilemmas the United States is struggling with are the following: (1) How is it possible that the United States has enjoyed a degree of dominance over its nearest rivals not seen since the Roman Empire, yet has failed in so many of its recent foreign policy endeavors, not only in Iraq but throughout the Middle East, East Asia, Latin America, and other regions? (2) How can the United States promote democracy, human rights, and respect for life when it is engaged in a "long war" against an enemy who may well be planning the next 9/11 attack against the U.S.

homeland and does not observe any conventional rules of engagement or any canons of civilized behavior whatsoever? Can the United States, for example, afford to resist the targeting of civilians if terrorists hide behind civilians? (3) How can the United States perform, in the words of some observers, the role of "sheriff of the posse" when it seems unwilling or unable to mobilize a grand, winning coalition in support of world order? (4) How does the United States offer leadership without appearing to be a domineering bully, that is, without projecting the image of not so much a sheriff but an outlaw, "rogue" state? (5) How can the United States become more of a multilateral player without potentially jeopardizing its sovereignty and national interests? Assorted schools of thought, including neoconservatives, liberal internationalists, and realists, have offered insights into these kinds of questions, although the answers remain elusive.

I start with a broad-brush portrait of the contemporary international system that forms the backdrop for this investigation, a system that presents both opportunities and constraints for American foreign policymakers. I then discuss some intellectual problems that the student of foreign policy encounters in the study of foreign policy in general and U.S. foreign policy in particular, suggesting some modes and tools of analysis that one might utilize; most of us are quick to criticize policymakers and to offer our favorite bromides for saving America, if not the planet, before we have adequately done the painstaking work of analyzing with some degree of rigor what the sources of the problems are and what outcomes are feasible. The latter "theoretical perspective" on foreign policy is followed by a "historical perspective," as I briefly trace the history of U.S. foreign policy "from George W. to George W." Having equipped the reader with an analytical and historical framework for thinking about American foreign policy, the book then proceeds to its core task of examining contemporary U.S. foreign policy dilemmas, first surveying the various competing schools of thought and the critiques and prescriptions offered by each, and secondly focusing on five specific case studies that illustrate the special quandaries experienced by the United States today. I wrap up with some concluding thoughts about future directions that U.S. foreign policy might take, including a "new multilateralism" approach that would address critics' calls for a more moral, legal, and smart strategic vision, granted that—as with any foreign policy advice these days—following such a path is easier said than done.

I have tried to subject American foreign policy to a lively, engaging, concise treatment while drawing on the latest scholarship and addressing "real world" concerns, keeping with the mission of the *Dilemmas in World Politics* series. I have distilled what I think are the key concepts and issues surrounding the study of American foreign policy. At the end of each chapter, the reader will find Discussion Questions, and at the rear of the book are Suggested Readings for further exploration of this topic. Few topics would seem more worthy of additional thought than America's role in the world, especially from current undergraduate and graduate students, and citizens in general. Former U.S. Secretary of State Henry Kissinger maybe said it best when, as the post–Cold War era was dawning in the 1990s, he remarked that the major challenge facing the United States was to define a role for itself in a world which "for the first time in her history . . . she cannot dominate but from which she cannot simply withdraw." That remains in many ways the central challenge of American foreign policy.

I need to thank many people for helping to bring this project to fruition. First, I dedicate the book to my wife, Ruth, who is the "hegemon" in our household, in the best sense of the term, having been the mother of all mothers to our children and having provided the glue to our family over the years. I want, also, to thank my brother Stuart, the deputy chief historian in the Office of the Secretary of Defense at the Pentagon, whose willingness to share his knowledge about the historiography of American foreign policy added immensely to my own understanding of how contemporary policy compares with the past. My students, too, are owed a debt of gratitude for their constant stimulation, asking good questions and demanding replies, which forced me to engage in further reflection, even as I reminded them that the main purpose of education is to learn to cope with ambiguity. Finally, I wish to express my deep gratitude to Steve Catalano, the executive editor at Westview Press, who enthusiastically supported the project from the start and expertly shepherded it through to completion, with the help of Brooke Kush, Lori Hobkirk, and Meredith Smith.

I suppose I should be grateful as well to a world that offers such a rich set of problems to write about, but I would much prefer that it be a quieter place and that Gulliver's travails be fewer in number. I recall, in 1986, attending a scholarly meeting that featured two American diplomats and two Soviet diplomats speculating about the future of U.S.-Soviet relations, where one of the Russians quoted what he said was an old Romanian proverb: "It's always hard to predict anything, especially the future." Ever since, America along with much of humanity has found itself lurching between euphoria one moment and despair the next. We can always hope for a happy medium. That will depend upon a wise foreign policy leadership and an educated public that encourages such leadership. This book hopes to contribute in at least a small way to that prospect.

J. Martin Rochester
St. Louis, Missouri
August 2007

1

Gulliver's Travails

America and the World

If America's current global predominance does not
constitute unipolarity, then nothing ever will. The sources
of American strength are so varied and so durable that the
country now enjoys more freedom in its foreign policy
choices than has any other power in modern history.
Today the United States has no rival in any critical
dimension of national power. There has never been a
system of sovereign states that contained one state with
this degree of dominance.

—Stephen Brooks and William Wohlforth,
Foreign Affairs, July/August 2002

Is the American empire mightier than any other in history,
bestriding the globe as the Colossus was said to tower over
the harbor of Rhodes? Or is this giant a Goliath, vast but
vulnerable to a single slingshot from a diminutive, elusive
foe? Might the United States in fact be more like Samson,
eyeless in Gaza, chained by irreconcilable commitments
in the Middle East [and elsewhere] and ultimately capable
of only blind destruction?

—Niall Ferguson, *Colossus*, 2004

In March 2003, the United States sent more than one hundred thousand troops into Iraq and mounted a "shock and awe" aerial bombing campaign over Baghdad that was aimed at overthrowing Iraqi dictator Saddam Hussein. Within a month, Hussein's enormous statue in the center of the capital city was taken down, and by May 1 that same year, on board the USS *Abraham Lincoln*, President George W. Bush declared victory, with fewer than two hundred American combat fatalities suffered during what came to be known as the Second Persian Gulf War (dubbed "Operation Iraqi Freedom" by Washington). The war had gone well. Peace would be a different matter, however, with U.S. forces remaining bogged down in a brutal, protracted postwar insurgency through 2007, with little end in sight.

The Iraq conflict will eventually end, but the problems that gave rise to the intervention and the issues raised by the war are symptomatic of much larger phenomena that are likely to continue to preoccupy American foreign policymakers for much of the early twenty-first century. This book attempts to engage the reader in an examination of American foreign policy. It is mainly focused on the present, although I provide some historical perspective in order to add necessary context, and I indulge in some speculation about the future in order to enhance relevance. The central questions to be discussed are: How would one characterize current U.S. foreign policy compared with the past? What factors account for U.S. foreign policy behavior? What are the pros and cons of the present policy? And what foreign policy options might the United States pursue in the near term? In other words, how would you, the reader, *describe* U.S. foreign policy? How would you *explain* it? And how would you *evaluate* it and *prescribe* possible alternatives? I am particularly interested in exploring the difficult foreign policy choices—*dilemmas*—that confront the United States today in a post–Cold War environment that is arguably more complex, if not more dangerous, than the Cold War system that lasted for a half century after World War II.

A WORLD OF TROUBLES

If there is a single country whose foreign policy is most worth analyzing, if only for its potential impact on the rest of the planet, the United States stands out as the number one candidate. As the above epigraph by Brooks and Wohlforth points out, the United States today, at least on paper (based on military, economic, or any other standard criteria used to measure power), gives the appearance of Gulliver in a world of Lilliputians, resembling the main character in Jonathan Swift's famous fictional account of a man abroad who physically towers over his foreign hosts. Following the decline of its erstwhile Cold War rival—the Soviet Union—the United States would seem to have no serious challenger as a "great power." To quote Richard Haass, the United States is "the first among unequals."[1] Haass puts it even more plainly when he says that "the United States is the 800-pound gorilla, whether it is in the room or not."[2] However, as the Niall Ferguson epigraph suggests, American strength may be illusory. Power is best understood not as a commodity whose possession alone confers influence but rather as a relationship that consists in the ability to get someone to do something they would

CARTOON 1.1 Gulliver's Travails. CREDIT: GULLIVER'S TRAV-
ELS, ILLUSTRATIONS BY MILO WINTER. RAND McNALLY, 1936

not otherwise do.[3] In the post–Cold War world, the United States, like Gulliver, reminds one of a pitiful giant, whose hands are tied by forces it seems unable to control, Iraq serving as a metaphor for American frustrations experienced all over the globe.

One might rightly ask, where is the United States getting anybody to do its bidding? Mexico, where Washington has been unable to get cooperation to secure the border and stem the tide of illegal immigrants that had exceeded twelve million by 2007? The Middle East, where, in addition to the Iraq problem, Washington has been unable to broker peace between the Israelis and Palestinians, has been unable to thwart the threat posed by al-Qaeda and Islamic terrorism, and has failed to convince Iran to renounce its nuclear weapons ambitions? East Asia, where the United States has experienced similar struggles in trying to prevent a petty despot in North Korea from developing nuclear weapons technology, and where China continues to test American resolve in support of Taiwan's autonomy from Beijing? Africa, where genocide in Sudan and the persistence of dictatorships in Zimbabwe and elsewhere on the continent run counter to the U.S. efforts of promoting human rights and democracy? Latin America, where a growing number of left-wing regimes, particularly in Venezuela, thumb their noses at what they see as another chapter in American imperialism? Russia, whose recent votes on the United Nations Security Council have been mostly hostile, or at best indifferent, to U.S. interests? Europe, where the French and many other North Atlantic Treaty Organization (NATO) allies are often critical of American foreign policy and have resisted Washington's worldview on issues ranging from reduction of agricultural trade barriers to global warming to the formation of a new International Criminal Court aimed at punishing war crimes? And, of course, at home there is the fearful prospect of possibly another attack like 9/11.

During the Bush presidency, there were headlines such as "For Bush, A World of Worry: Abundant Troubles but Few Solutions." As the Bush presidency was nearing its end, another headline expressed anguish over "After Bush: How to Restore America's Place in the World."[4]

To be sure, the United States is not without power. It has achieved some successes since the Cold War, which ended in 1990—for example, in stopping Saddam Hussein's aggression against Kuwait in the First Persian Gulf War in 1991 (the United States suffered fewer than 150 battlefield fatalities in forty-eight days of fighting) and in stopping Serbian president Slobodan Milosevic's ethnic cleansing of Albanians in Kosovo in 1999 (the United States had no combat deaths despite flying some ten thousand sorties for seventy-eight days). However, one could argue that the real test of power is not so much the capacity to engage in raw coercion as the capacity to persuade others short of the actual use of armed force, either by simply threatening to use force or, better yet, offering positive incentives to cooperate, or convincing through sheer moral suasion.

Take, for instance, the case of Kosovo, where the United States was not strong enough to deter Serbia from engaging in the genocidal behavior of which Washington disapproved. As one observer noted:

When U.S. diplomat Richard Holbrooke met with Milosevic [whose country had a population 3 percent the size of the United States with a GNP only 0.2 percent that of the United States, and a defense budget $270 billion smaller] in October 1998 to negotiate the status of Kosovo, Holbrooke tried to impress the Serb leader by bringing along Air Force Lieutenant General Michael Short. . . . Milosevic greeted Short by remarking, "So you are the man who is going to bomb me." And when Short told the Serbian president that he had "U–2s in one hand and B–52s in the other, and the choice [of which I use] is up to you," Milosevic "just sort of nodded" . . . and chose to face war.[5]

Although the United States ultimately prevailed, as Milosevic was forcibly removed from power, the Balkans remained an ethnic powderkeg, and (in the view of many) the benefit of a fragile peace was achieved only at the cost of considerable harm to America's reputation; the bombings caused thousands of civilian deaths (the reliance on air power and the resulting collateral damage attributable mainly to the U.S. fear of committing ground troops), violated the UN Charter's proscription against aggression and noninterference in the internal affairs of other countries, and contributed to the world's growing perception of the United States as a bully who claimed to be a champion of international law while ignoring it when it conflicted with American goals. If this was evidence of a display of power, one wondered what weakness and failure looked like.

In Kosovo, Iraq, and elsewhere in contemporary international relations, power seems not what it used to be. True, throughout history, military might has never been an ironclad guarantor of successful exercise of influence. The axioms attributed to Frederick the Great (the eighteenth-century ruler of Prussia) that "diplomacy is only as good as the number of guns backing it up" and "God is always for the biggest battalions" have always proved a bit simplistic, as quantitative military superiority has not automatically assured effective diplomacy any more than it has assured long-term victory, when diplomacy has failed and given way to the resort to war. But these nostrums seemed somewhat more reliable as predictors of events in the past than they are today in an age when the threat to use armed force is irrelevant to a growing number of issues (such as getting countries to lift their restrictions on genetically modified food imports from the United States) and when, where it is relevant, huge arsenals can now often be neutralized by "asymmetrical warfare" conducted by numerically or technologically weaker foes (for example, in Iraq).

"IT'S FOREIGN POLICY, STUPID"

Frederick the Great might have added that a state is only as good as its leadership, as the quality of its statesmanship. Charles Kupchan sees this, and not the absence of power, as the critical problem afflicting the United States:

> America today arguably has greater ability to shape the future of world politics than any other power in history. The United States enjoys overwhelming military, economic, technological, and cultural dominance. America's military has unquestioned superiority against all potential challengers. The strength of the dollar and the size of its economy give the United States decisive weight on matters of trade and finance. . . . The information revolution, born and bred in Silicon Valley and the country's other high-tech centers, gives U.S. companies, media, and culture unprecedented reach. . . .
>
> The opportunity that America has before it also stems from the geopolitical opening afforded by the Cold War's end. Postwar periods are moments of extraordinary prospect, usually accompanied by searching debate and institutional innovation [for example, the creation of the Concert of Europe after the Napoleonic Wars in 1815, the League of Nations after World War I in 1919, and the United Nations after World War II in 1945], all . . . born of courageous and creative efforts to fashion a new order.

Despite the opportunities afforded by its dominance, America is squandering the moment. The United States has unparalleled potential to shape what comes next, but it has no grand strategy, no design to guide the ship of state. Rather than articulating a new vision of international order and working with partners to make that vision a reality, America has been floundering. The United States is a great power adrift, as made clear by its contradictory and incoherent behavior.[6]

Bill Clinton, when running for president in 1992, famously used the campaign slogan, "It's the economy, stupid," claiming that domestic economic issues seemed the most daunting challenges to the country at the time and that he was best equipped to handle those. These days, it would seem, "It's foreign policy, stupid," although it is not clear who is equipped to deal with the external challenges facing the United States.

Kupchan raises interesting questions, such as how much freedom or constraint does a country such as the United States have in its foreign policy, and how well-planned can any country's foreign policy hope to be? These are not new questions, however. This is not the first time the United States has been compared to the literary figure Gulliver, a shipwrecked soul reduced to a muscle-bound oaf who was clumsily trying to cope in a foreign environment whose inhabitants it physically dwarfed. In the immediate post–World War II period, following the wartime devastation of many European and Asian economies, and before the Soviet Union had acquired the atomic bomb and had joined America as a "superpower," the United States in some respects enjoyed an even greater power differential than today. As Harold Laski commented in 1947, "America bestrides the world like a colossus; neither Rome at the height of its power nor Great Britain in the period of its economic supremacy enjoyed influence so . . . pervasive. It has half the wealth of the world today in its hands, it has more than half of the world's productive capacity, and it exports more than twice as much as it imports."[7] One could have added that "Americans possessed 70 percent of the world's automobiles, 83 percent of its aircraft, 50 percent of its telephones, and 45 percent of its radios."[8] Yet then, too, for all the praise eventually given the Marshall Plan foreign aid program and other postwar efforts, Washington was criticized initially for erratic and misguided foreign policy behavior—the "lack of any general agreement" concerning "the basic purposes" of foreign policy—and for not taking advantage of its many strengths.[9] Similarly, during the Vietnam era of the 1960s, at a time when what was thought by some to be "the greatest power in the world" was unable to defeat "a band of night-riders in black pajamas,"[10] one could find books like *Gulliver's Troubles, Or the Setting of American Foreign Policy* that warned of U.S. policy "in crisis" and full of "incoherence and contradictions."[11]

If the United States often has been criticized in the past as a gangly giant lacking sure footing in foreign policy, there is something about the current era, as Kupchan argues, that seems to invite special scrutiny. Perhaps never before in the annals of foreign policy has there been such a disconnect between potential and performance; perhaps never before has an actor seemingly achieved so little with so much going for it.

One measure of the failure of American foreign policy in the post–Cold War era is the lack of respect enjoyed by the United States worldwide, even among its "friends."

PHOTO 1.1 President John F. Kennedy in the Oval Office: The dilemmas of foreign policymaking.
CREDIT: GEORGE TAMES/THE NEW YORK TIMES/REDUX

The dictionary equates respect with "esteem," which is defined as "deference, combined with admiration and often affection." We have already noted the lack of deference paid to Washington. There is probably even less admiration, and still less affection, toward the United States today than at any time in memory. Admittedly, the United States has long suffered an image problem, personified by the term "Ugly American," especially since the end of World War II, when America's superpower status invited resentment and envy. Such annoyance at times has boiled over into anger, for example during Ronald Reagan's presidency, when America's own Western European allies complained about the administration's "Rambo-like" cockiness and abrasiveness. Longitudinal data show that the percentage of foreigners with a favorable view of the United States was already plummeting by the late 1990s during the Clinton years.[12] However, none of this compares to the visceral disdain that George W. Bush's administration has engendered over what is perceived to be extraordinary hubris and insensitivity to the concerns of others. Again, one does not expect an eight-hundred-pound gorilla to be loved or to win a popularity contest; the current animus toward the United States perhaps is not unusual given the fact that there is now no other clear rival, since the eclipse of the Soviet Union, to share the spotlight and the blame for the world's problems. It is not surprising that a 2006 Pew Research Center survey of ninety-one thousand respondents in fifty nations found that more than seventy percent of non-Americans think the world would be better off if there were another superpower to keep the United States in check.[13] Nonetheless, it is striking when public opinion polls report that so many in the world, including in Western capitals, consider the United States "a greater threat to world peace than Iran or North Korea,"[14] so-called rogue states that have been in violation of the Nuclear Non-Proliferation Treaty that for more than thirty years has helped to avert a nuclear Armageddon.

"The problem," says Fareed Zakaria, "isn't that America is too strong, but that it's seen as too arrogant and insensitive."[15] As Michael Mandelbaum notes, "the foreign policy of the world's strongest country" in the eyes of much of the world "resembled the conduct of a schoolyard bully who randomly assaults others, steals the lunch money of weaker students, and generally makes life unpleasant wherever he goes. The United States was seen as the world's Goliath,"[16] a somewhat less flattering comparison than Gulliver. Just as Gulliver was able eventually to win over the Lilliputians and escape his chains through, in Jonathan Swift's words, "gaining favour by his mild disposition" and "gentleness and good behaviour," so also might the United States possibly overcome foreign relations failures through making better use of what Joseph Nye has called "soft power," that is, "getting others to want what you want" by "co-opting" rather than "coercing" them.[17]

Let us look more closely at the contemporary, post–Cold War international system, taking a bird's-eye view of the planet, of not only the power configuration but also other key features of global politics. These features represent constraints as well as opportunities that the United States faces as it seeks to overcome what appears to be a helpless hegemon condition.

AN OVERVIEW OF THE POST–COLD WAR INTERNATIONAL SYSTEM

The Berlin wall fell on November 9, 1989, symbolizing the end of the Cold War. Almost twenty years later—through the euphoria after 11/9 and the doom and gloom after 9/11—the U.S. ship of state still seems adrift, if not lost at sea, as Kupchan and others point out. Part of the problem is that, when the Soviet Union disappeared from the world map, so did the anchor that had helped to give American foreign policy its moorings for fifty years. To quote William Maynes in 1990, "the United States has lost more than an enemy; it has lost the sextant that provided direction for policy."[18] No buzzword emerged to replace "containment" of Soviet-led communism as the centerpiece of American foreign policy. But it was not just the absence of the Soviet Union that left America without any foreign policy compass. It was the absence of any systemic crisis, akin to World War I or World War II, that might have provided the necessary catalyst for "searching debate and institutional innovation" aimed at promoting a new world order; the "geopolitical opening" was there, but not the sense of urgency. After all, the Cold War was just that—a non-shooting war—and the Cold War era ended rather suddenly without a shot being fired. For the first time in memory, and perhaps ever, a fundamental transformation of the international system had occurred without major war as the engine of change.

The world the United States found itself in was a strange and, in many ways, far more complex place than anything the country had seen before. Henry Kissinger, writing at the same time as Maynes, remarked that the major challenge facing the United States in the post–Cold War era was to define a role for itself in a world which "for the first time in her history . . . she cannot dominate [in terms of being a superpower, as during the Cold War], but from which she cannot simply withdraw"[19] in terms of isolationism, which characterized America's posture toward the world through much of its pre–Cold War existence.

The events of 9/11 only reinforced the sense of American vulnerability and the fact that the United States was capable of neither superpower domination nor withdrawal to Fortress America. America is still attempting to get a handle on this brave new world and searching for its proper role in it.

There is general agreement that the relatively neat, tidy, **bipolar** era following World War II, which featured two superpowers engaged in a global competition leading two fairly cohesive blocs (the Western developed capitalist democracies of the First World pitted against the Eastern-bloc developed communist states of the Second World), separated by a Third World of "nonaligned" developing countries, is gone; trends in the direction of a more complicated system that were already partially discernible toward the latter stages of the Cold War have become more pronounced and have accelerated. This complexity is marked by at least four key properties: (1) a growing diffusion and ambiguity of power, with the term "superpower" in question and the term "power" itself increasingly problematical; (2) a growing fluidity of alignments, with the old East-West (communist versus noncommunist) and North-South (rich versus poor) axes of conflict giving way to West-West, South-South, and assorted other faultlines; (3) a growing agenda of issues facing national governments, with economic, environmental, energy, and other concerns competing for attention with traditional military-security issues, with the nature of "security" itself changing, and all this enmeshing states in ever more intricate patterns of interdependence; and (4) a growing importance of nonstate actors, including multinational corporations, intergovernmental organizations, and nongovernmental organizations, competing with states in shaping outcomes in world politics.

The Growing Diffusion and Ambiguity of Power

We have noted the following conundrum that is a central theme of this book: how can the United States at once be seemingly all-powerful in its possession of resources and, yet, so weak in translating these into successful influence?

On the one hand, we hear constantly that it is now a "unipolar" moment in which the United States, as the lone superpower left standing, resembles the Roman Empire at its peak, and is maybe even superior to Rome.[20] Paul Kennedy wrote: "Nothing has ever existed like this disparity of power. . . . No other nation comes close. . . . Charlemagne's empire was merely western European in its reach. The Roman Empire stretched further afield, but there was another great empire in Persia, and a larger one in China. There is, therefore, no comparison."[21] Stephen Walt wrote: "The end of the Cold War left the United States in a position of power unseen since the Roman Empire."[22] Timothy Garton Ash wrote: "Not since Rome has a single power enjoyed such superiority."[23] And Josef Joffe wrote: "Its power is more overwhelming than that of any previous hegemon since the Roman Empire."[24]

Such analyses are based on the fact that the United States "is the only Great Power in modern history to establish a clear lead in virtually every important dimension of power."[25] The United States alone accounts for forty percent of global military expenditures, outspending the next dozen or so countries combined, and has troops deployed in well over one hundred countries. The U.S. economy accounts for more than twenty-five percent of the planetary product and is approximately sixty percent larger than its nearest rival; the U.S. imports almost one-fifth of the rest of the world's exports, making access to the American market, as well as its foreign investment, much-desired. Regarding cultural influence, although the United States may be at risk of squandering its "soft power," "the top twenty-five highest-grossing films of all time [are] U.S. productions, even if one omits U.S. ticket sales and looks solely at foreign revenues. American consumer products and brand names are ubiquitous, along with U.S. sports and media figures."[26] In addition, "not only is English increasingly the *lingua franca* of diplomacy, science, and international business, but the American university system is a potent mechanism for socializing foreign elites," attracting more than a half-million foreign students annually.[27]

On the other hand, some scholars see **unipolarity** giving way to **multipolarity**. They point to several "power centers" that figure to be "the chief rivals" potentially capable of challenging or overtaking the United States in the twenty-first century, especially if American structural economic problems, such as trade and budget deficits and foreign debt obligations, force a retrenchment in the country's overseas commitments. One chief rival is China, representing one-fifth of the world's population and experiencing the highest economic growth rate of any nation over the past two decades (averaging between eight and thirteen percent annually), which in turn is fueling an increase in military spending. Still, China has its own vulnerabilities, notably environmental problems related to uncontrolled economic growth, population problems, and problems with its banking institutions and political institutions as the communist system makes the transition from a command economy and one-party state to a full player in an open world economy. A second possible rival is the Russian Federation—the main successor state to the Soviet Union—still the largest piece of real estate on the planet, blessed with oil and vast natural resources, and still in possession of thousands of nuclear weapons. However, the Russian Federation is also plagued by a declining population in poor health (partly related to the AIDS epidemic and rampant alcoholism), internal ethnic strife, and a Gross National Product now no larger than Brazil's. A third rival is Japan, with the second largest GNP in the world and the fourth largest defense budget. Japan's economy, though, has been somewhat stagnant, its population has been shrinking, and its military is limited by its constitution that technically allows only for a "defense force" and "renounces war as a sovereign right." In addition, Japan's lack of racial diversity and its ethnocentric attitudes limit its "soft power" appeal to other peoples. A final potential competitor and "pole" is the European Union (a group of twenty-seven countries led by Germany, France, and Britain), moving to consolidate a single market, and possibly further down the road a single European supranational state larger than the United States. Despite having a single currency and growing cooperation, the main impediments are lack of cohesion in EU-wide political institutions and loyalties, high unemployment and other economic problems related to bloated welfare states, an aging, dwindling population, and an antipathy toward major increases in military spending. India and some other states have been mentioned as well as possible "counterweights" to the United States.[28]

However, to talk of chief rivals may be missing the point, since the world may no longer be revolving around "great powers" quite as much as it has in the past. Indeed, the actual exercise of power has become so problematical and complex that calling today's international system multipolar might not do justice to the current dispersion of power in real terms. One could already see superpower slippage by the 1970s with the failure of both the United States and the Soviet Union to defeat "backward" peoples in Vietnam and Afghanistan and with the "oil crisis" episode in which a group of less developed countries—some of which were tiny "statelets" and all of which were devoid of the assets traditionally associated with international influence—threatened to bring the industrialized world to a standstill over petroleum price hikes and boycotts. It was said that "never before in history has a group of such relatively weak nations been able to impose with so little protest such a dramatic change in the way of life of the overwhelming majority of the rest of mankind."[29] These were harbingers of other setbacks and humiliations for the United States that were to follow in the next decades. The construction of a meaningful pecking order in international relations has become much more difficult lately. The United States may have the greatest range of power assets to be applied across the board, but resources seem less fungible than ever, and power is more fragmented and issue-specific.

The chief threat to United States security and well-being may no longer be from great powers but from not-so-great powers, such as North Korea and Iran, which lately have "defied the American hyperpower with impunity."[30] Although we are not there yet, as small or underdeveloped rogue states like North Korea possibly close in on acquiring ABC (atomic, bacteriological, and chemical) arsenals (particularly biological and chemical weapons—the "poor man's" **weapons of mass destruction** [WMDs] which are more readily obtainable than atomic weapons), the international system may become a "unit veto" system of the kind that was only fantasized about in the 1950s, where each state has the ultimate instrument of warfare.[31] Just as the six-inch-high Lilliputians stripped Gulliver of his watch and comb, ministates may be positioned to strip the United States of far more—of New York City or Washington, DC—with a dirty radioactive bomb or other device.

It should be added that it is not strong states but weak, "failed" states (those, such as Somalia, whose governmental institutions have collapsed) that tend to offer the most inviting havens for terrorists. Terrorism itself has been called "the weapon of the weak."[32] Terrorists specialize in **asymmetrical warfare**, a form of combat aimed at negating a superior foe's military advantages and leveling the playing field by changing the traditional rules of engagement.[33] Terrorists are uninhibited by the conventional norms of war-fighting that armies generally are held to, such as limiting civilian casualties. Even though armies at times skirt the rules, they, unlike terrorists, rarely adopt a strategy of striking civilians as their prime targets and hiding behind civilians as defensive measures. Even more worrisome than rogue states getting nuclear weapons is the threat posed by "super-empowered"[34] individuals and groups acquiring them, such as Osama bin Laden and al-Qaeda. One can at least try to deter WMD strikes from Tehran or Pyongyang by threatening to retaliate, but terrorist groups ordinarily do not have return addresses that permit deterrence to work.

Niall Ferguson concludes that, instead of unipolarity, we may be seeing "apolarity," that is, a power vacuum in which there is no great power or set of great powers to ride herd over the inherent anarchy of the international system.[35] Joseph Nye also recognizes that "the bad news for Americans in this more complex distribution of power in the twenty-first century is that there are more and more things outside the control of even the most powerful state." However, he argues that the solution is for the United States to "mobilize international coalitions to address shared threats and challenges."[36] This, then, leads us to examine the *alignment* configuration in the contemporary international system.

The Growing Fluidity of Alignments

John Mearsheimer, waxing nostalgic, has said that the Cold War gave a kind of "order to the anarchy of international relations."[37] If not order, there at least was clarity, as summed up by Former Israeli Foreign Minister Abba Eban: "The Cold War, with all its perils, expressed a certain bleak stability: alignments, fidelities, and rivalries were sharply defined."[38] Clarity itself became more muddled as the Cold War system progressed; tight bipolarity had given way to loose bipolarity by the 1960s, and the latter had been superceded by "bimultipolarity" by the late 1970s, perhaps best exemplified by the failure of the United States to persuade many of its allies (and even Puerto Rico) to boycott the 1980 Olympic Games in Moscow in protest against the Soviet invasion of Afghanistan despite President Carter calling the Soviet action "the greatest threat to world peace since World War II."[39] Still, to the very end of the Cold War, indeed well into the 1990s, the main categories that international law texts as well as most other international relations treatises comfortably fell back on in conceptualizing world affairs were Western, Marxist, and Third World perspectives. These trichotomous, polarizing tendencies of the Cold War have now been replaced by a far more complex set of relationships, with many sources of conflict and cross-cutting cleavages to be found in the post–Cold War world.

It is possible that the East-West conflict could be revived in some form if communism as a belief system is resuscitated by the failure of capitalism to deliver the goods in societies undergoing capitalist transitions, but for now Marxism-Leninism has been overtaken by "Market-Leninism."[40] Any East-West axis of conflict that might reemerge is more likely to be motivated by a Russo-Sino reaction to NATO expansion and other perceived U.S. ambitions than by rival ideologies. Mearsheimer has written about "the tragedy of great power politics," that is, the almost inevitability of a revival of balance of power politics through the creation of competing alliance systems that has characterized multipolar systems historically.[41] According to this logic, we may well see China not only seeking to join Russia—it already has declared a "strategic partnership" with Moscow and signed a treaty of "friendship and cooperation"—but also Japan and others in "resisting American hegemonism."[42] The former president of the EU Commission has said that "we are building new relationships, and it's clear it's a commitment for us and for China. Both of us want a multipolar world. This is a Chinese priority and it is a European interest." Russian President Vladimir Putin similarly has said, "We believe here in Russia, just as French President Jacques Chirac believes that the future . . . must be based on a multipolar world. That is the main thing that unites us."[43]

Although "the West" remains a powerful idea, built around shared values of capitalism and democracy, cracks have been appearing in the United States-Japan and NATO alliances. This is perhaps to be expected, given the demise of the common threat that was once posed by the Soviet Union and global communism that gave the alliances their main rationale. However, the cracks are also due to differences over policy ranging from handling of the Iraq War to handling of the North Korean nuclear proliferation problem. I noted earlier the low esteem in which the United States is held today even among many of its friends. While the NATO alliance was at times called "a troubled partnership"[44] during the Cold War, with France especially (under Charles de Gaulle) claiming "France has no permanent friends, only permanent interests," there was still a sense then of common purpose, and no American newspaper went so far as to talk of "our war with France."[45] There seems a widening gulf between the United States and Europe even in regard to basic cultural values. As one Italian commentator put it, "A collective apprehension about the United States seems the only glue that binds Europeans together. Scathing stories about the United States' death penalty, shootings in high schools, unforgiving markets, and lack of welfare abound in the European press. Cross the ocean and you will read about European gerontocracy, high unemployment, and very low defense budgets. There is no sign of a community forming between the two entities that the world insists on branding together as the West."[46] In the words of another European commentator, "We have gone from a Cold War configuration of one West and two Europes to a current world of one Europe and two Wests."[47] Adding further to the complexity is the talk of differences between "old Europe" (France, Germany, the Netherlands, and other Western European states that have often opposed American policies in Iraq and elsewhere) versus "new Europe" (Poland, the Czech Republic, the Baltic states, and former East European Soviet satellites who, with the United Kingdom and a few other Western European countries, have been part of the "coalition of the willing" and more supportive of American policies).

Just as the East-West conflict has disappeared, the North-South conflict—which came to compete for attention with the East-West conflict during the Cold War era— also shows signs of possibly losing its defining character despite the persistence of the rich-poor gap. Given the growing economic diversity within the developing world, Southern solidarity likely will be increasingly difficult to maintain as some of the more industrialized members gravitate toward the North. When more than one hundred members of the Non-Aligned Movement met for their annual summit in Havana in 2006, they had to search hard for a rationale for their continued existence. Venezuelan President Hugo Chavez called for alignment against the United States, asserting that "American imperialism is in decline. A new bipolar world is emerging. The nonaligned group has been relaunched to unite the South under one umbrella."[48] However, his words met with at best mixed reactions. Today, instead of a North-South cleavage, there is the first world and the "two-thirds world," the latter constituting what some now call the "Global South"—the collection of former communist states and third world, fourth world (super-poor), or middle-income less developed countries (LDCs) as well as newly industrializing countries (NICs) and next NICs trying to join the global elite. Some observers do worry that the fourth world, composed of roughly fifty states that the World Bank has labeled "least developed," combined with the tier of impoverished states just above them, may represent a major fault line threatening the industrialized world: "On one side of the fault line will be 'a relatively small number of rich, satiated, demographically stagnant societies.' On the other side will be 'a large number of poverty-stricken, resource-depleted nations whose populations are doubling every twenty-five years or less. . . . How those [two] relate to each other . . . dwarfs every other issue in global affairs.'"[49] Although economic cleavages clearly have the potential for major international strife, including providing breeding grounds for disaffected masses enticed by terrorist recruitment slogans, there are other cleavages that may be more volatile.

If the East-West and North-South conflicts were "the two dominant struggles of our time,"[50] in the last half of the twentieth century, what then are replacing them as the central global dramas? What new descriptive categories in the post–Cold War era might replace the vernacular of first, second, and third worlds and other such terminology that dominated discourse during the Cold War? Samuel Huntington, in his 1993 article "The Clash of Civilizations," argued that the East versus West axis of conflict would be replaced by the "West vs. the rest" axis, pitting Western culture against Islamic fundamentalism as well as militant Hinduism and other cultural traditions.[51] Huntington was reacting to Francis Fukuyama's widely cited 1989 article "The End of History?" which had argued that with the fall of the Berlin wall the world had witnessed the final triumph of Western, liberal-democratic, free-market principles against fascism, communism, and other competing ideologies and that there was a global consensus behind Westernization, modernization, and "globalization."[52] Huntington seems to have been more prescient than Fukuyama, although, aside from "the West" itself being somewhat divided and fractious at times, "the rest" are even more so, notably within Islam (as Sunnis, Shiites, and others have fought each other recently).[53] Perhaps "unalignment" is the order of the day.[54]

It is interesting that, despite many "chief rivals" criticizing the United States for its ostensible arrogance and hegemonic aspirations, there has been no actual counteralliance formed against the United States. Michael Mandelbaum frames the puzzle as follows:

> Sovereign states as powerful as the United States, and as dangerous as its critics declare it to be, were historically subject to a check on their power. Other countries banded together to block them. Revolutionary and Napoleonic France in the late eighteenth and early nineteenth century, Germany during the two world wars, and the Soviet Union during the Cold War all inspired countervailing coalitions. . . . Yet no such anti-American alignment has formed.[55]

As Stephen Walt notes, "The United States is still formally allied with NATO, and it has renewed and deepened its military relationship with Japan. . . . U.S. relations with Russia are sometimes contentious but still far better than they were during the Cold War, and relations with China [have] improved. . . . Similarly, United States' ties with India are warmer and deeper than ever before. . . . To date, at least, no one is making serious effort to forge a meaningful anti-American alliance."[56] Richard Haass hypothesizes that the reason why the formation of counteralliances has not occurred to balance the power of the lead state, as so often has happened throughout the history of the state system, is that "the twenty-first century is fundamentally different. For the first time in modern history, the major powers of the day . . . are not engaged in a classic struggle for domination at each other's expense. There are few contests over territory. For the foreseeable future, war between or among them borders on the highly unlikely and, in some cases, unthinkable."[57] Mandelbaum offers a further explanation, attributing the absence of any counteralliance to the fact that, notwithstanding the frequent rhetoric about American imperialism, the United States is perceived by its European allies, Russia, China, and most others as a relatively benign hegemon that, even if often brusque and bullying, is not a "predatory" state bent on global expansion.[58]

Some may question how truly benign the United States is. However, it is precisely the absence of tight, rigid polarization in the contemporary international system that may offer opportunities for the United States to, in Nye's words, "mobilize international coalitions to address shared threats and challenges." Whether the United States can seize such opportunities is open to question, but they are there. Most, if not all, states are potentially threatened by the disruptive effects of terrorism, energy shortages, the spread of diseases, and environmental decay. And their leaders all share a common wariness about the possible threat to state sovereignty posed by nonstate actors.

The Growing Agenda of Issues

Closely related to power and alignment trends, although potentially far more revolutionary in impact, is the increased blurring of the line between **high politics** (having to do with vital, core interests) and **low politics** (having to do with not so vital, noncore interests). In the contemporary international system, "national security" has taken on newer meaning, no longer equated almost exclusively with military issues. Although it may remain the overriding goal of nation-states, *security* has been broadened to include economic, ecological, and other *welfare* dimensions that have gained rising visibility on the agendas of governments. This trend is rooted in long-term historical processes: mass democracy and public demands for improved material well-being led to the growth of the welfare state in the twentieth century, while technology over time internationalized these concerns as it became clear that they could not be fully satisfied through unilateral national action. It was already apparent by the 1970s, as Stanley Hoffmann noted, that we were witnessing "the move from a world dominated by a single chessboard—the strategic-diplomatic one (which eclipsed or controlled all others)—to a world dispersed into a variety of chessboards."[59] There is now a global politics of poverty and plenty, of population, petroleum, pandemics, and pollution that impacts the developed and developing worlds alike.

That interdependence has become a cliché does not make it any less real a phenomenon. There is some disagreement over whether welfare issues have now achieved primacy over military issues. In the 1990s, as the end of the Cold War allowed globalization of the world economy to take off, finance ministers got the kinds of front-page newspaper headlines once reserved for defense ministers and foreign ministers. Playing on the famous nineteenth century Prussian military strategist von Clausewitz, economics was being called "the continuation of war by other means,"[60] particularly among highly developed societies, which seemed unlikely to wage shooting wars against each other given the destructiveness of armed combat in the nuclear age. Although there obviously had been considerable conflict during the Cold War, the period since 1945 was being called "the long peace,"[61] that is, the longest continuous stretch of time since the beginnings of the modern state system in the seventeenth century in which there had not been a single recorded instance of direct great-power exchange of actual hostilities.

The long peace has continued in the post–Cold War era and, as noted in the discussion of alignments, is unlikely to be broken anytime soon. However, the world obviously is anything but peaceful. Although September 11, 2001, has had the effect of restoring military concerns to the top of the agenda in the United States and elsewhere, the nature of such concerns has changed as the nature of war has changed. The history of international relations has revolved around **interstate** violence, particularly war between great powers. Not only is there an absence of great-power war today, but there is a dearth of interstate wars generally. While clearly some interstate wars still occur—for example, in addition to the 2003 U.S. invasion of Iraq, there are worries about U.S. confrontations with Iran and North Korea—they have been relatively infrequent in the post–Cold War era.[62] As Jack Levy has summarized the trends, "the twentieth century, and the second half-century in particular, marked a significant shift in warfare from the major powers to the minor powers, from Europe to other regions, and from inter-state warfare to intra-state wars."[63] In addition to the prevalence of **intrastate** violence, such as the recent civil wars involving ethnic and sectarian strife in the former Yugoslavia, Rwanda, and Somalia, there is the growing problem of **extrastate** violence, that is, the violence perpetrated by terrorist groups, often organized transnationally, such as al-Qaeda.[64] At times, all these different levels and forms of violence intersect and defy easy categorization, as has happened in Iraq. This is not a completely new phenomenon—certainly civil wars and terrorism have been part of the human condition for a long time—but what is new is their having replaced great-power interstate war as the central security problem of international relations.

Alongside the long peace we have "the long war"—the name the U.S. Pentagon has given the war on terror. The phrase "the long war" suggests the indeterminate character of the conflict and the sense that it may not have any ending insofar as it is hard to imagine the conquest of the last remaining terrorist. The current period may or may not be a transition era toward a more peaceful planet. The changing nature of warfare, along with the proliferation of a new agenda of issues competing for attention with war and peace concerns, adds greatly to the complexity of the post–Cold War straits through which the United States ship of state is trying to navigate. So, too, does the proliferation of a new cast of actors.

The Growing Importance of Nonstate Actors

The extrastate violence phenomenon is just one dimension of the growing visibility of **nonstate** actors on the world stage. Again, these actors are not altogether new, only gaining in importance.[65] Al-Qaeda is a nonstate actor, but so are the United Nations and the European Union (the latter two being intergovernmental organizations or **IGOs**), Human Rights Watch and the International Red Cross (nongovernmental organizations or **NGOs**), Toyota and McDonalds (multinational corporations or **MNCs**), and countless other actors, some of which are more benign than others. The UN Charter presumed a world of states as the basis for human organization. One of the major developments in the post–World War II era was, in fact, the tremendous proliferation of new states mainly precipitated by the decolonialization process whereby erstwhile colonies were granted their sovereign independence. The original UN membership had more than tripled by the time the Cold War ended in 1989, with another two dozen states added in the 1990s. However, the founders did not envision that many of these states would be of the cookie-cutter variety—microstates smaller in size than not only a typical American state but a typical American city and, in some cases, a typical American town. What was envisioned even less was the proliferation of *nonstate* actors and their growing importance if not autonomy in world politics, including subnational actors (e.g., the overseas trade missions maintained by virtually every state in the United States)[66] as well as transnational actors (e.g., the now more than three hundred IGOs, twenty thousand NGOs, and fifty thousand multinational corporations).[67] Relating to Hoffmann's chessboard imagery, world politics can be seen as a series of issue-areas in which outcomes are determined by a congeries of forces, including both state and nonstate actors.

For example, one cannot fully understand the dynamics of the 1992 UN Conference on Environment and Development held in Rio de Janeiro (the "Earth Summit") unless one takes into account, in addition to the interplay between Northern and

Southern governments, the variety of nonstate actors involved: the secretariats of the UN, World Bank, and other IGOs, nongovernmental scientific research bodies and global environmental advocacy groups, MNCs, and a host of other players. Although state-centric analysts would contend that IGOs are little more than fragile collections of states that tend to be dominated from a few national capital and that NGOs are no match for the power of governments, the point is not that nonstate actors played the decisive role in the conference, only that they were a not insignificant part of the equation that produced several new environmental agreements.[68] Likewise, whether one supports or opposes Bush administration policies relating to CIA secret prisons and harsh interrogation techniques, it is evident that human rights NGOs complicate U.S. foreign policy and American efforts to prosecute the war on terror when they monitor and publicize what they consider violations of the torture and POW provisions of the Geneva Conventions.

The rise of nonstate actors is captured in the following quote: "If the state remains at the centre of governance in the world, what has changed? In a word everything. Never have so many different nonstate actors competed for the authority and influence that once belonged to the states alone."[69] Some have gone so far as to speak of the "end of the nation-state" and "the end of sovereignty."[70] There is some disagreement among those who envision the demise of the nation-state as to whether the primary threat to its viability comes from *integrative* tendencies (the transnational links, perhaps best manifested by cyberspace, which are causing mounting "loss of control" and erosion of sovereignty) or *disintegrative* tendencies (the proliferation of so many small marginally self-sustaining polities, fueled especially by the surge of ethnic conflicts and separatist movements), or *both*.[71] Depending on which analyst one believes, we are witnessing the emergence of either a global village or the exact opposite—global villages.

Although it seems "state authority has leaked away, upwards, sideways, and downwards,"[72] one must be careful not to exaggerate the death of the nation-state.[73] When last checked, the United States, along with the United Kingdom and almost two hundred other such entities, still dominated the world map, demarcated by the dark boundaries we associate with sovereignty. States retain their formal independence despite becoming more interdependent. This is one feature of world politics that has not changed, even if the United States and other countries are having to formulate and conduct foreign policy in a much more complex setting today. A number of observers have suggested that the United States, no matter how much it may tower over other actors, cannot be the world's policeman, that at best it must settle for "the role of international sheriff, one who forges coalitions or posses of states and others for specific tasks."[74] Whether Gulliver can adapt to the strange new world that he finds himself in remains to be seen.

THE PLAN OF THE BOOK

Later chapters will consider the hard choices confronting the United States and the wisdom of various foreign policy approaches that might be adopted. However, before we can focus on American foreign policy, we need to examine foreign policy more generally. In order to understand the problems surrounding contemporary U.S. foreign policy, it is helpful, first, to develop a conceptual and analytical framework for thinking about "foreign policy" that can enable us to make basic sense of it, whether studying the United States or any other actor, a task I take up in Chapter 2. In Chapter 3, I trace the evolution of American foreign policy historically, especially since World War II, noting both continuity and change in not only foreign policy patterns but also the determinants shaping policy. In Chapter 4, I survey several different foreign policy schools of thought ("neocon" and others), examining major critiques of current American foreign policy and the prescriptions offered by various writers. Chapter 5 looks further into the contemporary policy debate, focusing on five issues (the war on terror, the Bush Doctrine and self-defense, control of weapons of mass destruction, humanitarian intervention, and the International Criminal Court) as case studies illustrating the special dilemmas experienced by the United States today. Chapter 6 is a concluding chapter that speculates about how the United States might fit into a future world order in which American interests and global interests converge.

DISCUSSION QUESTIONS

1. The United States has been called by many commentators "the greatest power on Earth since the Roman Empire," yet seems to be suffering foreign policy failures not only in Iraq and throughout the Middle East but in other regions of the world as well. What explains the apparent disparity between U.S. power on paper and the exercise of U.S. power in practice?
2. What is meant by "soft power"? How important is it in the successful conduct of foreign policy? Is U.S. soft power at an all-time low, or is the recent criticism of the United States, including by allies in Europe, merely an extension of long-term trends that can be traced at least as far back as "Rambo" Reagan and even well before that?
3. If you had to identify four key features of the contemporary, post–Cold War international system that constitutes the environment of American foreign policy today, what would they be? Would you say the current post–Cold War system is more dangerous than the Cold War system, or just more complex?
4. How would you characterize the distribution of power in the contemporary international system—unipolar, multipolar, or some other configuration? Is the main threat to U.S. security likely to come from "great powers" or weaker powers, especially "failed states" that are havens for terrorism?
5. How would you describe the nature of alignments in the contemporary international system—increasingly flexible and fluid or polarized? What "camps," if any, have replaced the "Western," "Marxist," and "Third World" blocs that dominated during the Cold War? What about the observation made by some that "we have gone from a Cold War configuration of one

West and two Europes to a current world of one Europe and two Wests"? What is meant by Samuel Huntington's "clash of civilizations" argument that the East-West axis of conflict during the Cold War has been replaced today by the "West vs. the rest" axis of conflict? Do you agree with Huntington? What accounts for the fact that, despite all the criticism of the United States as a "bully" and too-powerful hegemon, no formal counter-alliance has formed as yet against the United States, contrary to what classic balance of power theory would predict?

6. How would you characterize what issues are of greatest importance today on the foreign policy agendas of the United States and other countries? Do military security issues remain at the top of the agenda, or do they compete with a growing set of additional issues, including economic, energy, environmental, and other concerns? To the extent that national defense remains the primary concern of foreign policymakers, how has the security issue-area changed, in the wake of what is called "the long peace" and "the long war"? Discuss trends in interstate, intrastate, and extrastate violence.

7. How would you describe the nature of the actors in the contemporary international system? Are nonstate actors increasing in importance relative to nation-states? If so, what kinds of nonstate actors are impacting international affairs? IGOs? NGOs? MNCs? How so?

8. Would you characterize the dominant trend in today's world as integration (centralization) or disintegration (decentralization)? Are we witnessing the creation of "the global village" or, instead, "global villages"? Because of transnational forces such as globalization and subnational forces such as ethnic tensions, is national sovereignty at risk? Is it possible we are witnessing the beginning of the end of the nation-state as the primary form of human political organization? How will all this affect the United States in the future? Specifically, how does this affect U.S. foreign policy?

2

Thinking About Foreign Policy

Analyzing the Iraq War and Other Decisions

Politics is harder than physics.

—**Albert Einstein**

In this chapter, we will discuss a number of intellectual problems one encounters in the study of foreign policy. A framework for analyzing foreign policy will be presented and will then be applied to a particular case: the United States' decision to invade Iraq in March 2003.

WHAT IS FOREIGN POLICY?: DEFINITIONAL PROBLEMS

Trying to define **foreign policy** is reminiscent of the judge in the obscenity case who said, "I can't define it, but I know it when I see it." We all sort of know what is meant by the term. Or do we? One author writes that the analysis of foreign policy deals with "the intentions, statements and actions of an actor [normally, a state] . . . directed toward the external world and the response of other actors to these intentions, statements, and actions."[1] If the word "foreign" puts the emphasis on the international arena as the target of action, the word "policy" implies conscious, purposeful decision as a basis for action. In an international relations textbook, I have defined foreign policy as "a set of priorities and guides for action that underlies a country's behavior toward other states and includes both the basic goals a national government seeks to pursue in the world and the instruments used to achieve those goals."[2] Other texts offer similar definitions of foreign policy: "a guide to action taken beyond the boundaries of a state to further the goals of the state"[3] or "the strategies used by governments to guide their actions in the international arena [that

21

involves] . . . spelling out the objectives . . . and the general means by which they intend to pursue those objectives."[4]

All this begs the following question: Exactly how thoughtful is any country's foreign policy? Indeed, does any country, including the United States, actually have "a foreign policy," if that is defined as a carefully construed and faithfully implemented "guide" to action in world affairs? Six months after Ronald Reagan entered the White House, a newspaper ran the headline "Reagan Pressed to Spell Out Foreign Policy."[5] A year into his presidency, Reagan's successor, George H. W. Bush, also was being criticized for passively reacting to events rather than trying to shape them, until at least one headline proclaimed: "A Bolder Bush Foreign Policy Emerges."[6] Likewise, Bush's successor, Bill Clinton, was criticized for lack of foreign policy direction, with one magazine running a story entitled "The Clinton Foreign Policy: Is There a Doctrine in the House?"[7] I have already noted the lament of Charles Kupchan and others that, under the current administration of George W. Bush, the United States has "no grand strategy, no design to guide the ship of state." It is likely that the next American president will face similar criticism.

The above headlines conjure up images of foreign policy as being a single, overarching, deliberate "plan"—a master blueprint containing an explicit set of ends and means, into which all smaller decisions are fitted. References are commonly made to the "architects" of American (or, say, Russian or Iranian) policy. National leaders themselves like to reassure their citizenry that they have a plan, and they often accuse their counterparts in other states of having their own policy "designs." However, to what extent does this square with reality?

Among those who have questioned whether states have such blueprints in any meaningful sense is Henry Kissinger (at least before he was to become U.S. Secretary of State under President Richard Nixon):

> The most frequent question that is asked . . . by people who are concerned with international affairs and have not seen policy made is, 'What is American policy?' . . . [People] attempt to give a rationality and consistency to foreign policy which it simply does not have. I have found it next to impossible to convince Frenchmen that there is no such thing as an American foreign policy, and that a series of moves that have produced a certain result may not have been planned to produce that result. Foreigners looking at American policy have a tendency to assume that anything that happened was intended and that there is a deep, complicated purpose behind our actions. I wish this were true, but I don't believe that it is. . . . In fact, . . . this is probably the case with the Soviet Union also.[8]

Kissinger is overstating the case a bit. As will be discussed in Chapter 3, Franklin Roosevelt, for example, had what he considered a "Great Design" for the post–World War II period, in which the centerpiece was an active internationalist role for the United States. Later American presidents invoked the "containment doctrine," "détente," or "human rights" as guiding principles of their foreign policy during the Cold War. Searching for new catchwords or phrases to define American foreign policy in the post–Cold War era, George H. W. Bush spoke of "the new world order," and Bill Clinton spoke of "enlargement" of the number of free markets and democracies. These themes represented, at least to some extent, an attempt to give an overall rationale to U.S. foreign affairs. Indeed, every U.S. president has felt compelled, either in his inaugural address or in his first State of the Union address, to outline how the nation's foreign policy would be charted over the next four years. Similar pronouncements can be found in major addresses of leaders in other countries.

It is not that leaders make no attempt to develop a comprehensive framework for action. The thrust of Kissinger's remarks is that no matter how much a leadership tries to conceive and adhere to a single, overall foreign policy, it inevitably finds itself having to make decisions about more discrete matters—in the case of the United States, whether to support Russia's admission into the World Trade Organization, whether to sell more cluster bombs to Israel, whether to give territorial asylum to a dissident writer from China, as well as a host of other concerns. As Roger Hilsman has noted, "Very often policy is the sum of a congeries of separate or only vaguely related actions."[9]

Foreign policy perhaps is best thought of not as a single driving philosophy or game plan but, more realistically, as a series of hundreds of decisions that have to be made, which may or may not hold together in a coherent fashion. These myriad decisions confronting a national government can be categorized in a number of ways. One way to classify foreign policy decisions is according to **issue-area**—national security policy, economic policy, and so forth. Although national security issues traditionally have attracted the greatest attention from foreign policy analysts, increasingly economic, environmental, and other nondefense issues are competing for attention. Another typology is based more on the **situational setting** in which decisions are made rather than on the substantive content of the decisions. For example, some decisions are crisis as opposed to noncrisis decisions. Both the issue-area and the situational setting will heavily influence "who makes foreign policy decisions and how."[10]

Regarding the situational typology, at least three types of decisions can be identified. What could be called **macro-decisions** conform most closely to what is ordinarily implied by the term "policy." Some of the most important foreign policy decisions that a government must make relate to such matters as level of defense spending, level and type of foreign aid to be given or sought, arms control policy, and international trade policy. For a country such as the United States, with diverse global interests, macro-decisions also must be made on Middle East policy, Asian policy, Latin American policy, etc. More limited, but still fairly significant decisions might have to be made regarding, say, a reevaluation of relations with China or the terms of peaceful nuclear technology transfer to less developed countries. These can be labeled macro-decisions in the sense that they involve relatively large, general concerns and are meant to establish rough guidelines to be applied to specific circumstances as they arise. These decisions normally occur in a setting in which (1) the need to make a decision has been *anticipated* and is not in response to some sudden, surprise occurrence in the environment; (2) there is a relatively *lengthy time frame* in which to reach a decision; (3) the decision involves a *major*, if not grave, concern; and (4) a *large variety of domestic political actors* inside and outside the government can become involved in the decision-making process, although the decision may ultimately be made by top-level officials.

Many other foreign policy decisions, in contrast, can be labeled **micro-decisions**, which are more administrative in nature. The bulk of foreign policy decisions made by a government are of this type. "The American State Department on any one day receives about 2,300 cables from American diplomatic and consular officials abroad . . . requesting directions or seeking permission to make certain decisions in the field. But . . . the Secretary of State will read only . . . 2 percent of the total. The State Department also sends out approximately 3,000 cables daily; . . . of these, the Secretary of State may see only six, and the President will have only one or two of the most important communications referred to his office."[11] Micro-decisions may or may not involve the element of surprise and may or may not allow for lengthy deliberation. Such decisions by definition normally involve concerns that (1) are relatively *narrow in scope*, (2) are *low-threat* in seriousness, and (3) are handled at the *lower levels of the government bureaucracy*. An example might be the determination of seating arrangements at a diplomatic reception for a visiting dignitary. Although such decisions by themselves are unlikely to have significant consequences, taken together they can add up to important foreign policy developments. (For example, a minor diplomatic incident may be created by an errant choice of dining utensils, as happened when some "made in Taiwan" chopsticks turned up at a Carter White House dinner honoring officials from mainland China.)

One special category of decisions that has attracted the attention of many scholars involves crisis situations. **Crisis decisions** are made in situations normally characterized by (1) a *high degree of threat* and potential gravity; (2) some element of *surprise*, at least in regard to timing; (3) a *finite time interval* in which to reach a decision, or at least a felt sense of *urgency*; and (4) involvement of the *very highest level* of the foreign policy establishment in the decision process (often in a small group setting). Michael Brecher has defined a crisis as a situation entailing perceptions of "threat to basic values, finite time frame for response, and the likelihood of involvement in military hostilities."[12] Although a crisis tends to be associated with a short response time, some crises can drag on for a long time (such as the "Iranian hostage crisis" faced by the Carter administration in 1979–1980, which lasted 444 days). At a minimum, a crisis entails a sufficiently serious problem to command the intense, sustained attention of the top leadership. One such situation, the Cuban missile crisis, may well be the most studied single case of crisis decision-making in history.

Some argue that much of what passes for foreign policy is really crisis management, that is, responding to the latest events as they unfold. At times, multiple crises can occur simultaneously and compete for attention, as in the case of the bombing of the barracks of a U.S. Marine peacekeeping force in Lebanon and the American invasion of Grenada within the same week in 1983. However, it is a mistake to depict the foreign policy process as consisting of one round after another of crisis management. Foreign policymakers do not spend all their time lunging from one crisis to another any more than they do sitting at their desks pondering grand designs and stratagems.

In the foreign policy process, the various types of decisions—macro, micro, and crisis—blend together, often imperceptibly. Some decisions, such as the Kennedy administration's commitment of ten thousand American troops to Vietnam as advisory counterinsurgency personnel in 1961, can set in motion a plethora of smaller administrative decisions, breed more than one crisis, and even come to dominate a country's foreign policy agenda for more than a decade—beyond anyone's expectations or intentions.

HOW TO ANALYZE FOREIGN POLICY: ALTERNATIVE MODES OF INQUIRY

Regardless of whether one is interested in examining a country's broad foreign policy orientation and behavior patterns (internationalist versus isolationist tendencies) or in examining a specific foreign policy decision (the Kennedy administration's decision to impose a naval blockade around Cuba during the 1962 Cuban missile crisis), there are several possible types of analysis one might undertake. As Deborah Gerner states:

> Foreign policy analysis can be *descriptive*, establishing the facts regarding foreign policy decisions that are made. . . . Alternatively, by focusing on the external, societal and governmental roles and individual inputs affecting the foreign policy process, research efforts may attempt [to *explain*] *why* certain decisions and actions are taken. In contrast to these approaches, foreign policy *evaluation* [italics mine] considers the consequences of foreign policy actions and assesses whether these . . . were desirable and achieved.[13]

In other words, there are several different purposes that can be served by the study of foreign policy. Four are suggested by Gerner's statement. The first two purposes are **empirical** in nature: (1) *descriptive* analysis simply seeks to describe some behavior or occurrence and to give an accurate characterization of it (for example, does the United States tend to follow a unilateralist, go-it-alone policy, or is the U.S. policy better labeled multilateralist?); and (2) *explanatory* analysis seeks to go beyond mere description—beyond merely reporting a fact—and accounts for its existence, that is, establishes causal links between various determinants (variables) and behaviors or decisions (for example, to the extent the foreign policy of the George W. Bush administration can be called unilateralist, is it due to Bush's personal worldview or to domestic or international factors?). Two other types of analysis are **evaluative** in nature: (1) *normative* analysis entails making value judgments about foreign policy (was the U.S. bombing of civilians during the Kosovo war morally and ethically right?); and (2) *prescriptive* analysis involves foreign policy problem-solving and offers advice as to a future course of action (is U.S. Middle East policy flawed, and, if so, what other options might be recommended for consideration?). These four **modes of inquiry** are summarized in Figure 2.1.

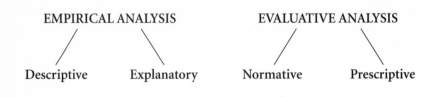

EMPIRICAL ANALYSIS   EVALUATIVE ANALYSIS

Descriptive   Explanatory   Normative   Prescriptive

Figure 2.1 Modes of Inquiry

Although these are distinct intellectual tasks aimed at very different analytical objectives, they are all somewhat interrelated and would seem to build on one another.
For example, a person presumably would not want to explain some reality before
having their basic facts straight; and that same person would not want to reach normative or prescriptive conclusions until having a deeper understanding of the problem or situation being critiqued. Many people engage in all these modes of analysis,
often all at once. There is a tendency to make a "mesh" of things. Most of us prefer to
concentrate on normative and prescriptive analysis more than on descriptive and explanatory analysis because debating the great moral issues of the day (determining
who the good guys and bad guys are) and solving the world's problems seem inherently more interesting than getting a firm handle on what is happening and why. Applying knowledge somehow seems more fun than acquiring it in the first place. For
the average person, normative and prescriptive analysis lends itself more easily to
discussion over a glass of beer after a hard day's work, although scholars and practitioners, too, at times have been known to mix up empirical and evaluative judgments. In this book, we will engage in all four modes of inquiry in the hope that the
reader will come away with a sharpened ability to analyze foreign policy problems
empirically and, ultimately, to evaluate or propose remedies for these problems,
especially as they relate to the United States.

DOING EMPIRICAL
ANALYSIS OF FOREIGN POLICY

Here, I am particularly interested in discussing the difficulties observers experience
in trying to explain why things happen as they do in international affairs. Arnold
Wolfers once noted that "as in all fields of human activity, decisions and actions in
the international arena can be understood, predicted, and manipulated only insofar
as the factors influencing the decision can be identified and isolated."[14] Admittedly,
this is easier said than done. In the case of the United States, John Ikenberry has remarked that its foreign policy "covers so much history and so many events that it
seems capable of sustaining many interpretations, even contradictory ones, at the
same time. Scholars are drawn to the study of foreign policy in efforts to develop

powerful and satisfying accounts of the forces that shape policy. Yet very little agreement can be found over what those forces are and how they operate. The student of foreign policy is left with an array of historical cases and lots of theories."[15] Such perplexity about the "forces" in which foreign policy is rooted has also been expressed about most other states as well. For example, Winston Churchill, as British prime minister during World War II, grappled with the same sorts of questions and offered his own answer concerning the behavior of the Soviet Union: "I cannot forecast to you the action of Russia. It is a riddle wrapped in a mystery inside an enigma; but perhaps there is a key. That key is Russian national interest."[16]

Notwithstanding the complexity of trying to unravel foreign policy behavior, we are obliged to try, as Wolfers argues above. Graham Allison, in his classic case study of the Cuban missile crisis—arguably "the most dangerous event in human history"[17]—provides an especially poignant reminder of why it is worthwhile subjecting foreign policy to careful investigation and reflection:

> For thirteen days of October 1962, there was a higher probability that more human lives would end suddenly than ever before in history. Had the worst occurred, the death of one hundred million Americans, over one hundred million Russians, and millions of Europeans as well would make previous natural calamities . . . appear insignificant. Given the probability of disaster—which President Kennedy estimated as "between one out of three and even"—our escape seems awesome. . . . That such consequences could follow from the choices and actions of national governments obliges students of government as well as participants in governance to think hard about these problems.[18]

In *Essence of Decision: Explaining the Cuban Missile Crisis*, Allison endeavors to explain a specific U.S. foreign policy action—a crisis decision—rather than try to explain American foreign policy as a whole during the Cold War. The facts of the case are generally agreed upon. Having discovered in October 1962 that the Soviet Union was installing offensive nuclear weapons on the island of Cuba, ninety miles from the U.S. mainland, the Kennedy administration decided during the course of thirteen days to enforce a naval blockade against Soviet ships that were sailing toward Cuba and carrying equipment that would complete the installation. The United States ultimately succeeded in forcing the Russian ships to turn back to the Soviet Union and to remove the missiles from Cuba. To quote then-Secretary of State Dean Rusk, "We're eyeball to eyeball and I think the other fellow just blinked."[19] Allison offers three different "explanatory models"—three different "cuts of reality"—that might account for U.S. foreign policy behavior during the crisis.

The first model that he uses, a **rational actor model**, is one that is based on the same national interest concept that Winston Churchill alluded to in explaining Russian behavior and that, in fact, is often relied on to explain most countries' foreign policy behaviors. Those attempting to understand foreign policy—practitioners, scholars, and laypersons alike—commonly view foreign policy as the work of a *unitary* actor, which is a national government that acts on behalf of a nation-state. Every

CARTOON 2.1 Foreign Policy and International Relations Made Simple: The billiard ball model. CREDIT: JOSH KORENBLAT

day we hear references in conversations and news reports that "the United States" or "Washington" (or "France" or "Paris") has decided something or done something in the international arena. These are not just convenient shorthand expressions but a reflection of a natural tendency to reify the nation-state, that is, to attribute human qualities to a collectivity. According to this conventional states-as-actors perspective, states can be thought of as **billiard balls**, colliding with one another and reacting to each other's moves like billiard balls on a pool table (see cartoon 2.1).[20] Put another way, states are viewed here as if they were monolithic "black boxes" cranking out foreign policy decisions based on rational calculations aimed at maximizing the national interest, with the observer not having to look beneath the surface at the internal dynamics of the policymaking process, whether it be the individual decision makers themselves or their domestic environment. It is presumed here that all states, no matter who their leaders are (Joseph Stalin, for example, or Winston Churchill), and no matter whether they are democratic or nondemocratic polities, tend to operate in accordance with the dictates of *Realpolitik*, each driven by similar impulses regarding the promotion of national security, power, and wealth.[21]

Applying the rational actor model to the "missiles of October" crisis, Allison notes:

> For example, on confronting the problem posed by the installation of strategic missiles in Cuba . . . [the] analyst frames the puzzle: Why did the Soviet Union decide to install missiles in Cuba? He then fixes the unit of analysis: governmental choice. Next, he focuses attention on . . . goals and objectives of the nation or government. And finally, he invokes certain patterns of inference: if the nation performed an action of this sort, it must have had a goal of this type. The analyst has "explained" this event when he can show how placing missiles in Cuba was a reasonable action, given Soviet strategic objectives.[22]

According to this model, the Kennedy administration, having (a) defined the situation as a high-threat problem posing major security risks to the United States, (b) specified the goal as the removal of Soviet missiles, (c) considered an exhaustive menu of possible means of response, ranging from diplomatic efforts through the United Nations to all-out use of military force, and (d) weighed the costs and benefits of each option, finally settled on the blockade decision as the one likely to maximize its own "strategic objectives." The rest, we are told, is history.

A good deal of international relations can be understood in these simple, parsimonious rational actor terms. However, clearly there are many other nonrational factors that also can affect foreign policy. As one author comments, "A natural assumption is that governments—including that of the United States—tailor their national security decisions to what is happening abroad or what they hope to achieve abroad. The truth is more complicated. The decisions and actions of governments result from the interplay among executive and legislative organizations, public and private interests, and, of course, personalities. This interplay becomes a determinant of foreign policy no less than events abroad."[23] We have already noted that the entire foreign policy establishment does not become activated every time there is a foreign policy decision to be made; depending on the issue-area and situation, certain persons rather than others will become involved.

In this vein, Allison suggests a second model—the **governmental politics model**—that treats foreign policy not as the deliberate response of a single-minded government to a strategic threat or opportunity outside its national borders but, instead, as the resultant of bargaining and compromise among different officials within the government who see the situation from competing bureaucratic and other perspectives. Allison points out that the members of ExCom, the small group of high-level advisors (Secretary of Defense Robert McNamara, Chairman of the Joint Chiefs Maxwell Taylor, Air Force General Curtis LeMay, CIA Director John McCone, and others) that President Kennedy convened to deal with the Cuban missile crisis, disagreed among themselves as to the gravity of the threat, as where one "stood" depended on where one "sat" in the bureaucracy and which "face" of the situation one saw. (Theodore Sorenson, one of Kennedy's closest advisors, is said to have warned, "We have to do something, since if we don't, the Republicans will murder us in November," referring to upcoming congressional elections.) Allison adds a third explanatory model, the **organizational process model**, which leads one to interpret the Cuban missile crisis decision as the outcome of various organizational procedures and routines that affected the collection and analysis of intelligence data and other aspects of the decision process.

In positing alternative explanations beyond the rational actor account of the Cuban missile crisis, Allison was identifying more subtle factors that are frequently overlooked, focusing our attention on flesh-and-blood human **decision makers** (possessing personality quirks, self-interest motivations, divergent perceptions, and other **idiosyncracies**) responding to stimuli not only from their **external environment** (threats and opportunities in the **international system**) but also from their **internal environment** (public opinion, electoral, interest group, and other **domestic political pressures**). These sets of variables, operating at different "levels of analysis," are depicted in Figure 2.2.

Among the first scholars to suggest that causation in international affairs could be understood in terms of **levels of analysis** was Kenneth Waltz, who in his 1959 *Man, the State, and War* argued that if one wished to explain why wars occur, one might examine world politics through three different "images": the individual (the personality and other characteristics of leaders), the state (political, economic, cultural, and other characteristics of the nation-state), and the state system (the balance of power and other characteristics of the international system).[24] Waltz, sounding very much like a "billiard ball," *Realpolitik* thinker, concluded that the *system level* provided the most important explanations of foreign policy behavior—including war decisions—since, in his judgment, it contained "constraints and imperatives to which all individuals and states, regardless of their uniqueness, must abide."[25]

In Chapter 1, I spent considerable time discussing the shape of the contemporary international system precisely because systemic characteristics are important. However, so are other sets of variables. Domestic-level and individual-level variables have tended to get overlooked, relative to international system–level variables, because the very definition of foreign policy steers us to the system level and, in part, because the former are rarely if ever mentioned by a government as the official explanation of a foreign policy decision. When was the last time you heard a leader say he or she made a particular foreign policy decision because "I wanted to get reelected" or because "I have an authoritarian personality"?

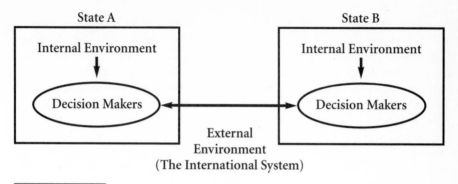

FIGURE 2.2 Foreign Policy and International Relations Made More Complicated: An alternative to the billiard ball model

Regarding *domestic-level* factors, one of the reasons Henry Kissinger said that foreign policy cannot be as neatly conceived and executed as one might wish is precisely because of the constraints imposed on decisionmakers by not only their external surroundings but also their domestic surroundings.[26] Noting the recent complaints about American bullying, Kissinger explains that "what is presented by foreign critics as America's quest for dominance is very frequently a response to domestic pressure groups," such as the Cuban lobby, Jewish lobby, textile industry lobby, or some other interest group.[27] Echoing Kissinger, Stanley Hoffmann has remarked, "I [do not] think that the French [as well as leaders of other states] have sufficiently understood the importance of domestic factors. If there is one country in which one cannot understand foreign policy without linking it to domestic politics, it is the United States."[28] As just one example, some observers went so far as to attribute the U.S. bombing of Afghanistan and Sudan in 1998, seemingly aimed at destroying al-Qaeda terrorist training camps, to a desire to improve the Clinton administration's poll ratings in the wake of the Monica Lewinsky scandal. The foreign policy of many other countries, as well, has been linked to internal pressures of the sort depicted in the 1997 movie *Wag the Dog*, where a leadership's unpopularity at home can lead it to manufacture a conflict against external scapegoats in the hope of producing a "rally around the flag" effect. The animosity many Middle East governments harbor toward Israel often is explained as a calculated attempt by shaky regimes to divert attention from their own failure to satisfy the political and economic longings of their populations.[29]

Although nondemocratic regimes need not worry about public opinion and other domestic political pressures quite as much as more open, democratic governments, internal factors always operate to some extent in foreign policymaking even in dictatorships. For example, at one point during the Cuban missile crisis, Soviet leader Nikita Khrushchev, anxiously awaiting President Kennedy's reaction to his latest proposal for defusing the crisis and wondering why there was a delay, is reported to have sighed, "I guess he [Kennedy] has his bureaucracy to contend with also."[30] One of the

most striking examples of **bureaucratic politics** in the Soviet Union was the competition between different subunits within the Kremlin's defense ministry in developing weapons systems. As one article noted, "New Soviet missiles seem to be born as
quadruplets. In the 1960s, they deployed the SS 7–8–9–11 missiles; the 1970s generation was the SS 16–17–18–19 missiles. In the 1980s, they deployed another generation of four missiles. Why always in fours? U.S. experts say that the organization
that designs Soviet missiles has four separate design bureaus, and that each is allowed
to design a new generation."[31] When, in 1990, Secretary of Defense Dick Cheney said
that "the United States believed that the Soviet Union was developing four new long-
range nuclear missiles," and he "expressed concern about the Soviet missile program"[32] to Soviet leaders, one wonders if he was aware that the Soviet program
possibly had less to do with deep geopolitical strategic designs against the United
States than with the more innocuous internal politics of Soviet national defense.
More recently, when President George W. Bush and Russian President Vladimir
Putin were asked if they could "say with certainty that your teams will act in the same
spirit" of cooperation that the two men seemed to exude, Bush's reply that "sometimes the intended [policy] doesn't necessarily get translated throughout the levels
of government [due to] bureaucratic intransigence" was echoed by Putin's words:
"Of course, there is always a bureaucratic threat."[33]

Just as one should not exaggerate the importance of systemic factors as sources of
foreign policy, domestic factors also should not be exaggerated. Both groups of structural determinants, along with the personal attributes of the decision makers themselves, are part of the puzzle of explaining foreign policy. At least one ExCom
participant in the Cuban missile crisis insisted that the group functioned "as fifteen individuals on our own, representing the President and not different departments."[34] A
vast literature has developed in the international relations field that has focused attention at the *individual level* of analysis, on such variables as personality traits, cognition,
group dynamics, and a host of other psychological phenomena.[35] Typical of this literature is the observation that Washington and Moscow "stumbled into a nuclear crisis"
in October of 1962 because policymakers in both countries "acted on the basis of perceptions deeply informed by their own historical perspectives and experiences, largely
oblivious to the fact that their counterparts' perspectives and experiences were radi-
cally different in important respects. By . . . assuming that others saw the world the
same way they did," they came close to a colossal miscalculation.[36]

Regarding individual-level variables, simplistic analysis should also be avoided. For
example, even though Adolph Hitler is often blamed for causing World War II, many
scholars argue that an excessively harsh peace treaty following World War I and the
subsequent economic depression in Germany would have produced a German desire
for revenge, no matter what leader had come to power in Berlin. The Cuban missile
crisis itself has produced some exaggerated accounts of the importance of individual
players, none greater than Attorney General Robert Kennedy's observation that if six
of the fourteen men in ExCom had been President of the United States, the world
would probably have blown up[37]—which, in paying tribute to his brother John's handling of the crisis, takes the "great man theory of history" to a new level. Although

PHOTO 2.1 President Kennedy Meeting with His Cabinet During the Cuban Missile Crisis in October 1962: How important are individuals in determining foreign policy? CREDIT: CORBIS

President Kennedy's personal qualities, including his "private ills"—the "crippling back pain" due to Addison's disease that required twice-a-day cortisone shots and no doubt afflicted him during the missile crisis, perhaps rendering his mental faculties less than 100 percent[38]—deserve to be part of the story of "the thirteen days," it is questionable whether the study of so-called biopolitics[39] offers more than secondary insights into U.S. foreign policy.

Although Figure 2.2 indicates that all foreign policy determinants boil down to a country's external environment (Level I) and internal environment (Level II), mediated by—seen through the eyes of—whatever individuals are involved in the decision-making process (Level III), many scholars have tried to offer still more elaborate explanatory schemes.[40] For example, James Rosenau has proposed a fivefold scheme that includes the following "inputs": systemic sources, societal sources, governmental sources, role sources, and idiosyncratic sources.[41] Rosenau applies his scheme to another foreign policy decision reached by the Kennedy administration: the Bay of Pigs decision in 1961 to train Cuban exiles for an invasion of Cuba aimed at overthrowing communist dictator Fidel Castro, which proved to be "a perfect failure."[42] It is worth quoting Rosenau at length for the rich series of questions he poses:

To what extent was [the decision to go ahead with the plan] a function of the idiosyncratic characteristics of John F. Kennedy . . . ? Were his youth, his commitments to action, his affiliation with the Democratic Party, his self-confidence, his close election victory—and so on through an endless list—relevant to the launching of the invasion and, if so, to what extent? Would any President have undertaken to oust the Castro regime upon assuming office in 1961? If so, how much potency should be attributed to such role-derived variables? Suppose everything else about the circumstances of April 1961 were unchanged except that Warren Harding or Richard Nixon occupied the White House; would the invasion have occurred? Or hold everything constant but the form of government. Stretch the imagination and conceive of the U.S. as having a [parliamentary] system of government with Kennedy as prime minister; would the action toward Cuba have been any different? Did legislative pressure derived from a decentralized policy-making system generate an impulse to "do something" about Castro, and, if so, to what extent did these governmental variables contribute to the external behavior? . . . Assume once more a presidential form of government. . . . Imagine the Cuban situation as arising in 1921, 1931, or 1951; would the America of the roaring twenties, the depression, or the McCarthy era have "permitted" . . . a refugee-mounted invasion? . . . Lastly, hold the idiosyncratic, role, governmental, and societal variables constant in the imagination, and posit Cuba as 9,000 rather than 90 miles off the Florida coast; would the invasion nevertheless have been launched?[43]

In short, the analyst must always be careful to consider a complex array of variables in order to arrive at a full account of why states and statesmen behave as they do, whether trying to explain a specific foreign policy decision, such as the Cuban missile crisis or Bay of Pigs case, or trying to understand a country's broader foreign policy behavior patterns, such as the American effort to contain the Soviet Union during the Cold War. One also needs to keep in mind the earlier distinctions we made between different modes of inquiry, since sloppy thinking can result from mixing up empirical analysis ("is" questions) with evaluative analysis ("ought" questions).

DOING EVALUATIVE ANALYSIS OF FOREIGN POLICY

Evaluative analysis engages the student of foreign policy in making normative and prescriptive judgments, that is, in examining whether some decision or behavior *ought* to have been undertaken, and whether some other foreign policy option(s) *ought* to have been pursued in its place or should be pursued in the future. It is one thing to ask: why did the United States blockade Cuba in 1962, or train Cuban exiles to invade Cuba in 1961? It is quite another to ask: *should* it have done so?

There are a number of criteria one might employ that can aid normative analysis of foreign policy and, in the process, help inform prescriptive recommendations as to alternative courses of action. Three, in particular, come to mind. First, was the decision/behavior **legal**, that is, was it compatible with international law? Second, was it **moral**, that is, was it consistent with basic canons of ethics relating to fairness, justice, and humanitarianism? Third, was it **smart**, that is, was it wise in terms of making practical sense in advancing national security and other national interests?

Applying these criteria to the Cuban missile crisis decision, was the blockade legal? Probably not, according to most international lawyers, since under the United Nations Charter (a treaty that the United States is a party to) one cannot engage in the use of armed force (which a naval blockade technically amounts to) unless one is acting in "self-defense" or "collective security" against an armed attack. This was something that neither Russia nor Cuba had committed. Was the decision moral? It was questionable, if only because the United States seemed to be operating with a double standard in that Washington was demanding that the Soviets remove their missiles ninety miles away from the American mainland, even though Washington, to the Soviets' consternation, had placed Jupiter missiles next door to the Soviet Union in Turkey. Was the decision smart? Although many consider the decision John Kennedy's finest hour as president, it could have turned out to be the ultimate disaster had Moscow not "blinked" first and Khrushchev not agreed to back down. As noted above, Kennedy himself estimated the odds of a possible nuclear war as "between one out of three and even." Secretary of Defense McNamara was among those who argued it was not worth going to the brink of war, since the Soviet missiles in Cuba did not measurably increase the threat that was already posed by Soviet intercontinental ballistic missiles (ICBMs) that could be fired from thousands of miles away. In McNamara's words, "A missile is a missile. It makes no great difference whether you are killed by a missile from the Soviet Union or Cuba."[44] The Cuban missile crisis reminds us that, no matter how sound a government's decision might seem, its wisdom ultimately depends on what reaction it elicits from the *other* side. One can rightly ask whether there were better options than the blockade that the Kennedy administration might have taken. One can ask similar questions about the Bay of Pigs decision, which is open to much more criticism, given the fact it was one of the worst "fiascoes" in U.S. foreign policy history.[45]

Recall that there is a tendency to make a mesh of things, at times blending statements about how countries behave with how they maybe should behave. Reflecting the cynicism harbored by many observers of world affairs, it is frequently said that "morality has no place in foreign policymaking." It is not always clear whether such statements mean morality *does not* play any role in foreign policy decisions or *should not* play any role in foreign policy decisions. Again, the first question is an empirical one: to what extent, if any, do ethical considerations, as opposed to cold, hard calculations of self-interest, influence foreign policy? The second is a normative and prescriptive question: to what extent, if any, should ethical decisions be allowed to enter the decision calculus?[46]

Regarding the first question, although ethical principles often are sacrificed to self-interests in the affairs of states, one can cite many examples in the case of the United States and other countries in which decision makers have taken action that on balance contributed little to national interests and may have even entailed considerable national sacrifice. For example, the decision by the United States to help its NATO allies with military support during the civil war in the former Yugoslavia during the 1990s in the name of "humanitarian intervention"—to end the slaughter of Muslims in Bosnia and later in Kosovo—seemed driven by purely selfless motives, even though at least one observer claimed it was done mainly to "provide American and NATO troops with an opportunity for target practice."[47] If one is prepared to read ulterior motives into every foreign policy action, then admittedly one is not likely to find many instances of genuine altruism. Earthquake and other international disaster relief efforts will be dismissed as world public relations gimmicks, the keeping of commitments and promises will be dismissed as crass ploys to maintain one's credibility, and so forth. So-called **constructivist** theorists maintain that there are some behaviors that states engage in, such as humanitarian intervention, which simply cannot be explained as rooted in material interests but owe instead to internalization of powerful *ideas* and *norms* similar to those that ended slavery and colonialism.[48]

Although moral pronouncements often can cloak self-serving decisions, there is evidence that even in crisis situations—when one would expect practical considerations to override all else—ethical concerns may be seriously weighed in the decision making process. One can question the morality of the Cuban missile crisis decision; but Irving Janis, among others, has noted that moral issues were at least given explicit attention by ExCom:

> During the Cuban missile crisis, members of the Executive Committee explicitly voiced their concerns about the morality of the policy alternatives they were considering. . . . For example, on the second day of the crisis, George Ball [Undersecretary of State] vigorously objected to the air-strike option, arguing that a surprise attack would violate the best traditions of the United States and would harm the moral standing of the nation. . . . Robert Kennedy continued the argument, calling attention to the large toll of innocent human lives that would result. . . . He emphasized this moral stance by stating that he was against acting as the Japanese had in 1941 by resorting to a "Pearl Harbor in reverse."[49]

Regarding the question of whether ethical considerations should be included in the decision calculus, it is true that any statesman who tries to act ethically in world affairs faces great difficulties. First, one cannot assume that actions taken on moral grounds will be appreciated by others as such, especially in a system with such sharp cultural differences as the international system. Secondly, one cannot assume that one country alone, by its example, can move others to act morally if they are not so inclined. It is easy to become a martyr to morality if, say, you withhold arms exports or other goods from countries engaged in human rights violations, only to see your companies lose business to firms in other states whose governments are not so queasy about such transactions. Still, doing "the right thing" need not damage one's interests and, indeed, at times can benefit a country. This applies not only to acting in an ethical fashion but also obeying rules of international law since violating these may undermine certain legal norms that a country may later need to rely on and wish to invoke.[50] It could be argued that the United States, with more embassies, corporations, and global presence than any other actor, has the greatest single stake in forging a world order based on the rule of law.

Perhaps nothing illustrates better the tendency to confuse empirical and evaluative analysis than the age-old debate involving the "realist" and "idealist" schools of international relations.[51] The **realist** (*Realpolitik*) school is closely associated with the rational actor model, insofar as it treats world politics as a game played by sovereign nation-states competing in an anarchic international system, without any central authority to provide order, and hence concerned above all else with their national security. Realists, then, tend to see world politics as the struggle for power and pursuit of self-interest, characterized mostly by interstate conflict. The **idealist** school (often called the **liberal** school), in contrast, tends to focus attention on legal-formal aspects of international relations, such as international law and international organization, and on moral concerns such as democratization and human rights. Liberals contend that realists underestimate the potential for human progress and interstate cooperation through states "pooling" their sovereignty, based on mutual interests, and engaging in global institution-building, creation of universal norms, and the development of "regimes" governing everything from regulation of transnational air traffic and postal flows to nuclear weapons proliferation.

Realism and idealism both purport to offer an empirical theory explaining how the world actually works, including what drives U.S. foreign policy. As one commentator notes, "in trying to isolate basic motivations in the history of American foreign policy, historians and political scientists [have] argued over whether policy historically could be explained best through . . . idealism or realism."[52] However, realist and idealist analyses of American foreign policy often have been more evaluative than empirical in nature; that is, they have admonished policymakers for *not* acting in accordance with what reality would dictate, with failing to conform to their predictive models! Realists complain about U.S. foreign policy being too moralistic and in need of firmer anchoring in realist principles,[53] while idealists complain about it being too self-centered and in need of liberal rethinking.[54] In other words, realists and idealists often are interested more in how countries such as the United States *should* behave than in how they actually behave, although their prescriptions claim to be based on the laws of politics deduced from the evolving science of international relations. Realists, believing that the world is something of a jungle in which institutions such as the United Nations "don't matter"[55] and foreign policymakers are foolhardy to get too hung up on matters of law and morality, tend to evaluate foreign policy decisions mostly in terms of whether they are smart. Idealists tend to be more willing to weigh legal and moral issues. It is not always clear which hat, the empirical or the evaluative one, the analyst is wearing.

As Robert Osgood has noted, not only have realism and idealism often blended in shaping American foreign policy, but there are good reasons to want to include both points of view in formulating policy. In discussing "the expediency of idealism," he comments: "A true realist must recognize that ideals and self-interest are so closely interdependent that, even on grounds of national expediency, there are cogent arguments for maintaining the vitality of American idealism." Calling to mind the concept of "soft power," he observes that "ideals are as much an instrument of national power as the weapons of war. All manifestations of national power . . . operate by influencing the thoughts and actions of human beings, whether by frightening them or by converting them. . . . The strength of America's moral [and, one could add, law-abiding] reputation are as vital a factor in the power equation as planes, ships, and tanks."[56]

A fundamental problem confronting policymakers is that it is often hard to know whether realist or idealist tenets will produce better results in a given situation. Idealism, if carried too far, can lead to either naïve sentimentality (for example, British prime minister Neville Chamberlain's noble but futile efforts to "talk" and make concessions to Hitler at Munich in 1938 in a desperate attempt to avert war, which only emboldened Nazi Germany to invade Poland a year later, triggering World War II) or reckless, messianic crusades against evil (for example, what some see as George W. Bush's campaign to impose democracy in the Middle East). Realism, if carried too far, not only can leave one without any moral compass but also—should excessive emphasis be put on stick (tough) rather than carrot (accommodative) approaches to interstate bargaining—can lead to missed opportunities for improved cooperation and peaceful conflict resolution (for example, the loud saber-rattling among the European powers that accompanied the assassination of Archduke Ferdinand of Austria in 1914, precipitating World War I, "the war nobody wanted"[57]). Monday morning quarterbacking (second-guessing) is a favorite pastime of foreign policy critics who have the benefit of 20–20 hindsight. This does not mean that foreign policymakers should not be held up to scrutiny; it only means that in doing so, one must remember that, just as trying to explain and understand foreign policy behavior involves great complexity, so, too, are foreign policymakers faced with complex choices when it comes to deciding on a course of action.

A CASE STUDY OF THE US
DECISION TO INVADE IRAQ IN 2003

In this chapter I have offered a framework for thinking about foreign policy that contains (1) an *empirical* component, namely describing and, more importantly, explaining foreign policy behavior by examining "source" variables found at three levels of analysis, including the international system (external environment), the nation-state (internal environment), and the individual (decision-maker) level; and (2) an *evaluative* component, namely engaging in normative analysis by asking if the behavior meets certain criteria (for example, whether it is moral, legal, and smart), and prescriptive analysis by considering alternative policy options. Let us apply this analytical framework to the U.S. decision to invade Iraq in 2003. The purpose of this exercise is to help the student of foreign policy develop the habit of thinking about foreign policymaking—American or otherwise—in a more systematic, sophisticated, and thoughtful manner.

The Facts of the Case

As noted at the outset of this book, on March 20, 2003, the United States invaded Iraq, initiating a "shock and awe" aerial bombardment campaign, accompanied by the dispatch of more than one hundred thousand ground troops (assisted by one British division). As one writer described the war effort:

> On April 9, 2003, one year after the larger-than-life statue of Saddam Hussein was erected in Baghdad's Firdos Square to mark the dictator's sixty-fifth birthday, it was pulled down by exuberant Iraqis with the help of U.S. marines and an armored recovery vehicle. Five days later, the Pentagon announced the end to major combat operations, which had commenced just one month before. Saddam Hussein's whereabouts were unknown, but his tyranny had been overthrown, and the ease with which this had been accomplished belied all but the most optimistic combat scenarios banded about before the war. No weapons of mass destruction had been used on the battlefield; there was no widespread torching of Iraq's oil wells; the American and British infantry had not become bogged down in bloody urban combat; no campaign of terrorist strikes against Western targets had materialized; and the Arab street had not risen up to overthrow friendly [pro-Western] regimes in the Middle East. By the time President George W. Bush made his triumphant . . . appearance aboard the USS *Abraham Lincoln* on May 1 to declare victory, coalition forces had suffered fewer than two hundred combat fatalities [139 American and 33 British deaths] and Iraqi casualties (military and civilian) . . . seem to have been lower than many feared. In the aggregate, the war itself had been relatively painless by historical standards.[58]

The same writer notes the problems that were to be experienced in the "postwar" phase of Operation Iraqi Freedom:

> All was not well, however. At the United Nations, the United States and Britain had shown a willingness to embark on a course of action in glaring opposition to the wishes of the majority on the Security Council. American pre-war and wartime diplomacy had ruffled the feathers of long-time allies in Western Europe and set off a wave of anti-Americanism there. . . . In Baghdad, as the many icons of Saddam came crashing down, so too did law and order. . . . The capital descended into a state of chaos, quickly wearing out the welcome that had greeted Baghdad's liberators. Few expected postwar stabilization and reconstruction to be easy, but reality still had a way of dissipating much of the euphoria accompanying the military victory. By mid-summer, occupation forces were coming under attack by guerrilla bands of Ba'ath loyalists, foreign jihadists [and others] . . . and had suffered as many casualties since the fall of Baghdad as before it.[59]

By 2007, despite Saddam Hussein's capture and execution and the establishment of a freely elected Iraqi government under a new constitution, the situation had deteriorated further. Joined by troops from several other nations (what President Bush called "the coalition of the willing"), the United States was attempting to deal with a situation that appeared to be spiraling out of control. Iraq was on the brink of civil war, bitterly divided along ethnic and sectarian lines between its Shiite population predominating in the southern part of the country, the Kurds in the north, and the Sunnis in the "Sunni Triangle" around Baghdad and the midsection of the country (the latter being the group that Saddam's Baathist Party had drawn its strength from and that had dominated the Shiites and Kurds under Saddam's rule). Thousands of Iraqis were being killed monthly in internecine violence. With more than 3,500 American combat fatalities in the postwar period, the Iraq War was drawing comparisons with the Vietnam War "quagmire" several decades earlier. On the domestic front, the Iraq War was becoming increasingly unpopular with the American public, as President Bush's approval ratings plummeted to new lows.

In order to understand the decision by the Bush administration to initiate the Second Persian Gulf War, it is necessary to provide some brief historical background on the First Persian Gulf War. In the latter case, Iraq under Saddam Hussein had invaded neighboring Kuwait in August 1990, attempting to annex that country, based on a historical claim that Kuwait had once been part of Iraqi territory before achieving its independence. Had Hussein succeeded in his conquest, he would have been in control of more than 10 percent of the world's oil supply and would possibly have been positioned to threaten Saudi Arabia, which had the most oil reserves in the world.

President George H. W. Bush, the father of George W., was able to convince the United Nations Security Council to pass Resolution 678 in November 1990, authorizing UN member states to "use all necessary means" to end Iraq's aggression and restore Kuwait's sovereignty. The resolution was passed in accordance with Chapter VII of the UN Charter, which permits the use of armed force by member states as part of a "collective security" operation to punish aggression. (Among the five permanent members of the Security Council having veto power under the UN Charter, the United States, Britain, France, and Russia all supported the resolution, with China agreeing to abstain rather than use its veto.) Once the January 15, 1991, deadline passed without Iraqi withdrawal from Kuwait, a U.S.-led force of more than five hundred thousand troops (Operation Desert Storm), composed of contingents from many countries including several Arab states, launched a six-week offensive that terminated Iraq's occupation. The near-universal coalition had succeeded in punishing blatant aggression in a rare show of collective security as envisioned by the UN's founders, although, since "regime change" in Iraq had never been the goal of Desert Storm, Saddam was allowed to remain in power.

UN Security Council Resolution 687 contained the terms of the cease-fire to which Saddam agreed. Iraq was expected to disclose and eliminate any weapons of mass destruction (WMD) capabilities it possessed (destroying any chemical, biological, or nuclear weapons stocks as well as development facilities), renounce any future WMD development, and allow UN inspectors into Iraq to monitor chemical and other plants for purposes of verifying compliance. (It was assumed that Iraq had chemical weapons since Saddam had used them previously against Iran in the Iraq-Iran War of

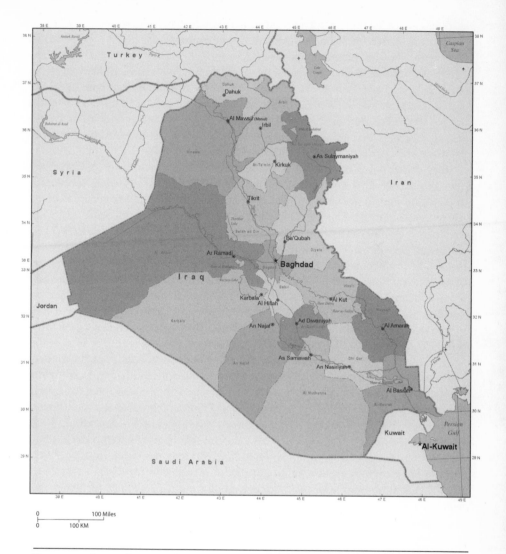

FIGURE 2.3 Iraq and Its Neighbors

the 1980s and on other occasions as well, and it was suspected Iraq also had active biological and nuclear weapons programs.) In addition, under Resolution 687, economic sanctions that had been instituted following Iraq's attack on Kuwait were to be continued until Iraqi disarmament was completed. In order to minimize harm to Iraqi civilians, the economic sanctions were modified to allow Iraq to sell limited amounts of oil so that medicines, food, and other essentials could be purchased. (The latter was expanded into an "oil for food" program, which permitted member states to import Iraqi petroleum, with payments placed in escrow under supervision of a UN committee that would dispense the monies for humanitarian relief.) Finally, another resolution, Resolution 688, demanded that Saddam end "repression of the Iraqi civilian population," particularly the Kurds in the north, who had attempted to revolt against Saddam's rule in the wake of his defeat in Kuwait only to be crushed by Iraqi troops. The United States and Britain interpreted Resolution 688 to allow them to create a "no-fly zone" that prohibited Iraqi planes from flying over Kurdish villages above the thirty-sixth parallel.

More than a dozen other UN Security Council resolutions were passed over the next decade ordering Iraq to comply with various UN demands. Saddam proceeded to play a cat-and-mouse game, ignoring or at best half-heartedly honoring his UN obligations, especially with regard to the team of UN inspectors (UNSCOM), who were not given full, unfettered access to facilities suspected of housing WMD research and development programs. By 1998, UNSCOM had become so frustrated by the lack of Iraqi cooperation that it left the country, declaring to the UN Security Council that it was unable to perform its mandate and unable to determine whether or not Saddam had destroyed all WMD stocks and facilities. The Clinton administration became increasingly impatient with Saddam and considered a number of options ranging from military strikes to the funding of insurgents, but never fully committed to regime change, despite congressional passage of the Iraq Liberation Act in 1998 (signed by Clinton) that stated: "It should be the policy of the United States to support efforts to remove the regime headed by Saddam Hussein from power in Iraq and to promote the emergence of a democratic government to replace that regime."[60] According to one advisor in the Clinton White House, the Clinton policy was "whack-a-mole" (after an old penny-arcade game): "Saddam would stick his head up, and we'd whack him."[61] As one example of the limited, intermittent punishments the Clinton administration inflicted on Iraq, the White House ordered a cruise-missile attack against the headquarters of Saddam's intelligence service in Baghdad after the Iraqi leader was discovered plotting to assassinate former President Bush in 1993 during his visit to Kuwait. Such actions did little to force Saddam to alter his behavior as he continued to display contempt for the UN, at least partly because several Security Council members themselves were tiring of enforcing the economic sanctions that were hurting Iraq's people and were interfering with their own business dealings with Iraq.

Such was the situation George W. Bush faced when he arrived in Washington after the 2000 presidential election. At first, in keeping with his campaign theme of not wanting the United States to get overextended in taking on too many "nation-building" commitments in the Middle East, the Balkans, or elsewhere, Bush sought simply to pressure Security Council members to continue the sanctions effort. (During the campaign, Bush's running mate, Dick Cheney, appearing on NBC's *Meet the Press*, had implied that he and Bush did not seek to overthrow Saddam since the United States should not act as though "we were an imperialist power, willy-nilly moving into capitals in that part of the world, taking down governments."[62]) However, in the White House "every day news would arrive of another violation of the UN sanctions—civilian planes from Arab nations making direct flights into Baghdad, brazen exports of oil and imports of prohibited goods."[63] Pressure was building to "do something."

The "Eureka moment"[64] came on September 11, 2001, when the twin towers of the World Trade Center in New York City were destroyed along with some three thousand lives, as two planes flown by al-Qaeda terrorists crashed into the buildings, followed shortly thereafter by another plane crashing into the Pentagon near Washington, DC. One month after 9/11, the United States launched an attack on Afghanistan, whose Taliban government had been harboring Osama bin Laden, the head of al-Qaeda, and proceeded to eliminate that regime.[65] "In November 2001, as alliance soldiers combed through al-Qaeda safe houses in Afghanistan, computer records revealed that Osama bin Laden's network had been trying to acquire WMDs."[66] This, combined with a false alarm that al-Qaeda had smuggled a ten-kiloton nuclear bomb into New York City in October,[67] along with unexplained anthrax scares reported in Washington that fall, contributed to the Bush administration feeling a heightened need for regime change in Iraq as well, not because of any direct link of Saddam to the 9/11 attacks, but because of Saddam's suspected WMD programs and his connections with terrorist groups in the Middle East (he was reputed to have been paying the families of Islamic Jihad suicide bombers $25,000 each for attacks on Israeli civilians). In his State of the Union speech in January 2002, the President told Americans that Iraq (along with Iran and North Korea) was a member of "the axis of evil, arming to threaten the peace of the world. By seeking weapons of mass destruction, these regimes pose a grave and growing danger. They could provide these arms to terrorists. . . . I will not wait on events while dangers gather." Two months later, Bush is reported to have told National Security Advisor Condoleezza Rice "F___ Saddam. We're taking him out."[68]

Throughout 2002, the Bush administration attempted to make a last-ditch effort to forge a common front with other Security Council members in forcing Saddam to comply with UN resolutions or face military action; but only the United States, supported by the British, had the stomach for war. To the United States, the UN had its head in the sand in allowing Iraq to evade its obligations with impunity; to many UN members, the United States was far too trigger-happy and unwilling to allow diplomacy to runs its course, with Saddam being "boxed in" and "contained" by the international community, even if the threat was not entirely removed. In October 2002, the U.S. Congress passed a joint resolution giving the president authorization to use military force against Iraq should he choose to do so. In November, Washington was able to get the Security Council to vote unanimously in favor of a somewhat ambiguously worded Resolution 1441, giving Saddam a "final opportunity" to allow the inspectors back in to do their job and demanding he submit within thirty days "an accurate, full, and complete declaration" of his weapons programs, warning of "serious consequences" if he failed to comply. When Saddam continued to obstruct full cooperation and compliance, the United States tried at the eleventh-hour to get another Security Council resolution passed explicitly authorizing the use of armed force against Iraq, but failed to garner the necessary approval from France, Russia, and China, who all said they would veto the proposal.

On March 16, 2003, Vice President Cheney, appearing again on *Meet the Press*, said, "I think we are still in the final stages of diplomacy, obviously. . . . But there's no question we're close to the end, if you will, of diplomatic efforts. And, clearly, the president is going to have to make a very, very difficult and important decision here in the next few days." The next day, the United States issued an ultimatum: "Saddam Hussein and his sons must leave Iraq within 48 hours. Their refusal to do so will result in military conflict, commenced at a time of our choosing." On March 20, President Bush ultimately decided to pull the trigger and invaded Iraq.

Why Did the United States Invade Iraq?: An Empirical Analysis

Establishing a factually accurate, descriptive account of an event is part of empirical analysis. The preceding was a fairly conventional narrative of *what* happened. The question remains: *why* did it happen? A first-cut explanation, focusing on the *system level* and a rational actor, billiard-ball set of factors, goes something like this: "Three significant features make this war one of the most remarkable events in international relations. First, this is perhaps history's most unequal war, fought between the world's militarily most powerful state and a weak, militarily easily vulnerable and economically collapsing Arab state. Second, the administration justified the war on the grounds of a new specter of threats originating from Iraq's alleged programs of weapons of mass destruction (WMD). . . . Third [was] the Iraqi leader Saddam Hussein's alleged links to terrorist organizations . . . which [was] seen as a major threat to American interests worldwide."[69] In other words, the United States invaded Iraq because it *could*—"because it was easy,"[70] or at least it looked easy—and because there seemed compelling national interests at stake.

Regarding the latter, at a public rally in Cincinnati in October 2002, Bush articulated the core rationale that "we know that Iraq is continuing to finance terror and give assistance to groups that use terrorism to undermine Middle East peace" and "Iraq's weapons of mass destruction are controlled by a murderous tyrant who has already used chemical weapons to kill thousands of people."[71] That same month, in its National Intelligence Estimate, the CIA concluded that "Iraq probably would not be able to make a [nuclear] weapon until 2007 to 2009," but "if Baghdad acquires sufficient fissile material from abroad it could make a nuclear weapon within several months to a year."[72] As then National Security Advisor Condoleezza Rice remarked: "The problem here is that there will always be some uncertainty about how quickly he can acquire nuclear weapons. But we don't want the smoking gun to be a mushroom cloud."[73] A related goal was the hope that the overthrow of Saddam would help "drain the swamp," that is, change the landscape of the Middle East by producing the first Arab, Islamic democracy in the region that could serve as an alternative model to the dictatorial regimes under which terrorism had taken root. Although never clearly stated, there was also the ongoing concern about oil, and a friendlier regime in Iraq would likely help U.S. energy security. If "from the American point of view, the 1991 Gulf conflict [following Saddam's invasion of Kuwait] was, at its heart, a war to defend Saudi oil" from "a reckless, ruthless dictator,"[74] somewhat similar logic seemed to obtain in 2003.

The Pentagon's formally stated objectives included the following: "(1) a stable Iraq, with its territorial integrity intact and a government that renounces WMD development and use and no longer supports terrorism or threatens its neighbors; (2) success in Iraq leveraged to convince or compel other countries to cease support to terrorists and to deny them access to WMDs; (3) destabilize and overthrow the Iraqi regime and provide support to a new, broad-based government; (4) destroy Iraqi WMD capability and infrastructure; (5) protect allies and supporters from Iraqi threats and attacks; and (6) destroy terrorist networks in Iraq."[75]

Of course, the official explanation, couched as a rational calculation of costs and benefits in response to a threat in America's external environment, does not necessarily tell the full story. It is not that the Bush administration consciously lied and deceived the American public and the world into thinking there were WMDs in Iraq so that it could justify a regime change. Although many critics hold that view, given the failure to uncover such weapons in the postwar period, most evidence indicates there was genuine belief and concern in Washington that Saddam posed a threat. More to the point, however, there were other, more subtle, complex factors operating that might have added to the equation of going to war.

Some of these factors operated at the *nation-state level* of analysis, including the role of such *domestic political forces* as interest groups and public opinion. For example, some scholars argue that the "Jewish lobby" in the United States, whose clout has been credited with tilting America's Middle East foreign policy toward Israel over several decades, had been pressuring the administration to take a harder line against Iraq's support for anti-Israel terrorists long before 9/11.[76] Hardly anyone would suggest that the Jewish lobby alone dictated the war decision, but those pressures in combination with other factors may have been leading the United States down a path toward war, with 9/11 providing the spark and the excuse—the "divine surprise"[77]— needed to mobilize the public in support of the war. It is often said that public opinion in a country like the United States has a "dike and dam" effect on foreign policy; that is, the public tends to give leaders relatively wide decision latitude on foreign affairs, but at the same time sets parameters that constrain policy to some extent. Stanley Hoffmann writes that "the attitude of the American leaders [in March 2003] can be explained to a large extent by the support of public opinion. After September 11, there was a rebirth of a wounded and indignant patriotism, a rallying behind the president."[78] David Kinsella likewise notes that "the political climate had changed so drastically" after 9/11 "that a new set of military options for dealing with Saddam Hussein now seemed viable."[79] It was not so much a case of an unpopular president inventing a crisis to pump up his poll numbers as his using a crisis to facilitate the pursuit of certain goals felt to be of critical importance.

As significant as systemic and nation-state level variables were to driving the war decision, any explanation would be incomplete without taking into account *individual-level* factors. As noted earlier, "under certain circumstances, individual characteristics of major international figures can have important impacts on policy outcomes," and "crises and war are perhaps the most prominent of these circumstances."[80] At the most personal level, George W. Bush has been accused of going to war out of revenge against Saddam for plotting the assassination of his father. Although it is almost impossible to establish any definitive cause-effect relationship here, one would not be surprised to learn that the son had a visceral hatred for his father's nemesis, which might have contributed to his anxiousness in taking Saddam down. Still, to the extent that idiosyncratic variables played a role in the war decision, deeper personality traits might have had greater impact than a simple desire for family vengeance. In addition to domestic political factors noted above, Hoffmann discusses the younger Bush's personal qualities, observing that "there is a side to Bush that is direct and amiable," but "Bush is more than a little devious and often vindictive. . . . I would say that deep down he was determined to overthrow Saddam."[81] Much has been made of how Bush's insular background and deep-seated religious beliefs may have contributed to his unwavering, uncompromising stance, along with exaggerated optimism, toward the Iraq war and related issues. Comparing Bush with others around him, one observer notes: "With his strong religious faith, President Bush has a more upbeat, soul-saving Christian take on life than his somewhat Hobbesian vice president. Bush had something like a conversion experience after 9/11; he became a war leader with a providential sense of duty and destiny. . . . Father and son have very different worldviews and experiences. Bush Senior, a former ambassador to the United Nations and China and CIA director . . . is perfectly comfortable with foreign heads of state. Bush Junior, far less worldly, is much more a creature of Midland."[82]

If personal psychological dispositions, life experiences, belief systems, and the like shape foreign policy decisions, then what about the other individual players who made up Bush's version of ExCom, who were part of his "war council"?[83] About Vice President Cheney and his Hobbesian worldview, one commentator, delving into Cheney's personal reading habits, found that in the fall of 2002, Cheney was reading Victor Davis Hanson's book *An Autumn of War*, which suggested that "war is the natural state of mankind" and "great leaders face evil and deal with it," a viewpoint that Cheney said reflected his own philosophy. (Interestingly, John F. Kennedy had reportedly been reading on the eve of the Cuban missile crisis Barbara Tuchman's book *The Guns of August*, an account of how highly jingoistic leaders had stumbled into World War I, something Kennedy apparently was bent on avoiding in October 1962; if Kennedy's reading habits had the effect of moderating his hawkish tendencies, Cheney's seemed to have had the opposite effect, although, again, the analyst must be careful not to read too much into a leader's literary tastes!) Hanson "was impressed with Cheney's 'tragic view of mankind,' akin to the ancient Greeks. Cheney may have had more in common with the Lone Ranger than Pericles. 'It's more Wyoming, the code of the West,' said a top aide. . . . [The President and Vice-President, with their John Wayne dead-or-alive pronouncements] do sound like a couple sheriffs, telling the bad guys they have 10 minutes to come out of the bar or 'we're coming in to get you.'"[84] Like Bush, Cheney was "someone whose view of the need to get rid of Saddam Hussein was transformed by September 11."[85]

Secretary of Defense Donald Rumsfeld (the youngest DOD secretary, under President Ford in the mid–1970s, and the oldest, under President George W. Bush in the 2000s, serving with Cheney in both administrations), according to one observer, saw the war on terror as "an opportunity to reform the slow-moving, risk-averse Pentagon bureaucracy. A former fighter pilot and a restless, probing questioner, Rumsfeld had grown frustrated in his first few months in office trying to 'transform' the military to fight the wars of the 21st century. But a real war gave him the urgency he needed to make the military 'lean forward,' in Rumsfeld's favorite phrase. . . . Rumsfeld strongly believed that the United States was seen around the world as a paper tiger, a weak giant that couldn't take a punch."[86] Rumsfeld's worldview was reinforced by Deputy Secretary of Defense Paul Wolfowitz, a leading "neoconservative" thinker, who combined pessimism (realism) and optimism (idealism) in seeing the world as a dangerous place at the same time that it was one that could be transformed through American will to use its military might.

In contrast, Secretary of State Colin Powell "was one voice for restraint. Powell, a Vietnam veteran, had been a reluctant warrior as chairman of the Joint Chiefs, initially resistant to the invasion of Kuwait, in 1991, and to any engagement by military forces in the Balkans. . . . There was considerable disagreement within the administration over what might be accomplished at the United Nations. Powell apparently believed that Saddam could be forced to disarm without war—that a firm stand by the United Nations, backed by the threat of U.S. military power, could compel Saddam to back down and give up his WMDs."[87] At least early on, Powell felt that "though [the Iraqis] may be pursuing weapons of mass destruction, it is not clear how successful they have been. We ought to declare this a success. We have kept him contained, kept him in a box."[88]

Another member of the Bush "war council" was National Security Advisor Condoleezza Rice (who later became Secretary of State after Powell resigned). A former professor of political science at Stanford University and an expert on the Soviet Union during the Cold War, Dr. Rice offered a partial test of the hypothesis that many feminist scholars have posited: gender matters in foreign policymaking and, in particular, since women by virtue of their physiological makeup (lacking male testosterone and other such physical traits) and socialization (imbued with maternalistic, nurturing dispositions) tend to be less "aggressive" and "war-prone" than men, the presence of more females in high places in government will reduce the incidence of war. At least one feminist scholar was heard to remark after the American invasion of Afghanistan that "if George W. Bush had had more women on his war council," it would have been a "peace council."[89] Although we should be careful not to generalize from the behavior of the one woman in Bush's inner circle, she hardly lends support to the latter proposition, since she was by most accounts one of the loudest voices in support of a hard-line policy toward Iraq.[90] Whether male leaders, in fact, are inherently more aggressive than their female counterparts is an empirical question that could be subject to testing if more women were to assume leadership positions; the overall historical evidence on the role of women in world politics thus far has been mixed, suggesting that gender is just one variable among many that affects foreign policy.

The focus on the individual level of analysis risks attaching excessive importance to great men or great women as movers of history. As yet another example of perhaps overattention to idiosyncratic factors, one scholar states that "the British choice in Iraq [in joining the U.S. invasion] has been characterized as 'Tony Blair's War,' with many believing that the personality and leadership style of the prime minister played a crucial part in determining British participation. . . . I show how Blair's personality and leadership style did indeed shape both the process and the outcome of British foreign policy toward Iraq."[91] A British cabinet minister went so far as to say that, given the unpopularity of the war in Britain, "had anyone else been leader, we would not have fought alongside Bush."[92] Other scholars have noted how Blair's "operational code"—the lens through which he perceived world events—was colored in a way that led him to be more cooperative toward democracies than nondemocracies but not as "cooperative across regime-types" as a Bill Clinton.[93] Blair also was thought to have had a deep sense of religiosity not unlike Bush.[94] All of this may well have explained "why exactly did the British prime minister risk his political life for a plan of action against Iraq that was designed in Washington with American needs primarily in mind."[95] However, it may also have had to do with the "special Atlantic relationship" between the United States and the United Kingdom that had existed for decades, buttressed by the same strategic concerns about Saddam's WMDs that haunted the Bush administration, reflected in Blair's House of Commons speech two days before the Iraq invasion, when he said "based on all available evidence, the strong presumption is that about 10,000 liters of anthrax was not destroyed and may still exist."[96]

Irving Janis's theory of **groupthink** suggests still another explanation that helps to account for how both Bush and Blair, along with many members of their foreign policy team, seemingly misinterpreted the WMD intelligence in a way that exaggerated the size of Saddam's arsenal. Janis argued that in crisis situations in which small groups engage in foreign policymaking under great stress, the individual members of the group frequently lose their critical thinking capacities and end up distorting reality as they succumb to group conformity pressures, a tendency to defer to the group leader and act the way they think the leader wants, stereotypical images of the enemy, and other such impulses.[97] There is some evidence that groupthink was operating in the lead-up to the Iraq war. As Senator Pat Roberts, a member of the U.S. Senate Intelligence Committee responsible for investigating the handling of WMD intelligence, commented: "'Groupthink' caused the [intelligence] community to interpret ambiguous evidence . . . as conclusive."[98] Senate committee members agreed that "groupthink led to incorrect intelligence about Iraq's supposed chemical, biological, and nuclear weapons and pushed aside the doubts of dissenting analysts, an attitude that also permeated several big foreign intelligence services."[99] There is some debate over how much pressure the CIA felt to skew the intelligence in the direction they assumed President Bush wanted, but even Secretary Rumsfeld seemed to tacitly acknowledge the role of *group* perceptions in the decision-making process, when he told Congress in July 2003: "The coalition did not act in Iraq because we had discovered dramatic new evidence of Iraq's pursuit of weapons of mass murder. We acted because we saw the evidence in a new light, through the prism of our experience on September 11."[100]

There was no single moment in which the war decision was made; rather, according to one U.S. State Department official, "it was like water dripping."[101] In the end, we cannot know for certain what "caused" the war decision. However, based on the kind of analysis presented here, we can at least speculate intelligently about the variety and range of factors that may have produced the outcome. Likewise, we cannot know for sure what might be the best decision in a given situation; but we can at least try to think intelligently about such things by utilizing the kind of framework for evaluative analysis suggested earlier, something I attempt to do next as I apply it to the Iraq decision.

Why Did the United States Invade Iraq?: An Evaluative Analysis

When conducting what we have called normative analysis, we are inquiring as to whether the reasoning behind a decision meets certain criteria, such as: Was the decision moral, and was it legal? Also, was it smart? Judgments about morality and legality can become intertwined, although morality clearly has more to do with the question of "legitimacy" than with legality per se. Even judgments about the smartness of a decision, in terms of promoting national interests, can have some connection with morality and legality—recall Robert Osgood's point about "the expediency of idealism"—but there will often be a tension between acting morally and legally on the one hand and acting to maximize one's self-interests on the other hand.

In weighing the *morality* of the U.S. invasion of Iraq, one starts with the observation that Saddam Hussein was arguably as brutal a dictator as one could find on the planet. It is estimated he was responsible for more than three hundred thousand mass graves discovered by coalition forces upon entering Iraq.[102] He had state-of-the art torture chambers and allowed no dissent against his rule. Moreover, Iraq under Saddam was the first country to use lethal chemical weapons in an interstate conflict since World War I, in violation of the 1925 Geneva Protocol that banned the first use of nerve gas and other such munitions in warfare.[103] In addition to using chemical weapons against Iran during the Iran-Iraq war of the 1980s, Saddam used them against Iraqis as well. David Kinsella describes the level of his regime's brutality:

> From 1987 to 1989, the governor of northern Iraq, Ali Hassan al-Majid (Saddam's cousin), conducted a campaign of genocide and ethnic cleansing that took the lives of 200,000 Kurds and displaced another 1.5 million. The governor's liberal use of weapons of mass destruction earned him the moniker "Chemical Ali." In perhaps one of the most barbarous attacks in the history of brutality, Al Hassan ordered chemical strikes on the town of Halabja . . . killing more than five thousand Kurdish civilians with haunting efficiency.[104]

Saddam's Iraq was also the only country to have the brazenness to attempt to eliminate another United Nations member, when he tried to annex Kuwait in 1990.

Commenting on both the moral and legal transgressions committed by Saddam during the First Persian Gulf War, David Scheffer notes that "the record of Iraqi compliance with the laws of war . . . was dismal. Examples of Iraq's conduct include: the detention of foreign hostages in Iraq as 'human shields' . . . the placement of military targets within civilian areas . . . the torture of Kuwaiti civilians . . . [and] the mistreatment of prisoners of war from the coalition forces, including televised interrogations [all violations of the 1949 Geneva Conventions]. In addition, Iraqi armies burned 700 oil wells in Kuwait, causing massive atmospheric pollution."[105]

In short, Saddam was rightly seen as a ruthless dictator internally and a reckless aggressor externally, providing seemingly ample moral grounds for humanitarian intervention and regime change. After all, Saddam seemed at least as morally challenged as Slobodan Milosevic, the Serb dictator deposed by the Clinton administration a few years earlier. The fact that Saddam's worst transgressions had occurred in the 1980s and 1990s seemed moot to many, since only UN sanctions were inhibiting him from resuming that sort of behavior, and the sanctions were eroding due to Security Council laxity.

However, many observers raised some troubling moral questions about America's own behavior in the Iraq affair. There was, of course, the basic question of whether America had any moral right to intervene and impose its values on another country and people. Beyond that, there were other issues as well. First, Washington had supported Saddam and had even helped him acquire chemical weapons in the early 1980s, when the view was that he was preferable to the Islamic fundamentalist regime that had just come to power in Iran and had imprisoned fifty-two American embassy personnel in 1979; it seemed hypocritical to suddenly condemn him now as the world's worst tyrant. Second, the United States' shock and awe aerial bombardment campaign killed many civilians in Iraqi cities, and the subsequent insurgency that the American invasion spawned resulted in thousands more civilian deaths. Third, U.S. personnel were accused of committing atrocities at Baghdad's Abu Ghraib prison; "the public spectacle of U.S. soldiers and interrogators employing torture, intimidation, and explicit acts of sexual humiliation—recorded on film and available for viewing around the world—dealt a heavy blow to U.S. efforts to portray itself as a responsible global power with high moral ideals," and, according to one foreign newspaper, made it "impossible to regain moral authority."[106]

In response to these charges, Washington could argue that it had no alternative to backing Saddam initially against Iran as the lesser of two evils (just as it had backed bin Laden and al-Qaeda against the Soviet Union in Afghanistan in the 1980s); that its shock and awe campaign was more restrained than some media portrayed it, with the *New York Times* reporting that "the allies deserve credit for conducting the most surgically precise bombing effort in the history of warfare" as American commanders took "extraordinary steps to limit collateral damage," including collecting a "vast database of some 10,000 targets to be avoided, such as hospitals, mosques, and cultural treasures"[107]; that Washington was willing in Iraq to not rely solely on long-distance killing, unlike in Kosovo, but to commit ground troops to topple a dictator as swiftly as possible; and that the Abu Ghraib incidents were relatively isolated deviations from the normal protocols followed by the American military in its treatment of POWs, exceptions that might be excused by the messy nature of urban insurgencies and the dire necessity to collect intelligence from persons thought possibly to have terrorist connections. Although the Iraq war showed how morally murky world politics had become, it nonetheless did not absolve analysts from trying to make some rough moral judgments, good or bad, about U.S. behavior.

Aside from whether the United States had a moral right to undertake regime change in Iraq, there was the question whether Washington had the legal right to do so. Regarding the *legality* of the war, the Bush administration attempted to claim its behavior was legal based on three different arguments. First, and most importantly, it tried to argue that it was essentially engaged in a "collective security" operation under Chapter VII of the UN Charter, in that it was enforcing a series of more than a dozen resolutions passed by the UN Security Council that Saddam had flouted, and that both Resolution 687 in 1991 and Resolution 1441 in 2002 gave any member the necessary authority to carry out military sanctions against Iraq. At least one observer has said that the Iraq invasion "was legal, or in any event was surely closer to being legal than the Kosovo operation,"[108] since Russia never supported any Security Council resolution condemning Serbia and Milosevic. However, the problem with this argument is that the 1991 resolution applied to the previous war and the Bush administration was never able to get explicit approval in 2002 to use armed force, as the Security Council resolution only referred vaguely to "serious consequences" resulting from continued Iraqi noncompliance. The second argument, which became known as the **Bush Doctrine**, was that the United States had a right to engage in the *preemptive* use of armed force in "self defense" against any country, including Iraq, which was thought to possibly pose a threat to American security in the future. We will discuss the Bush Doctrine at greater length later, but suffice it to say here that the main counterargument was that the attack on Iraq was more a *preventive* war against a distant threat at best rather than a *preemptive* war against an immediate threat of the sort that could conceivably trigger the self-defense provision of the UN Charter. Finally, the Bush administration attempted to make the "humanitarian intervention" case, relying on an earlier assertion by UN Secretary-General Kofi Annan that the need to protect people from genocide and other gross human rights abuses must "take precedence over concerns of state sovereignty."[109] But this argument came up against the traditional view that international law grants "no general right unilaterally to charge into another country to save its people from their own leaders," a view backed by most state practice.[110]

Although Niall Ferguson has written that "considering the list of Saddam's violations of international law and his manifest contempt for the UN Security Council resolutions he had inspired—seventeen in just four years—the only mystery is why Iraq was not invaded before 2003,"[111] Annan himself called the U.S. invasion "illegal," as did most international lawyers.[112] If the war decision was morally and legally debatable, how about the wisdom of the decision? Was it *smart*?

A raw cost-benefit analysis would not suggest an affirmative answer. In terms of *costs*, aside from the substantial human costs (including more than three thousand

American soldiers killed and several thousands more wounded, along with thousands of Iraqi civilian casualties), the economic costs have been astronomical, totaling more than $300 billion by the end of 2006, most of which was borne by the United States.[113] The United States has also paid a price in terms of the war having had the unintended effect of enhancing Iran's power in the region (if only by weakening its chief rival in Iraq), inflaming further "the Arab street" against America and reinforcing perceptions of the United States as an imperialist country bent on occupying Muslim societies in the Middle East, furnishing a training ground for terrorists, and producing other strategic setbacks. As for the *benefits*, they are hard to identify, at least thus far, other than the removal of a tyrant and possibly the planting of seeds of democracy in Iraq. Regarding the comparisons with the Vietnam War, although United States fatalities in Iraq are not yet near the fifty thousand deaths suffered in southeast Asia, and the United States this time is less open to the charge of being on "the side of the landlords rather than the peasants" given the mass hatred of Saddam, nonetheless there is the sense that Americans are reliving a desert version of that jungle conflict.

It is still premature to pass final judgment on the war decision. Although it is looking dumber and dumber as time goes on, it looks somewhat more reasonable if one examines it at the time of the invasion itself. There were many observers who at the time shared Kenneth Pollack's view, stated in his *The Threatening Storm*, that "the only prudent and realistic course of action left to the United States is to mount a full-scale invasion of Iraq to smash the Iraqi armed forces, depose Saddam's regime, and rid the country of weapons of mass destruction."[114] True, many prominent "realist" scholars from the start opposed the war, with several dozen putting their signatures on a full-page anti-war advertisement published in the *New York Times* on September 26, 2002.[115] However, showing the complexity of the decision, many equally prominent scholars normally considered members of the "idealist" (liberal) school, known for dovish proclivities, at least initially supported going to war, persuaded by the need to overthrow a maniacal tyrant.[116] Early on, the latter scholars appeared to be vindicated, as polls taken in Baghdad in September 2003 revealed that almost two-thirds of the residents believed "the ousting of Saddam Hussein was worth any hardships they might have personally suffered since . . . the invasion."[117]

If you were George W. Bush sitting in the Oval Office in March of 2003, it would not be wholly unreasonable to take the view that in a post–9/11 world an American president no longer had the luxury of waiting for perfect or near-perfect intelligence before acting, and that there was every reason to believe Iraq either had WMD capabilities (at the very least chemical weapons) or, if programs had been suspended, they could be reconstituted quickly. The director of the CIA told the President it was "a slam-dunk" Saddam had such weapons.[118] Virtually every intelligence service in the world said as much. Typical was the statement by an analyst affiliated with the Carnegie Endowment for International Peace: "Iraq continues to possess several tons of chemical weapons agents, enough to kill thousands and thousands of civilians or soldiers."[119] Saddam himself cultivated such assumptions, when the twelve-thousand-page "full disclosure" report he submitted in response to Resolution 1441 appeared to be "nothing more than recycled reports, plagiarism, and outright lies."[120] Even if groupthink pressures had not been operating, the administration might well have concluded WMDs were present in Iraq, given the difficulty of locating weapons that could be hidden in basements and garages. On the inherent uncertainty of intelligence, one observer perhaps said it best when he noted "the laughable contradiction of the Senate Intelligence Committee criticizing the Bush administration for acting on third-rate intelligence [in going to war], even as the 9/11 Commission criticized it for not acting on third-rate intelligence [in failing to anticipate the 9/11 attack]."[121]

Ultimately, leaders cannot avoid being held accountable for intelligence failures and other policy failures, no matter the extenuating circumstances. If the WMD assumption ultimately proved flawed, what about the assumption that the United States could "drain the swamp" by installing democracy in a place like Iraq, with its many cleavages and no prior experience with democratic institutions? "Forging democracy at gunpoint" is not impossible, but is relatively rare—the U.S. invasion of Panama in 1989 and of Grenada in 1983 are often cited as among the few examples one can find of American armed intervention resulting in a degree of successful regime change.[122] Although the forging of democracy in Germany and Japan after World War II might also qualify as exceptions, they were special cases and did not pose quite the same challenge as a state torn by ethnic and religious strife. Of course, had better postwar planning been done by the Bush administration, it might have greatly reduced the problems that materialized after the invasion. For example, whereas Truman after WWII purged only the top leadership of fascist Germany and Japan and left many remnants of the old regime intact to help run the country, Bush purged almost all Ba'athists from the Iraqi military and police administration, thereby eliminating experienced personnel needed to keep order and, also, alienating much of the Sunni population. Other errors were made as well, notably underestimating the number of coalition forces needed to maintain security and reconstruct the country.

Evaluative analysis of foreign policy requires one not only to critique a decision but also to offer prescriptions—solutions. Stanley Hoffmann has said that Iraq "appears more and more like a huge kick into a poisoned ant hill, and all the options seem grim."[123] By 2007, these options seemed to be "go big" (expand the size of American troop strength), "go long" (plan for a phased withdrawal), or "go home" (withdraw immediately).[124] A special Iraq Study Group commissioned by Bush in late 2006 to proffer advice on the conflict examined four "alternative courses"— "precipitate withdrawal, staying the course, more troops for Iraq, and devolution [of Iraq] into three regions"—and dismissed all four, settling on "a new approach" that entailed "an external approach—building an international consensus" and "an internal approach—helping Iraqis help themselves."[125] The president was left to search for a way out, with debate raging in the nation's capital throughout the remainder of his term. We will leave prescriptive analysis to later chapters, as we focus on Gulliver's travails and examine the Iraq War in the context of larger dilemmas the United States faces today. Before looking at contemporary U.S. foreign policy in broad perspective, it is helpful first to get some historical perspective. Some concerns today are unique

CARTOON 2.2 Doing Prescriptive Analysis About the Iraq War. CREDIT: PATRICK CHAPPATTE

and unprecedented, but others seem like old wine in new bottles. The next chapter offers a quick history lesson in American foreign policy from George W (ashington) to George W (Bush).

DISCUSSION QUESTIONS

1. How would you define "foreign policy"? To the extent that foreign policy consists of a carefully conceived set of goals and strategies—a master plan that a country's leadership has for dealing with the rest of the world— would you say the United States has such a plan? Has it ever?

2. What are the main characteristics of "macro-decisions," "micro-decisions," and "crisis decisions"? Give examples of each, drawn from recent cases in U.S. foreign policy.

3. What are the various modes of analysis or inquiry one might engage in when examining foreign policy in general and U.S. foreign policy in particular?

What is meant by descriptive analysis? Explanatory analysis? Normative analysis? Prescriptive analysis? Which do you think is the hardest to do?

4. In attempting to understand and explain the foreign policy behavior of the United States or any other state, what are the various "levels of analysis" one might examine as one looks for possible determinants of behavior? Which level of analysis do you think is the most useful—the most powerful—in the search for explanations of foreign policy behavior in international relations in general and in U.S. foreign policy in particular?

5. What is meant by "the rational actor" or "billiard ball" model as an explanation of foreign policy? What are the merits and limitations of this model as an explanatory tool for understanding U.S. foreign policy decisions?

6. Would you label yourself a realist or an idealist (liberal) when it comes to your thinking about foreign policy and international relations? What do these labels mean?

7. Do countries take moral concerns into account in making foreign policy decisions? Should they? Do you feel the United States has behaved morally or immorally in its foreign policy behavior over the years? Give examples of what you think are moral decisions and actions taken by the United States versus immoral decisions and actions.

8. Do countries take legal concerns (international law) into account in making foreign policy decisions? Should they? Do you feel the United States has acted legally or illegally in its foreign policy behavior over the years? Give examples of what you think are legal actions taken by the United States, and what you think are illegal actions.

9. Do you think the decision by the United States to invade Iraq in March 2003 was moral? Legal? Smart? Why?

10. Apply the latter criteria to the following case:

It was reported in March 2007 that the CIA was holding the young sons of Khalid Sheikh Mohammed—the suspected mastermind of the 9/11 attack on the World Trade Center in New York City and a chief lieutenant of Osama bin Laden—in an effort to pressure Mohammed to talk and reveal information about future terrorist plots, hoping to prevent another major attack on New York or another large American city. Do you think this is moral? Legal? Smart?

Apply the criteria, also, to the case of the CIA running secret prisons where suspected al-Qaeda terrorists are being subjected to tactics bordering on "torture," in possible violation of the Geneva Convention and other international humanitarian norms, in order to extract what is hoped will be vital intelligence information. If you were President of the United States and could potentially save thousands of lives through this sort of policy, would you authorize it?

3

US Foreign Policy
from George W. to George W.
Patterns and Determinants

The great rule of conduct for us in regard to foreign
nations is . . . to have with them as little political
connection as possible. . . . Why, by interweaving our
destiny with that of any part of Europe, entangle our peace
and prosperity in the toils of European ambition . . . ?
It is our true policy to steer clear of permanent alliances
with any portion of the foreign world.

—President George Washington, 1796

We are participants, whether we would or not, in the life
of the world. The interests of all nations are our own also.
We are partners with the rest. What affects mankind is
inevitably our affair as well as the affair of Europe and Asia.

—President Woodrow Wilson, 1916

If we are an arrogant nation, they'll view us that way, but if
we're a humble nation, they'll respect us.

—George W. Bush, as a presidential candidate in 2000

**It is the policy of the United States to seek and support
the growth of democratic movements and institutions in
every nation and culture, with the ultimate goal of ending
tyranny in the world.**

—**President George W. Bush, 2005**

In the previous chapter, I noted John Ikenberry's observation that U.S. foreign policy often has been hard to describe or understand. Yet, along with a number of changes in American foreign policy behavior over time, there have been persistent, discernible *patterns*, including ongoing tensions between realist and idealist proclivities and between isolationist or unilateralist and multilateralist proclivities—dramas that are still being played out in the twenty-first century. This chapter traces the history of American foreign policy from the founding of the republic to the present, with special emphasis on developments since World War II. In the space of one chapter, we cannot possibly do justice to the history of American foreign relations; the intent is simply to provide a brief overview that highlights key events and trends that may shed some light on current concerns. In addition to examining shifting and enduring patterns of American foreign policy behavior, we also want to examine here the operation of various sets of determinants in shaping policy in different historical periods.

CONTINUITY AND CHANGE
IN AMERICAN FOREIGN POLICY

Henry Kissinger was not the first person to suggest that "there is no such thing as an American foreign policy."[1] George Harvey, the American ambassador to Great Britain in 1923, was quoted as saying "the national American foreign policy is to have no foreign policy."[2] Like Kissinger, Harvey was exaggerating the absence of any clearly thought out, identifiable set of objectives and strategies. Thomas Bailey, in his classic diplomatic history of the United States, first published in 1940, was more accurate in his assessment: "The plain truth is that the United States has always had fundamental foreign policies or objectives, whether farsighted or shortsighted, successful or unsuccessful. A half-dozen or so of them have persisted for well over a century. In some cases these objectives or policies, notably 'no-entangling alliances,' were pursued with a blind devotion long after the reasons for their existence had passed. . . . Few, if any, of the great powers can point to such a large body of traditional policy adhered to so tenaciously over so many decades."[3] Even with "the rise to globalism"[4] after 1945, when the "no-entangling alliances" policy was abandoned in an effort to contain the Soviet Union, there was still the residue of a go-it-alone habit that continues to this day.

There also has been "a constant oscillation"[5] between, on the one hand, the pursuit of American national interests narrowly and crassly defined and, on the other hand, the pursuit of broader, nobler, missionary-like goals. These contradictory impulses periodically, almost rhythmically, have produced wild swings in policy, representing in a sense an element of continuity but leading a former secretary of defense to complain that American foreign policy "lacks the steadiness that has been associated with great powers."[6] What has been called a "political culture of American exceptionalism"[7]—that is, the *idea* of America as "the city on the hill" that was somehow above the sordid power politics of the Old World of Europe and beyond—has made the United States especially susceptible to a moralistic foreign policy that often competes with—at times disguising—self-aggrandizement tendencies. As Robert Osgood has said, "The problem of reconciling national self-interest with universal ideals transcending the interests of particular nations forms a central theme of [the] study of American foreign relations."[8]

The realism versus idealism debate and the isolationism/unilateralism versus multilateralism debate are closely related, overlapping dialogues that have dominated U.S. foreign policy discourse from the beginning. Stanley Hoffmann notes how the two sets of "dilemmas" have intermingled:

> For more than a century after its independence, America's privileged geographic position was the main component of foreign policy: far enough from Europe and Asia to be safe and to be able to protect itself from involvement in any other nation's affairs; capable, at the same time, of extending its borders without any real opposition. A second component has been the American institutional system; it is the greatest representative of democracy.... Hence, America's rejection of the rule of force, which characterized European diplomacy ...; these features defined the particular mission of America. At the same time, this grand missionary definition left room for contradictions. First, the pretensions to universality were perfectly compatible with a defense of the national interest as fierce as that of other countries; the brutal behavior involved in American territorial expansion during the nineteenth and early twentieth centuries bear witness to this. Secondly, the fundamental contradictions came from the two very different forms that American exceptionalism has had.... The first form, less relevant once the U.S. grew in power, is isolationism, which resulted from the legacy of the Founding Fathers: not letting oneself be entangled in alliances. This is what led Woodrow Wilson to declare, when the First World War broke out, that the United States was too proud to fight because Americans considered themselves as a beacon for mankind and thus did not have to get involved in other nations' battles. The other form is more militant, aimed at guaranteeing a world safe for democracy by building international institutions [such as the League of Nations and the United Nations], good both for the promotion of American interests and for the accomplishment of its mission.... Those two forms of exceptionalism showed the same desire to protect and, in the second case, even to project those American values and institutions which made the U.S. unique in the eyes of Americans. Thirdly, let me add that the militant form of exceptionalism itself has two different faces: that of the sheriff

always ready to resort to force in order to crush the bad guys, to protect the little ones, and to insure the triumph of goodness . . . and the face of the missionary who wants to emancipate and to "lift" other nations.[9]

Osgood offers a similar profile of U.S. foreign policy:

Because the United States was relatively isolated from the pressures of world politics by virtue of its geographical and economic position, the American people were spared the necessity of testing their assumptions about American conduct and the conduct of other nations against the unpleasant realities of international relations. Consequently, they were encouraged to believe that the realities were perfectly consistent with their ideals. . . . With a mixture of self-righteousness and genuine moral fervor they interpreted their own history as the prime example of this truth and based their assertion of the American mission upon a faith that their lofty example would shed enlightenment abroad. . . . They tended to regard the society of foreign nations as something either to be avoided or to be uplifted rather than to be understood and lived with. Nevertheless, the American nation demonstrated that, while it was indeed inspired by an unusual degree of idealism, it was also strongly motivated by egoism and was, in fact, no more capable of completely transcending its self-interest than other nations.[10]

I have quoted Hoffmann and Osgood at length since the tendencies described above form the major threads of the historical treatment of U.S. foreign policy that follows in this chapter. It was not until 1986, with the Goldwater-Nichols Department of Defense Reorganization Act, that American presidents were required by law to report to Congress annually on their national security strategy and that a new administration was required to release its strategy publicly within its first five months in office.[11] Prior to 1986, the outlines of American foreign policy could be detected in various sources, including presidential inaugural addresses and State of the Union speeches, the occasional enunciations of doctrines, and assorted reports issued by the U.S. State Department and other agencies. We will refer to these statements throughout the chapter. Of course, before 1986, and since then, much of American foreign policy behavior was best manifested by deeds more than words. It is perhaps endemic to international relations that a country's words may never fully match its deeds, given the natural tendency for any country to want to portray itself as the most high-minded no matter how low its actual behavior. As Hoffmann and Osgood suggest, the United States especially has been prone to gaps between its rhetoric and its actions.

THE FIRST CENTURY OF US FOREIGN POLICY: THE LUXURY OF ISOLATIONISM

From the birth of the United States of America in 1787 until the late nineteenth century, American foreign policy tended to take its cues from the three leading "architects" among the Founding Fathers—George Washington, Thomas Jefferson, and Alexander Hamilton. George Washington, in his **Farewell Address** as president in 1796 (first published in a Philadelphia newspaper), warned against America entering into permanent alliances with other countries. He asked, "Why, by interweaving our destiny with that of any part of Europe, entangle our peace and prosperity in the toils of European ambition, rivalship, interest, humour, or caprice?" Washington elaborated: "It is our true policy to steer clear of permanent alliances with any portion of the foreign world. . . . [But] we may safely trust to temporary alliances for extraordinary purposes."[12] Washington was not so much proclaiming grand policy as he was merely reacting against the fact that the United States had become saddled with a Franco-American Treaty of Alliance that seemed to require the United States "forever" to guarantee French possessions in the Americas from foreign seizure. Nonetheless, Washington's words were to be invoked time and again by succeeding generations as if they were sacred scripture writ large over all U.S. foreign policy. Thomas Jefferson, in his presidential Inaugural Address in 1801, repeated Washington's admonition, urging that America be guided by the principles of "peace, commerce, and honest friendship with all nations, entangling alliances with none."[13] Well beyond America's first century, the United States was to heed these cautions, never joining a peacetime alliance until after 1945.

Washington and Jefferson initially were on somewhat opposite sides of the question as to whether the United States should honor its treaty of alliance with France, originally concluded during the Revolutionary War against Britain, and come to the assistance of Paris when war broke out in 1793 between republican France and monarchical Europe or instead remain neutral. Washington was against maintaining the alliance and getting embroiled in a European war even if it meant violating the treaty. Although a fundamental, seminal principle of international law was *pacta sunt servanda*—treaties, once signed and ratified, were to be obeyed—he tried to rationalize and excuse what was arguably America's first violation of international law in its history by claiming that the United States was no longer bound by the pact since it had been negotiated with King Louis XVI, whose regime was no longer in power and who himself had been beheaded following the French Revolution in 1789. Jefferson—who as Secretary of State was much more sympathetic than the president to the new radical regime in Paris, thinking it represented the march of freedom and democracy—reminded Washington that, technically, treaties were concluded between nations, not governments, and therefore under the "continuity of state" principle America's treaty obligations still existed. The United States ended up unilaterally abrogating the treaty, with Washington issuing a "Proclamation of Neutrality" that was to be observed as well by his successor, John Adams.

A related question was whether Washington should receive a diplomatic envoy from the new French republic, thereby officially recognizing the new government, which was undertaking a violent "reign of terror" against anyone considered an enemy of the state. Jefferson articulated what was to become the recognition policy of the United States through much of its first hundred years: "We certainly cannot deny to other nations that principle whereon our government is founded, that every nation has a right to govern itself internally under what forms it pleases, and to change these forms at its own will."[14] Confronted with one of the first instances of "bureaucratic politics" in America's history—Jefferson's Francophile tendencies were offset by the Francophobe tendencies of others in the president's cabinet, notably Secretary of the Treasury Alexander Hamilton—Washington did eventually opt to recognize the French government.

Hamilton became the leading advocate of not only a strong federal government *internally*, urging that power be redistributed from the state governments to the central government in Washington, DC, but also *externally*. He was the chief spokesman for a strong national defense as well as the development of a "strong state" capable of protecting "infant industries" from foreign trade competition through government-imposed tariffs and promoting the construction of a nationwide transportation infrastructure, aimed at generating commercial wealth that could support the defense establishment needed for national security. Jefferson, in contrast, preferred a "weak state," one that stressed limited government, which by implication meant a small defense establishment and a relatively pacifist foreign policy. One writer notes that there were "two opposing conceptions of foreign policy . . . at the very beginning of the history of the United States: a 'realistic position,' attributed to Alexander Hamilton and his followers [preoccupied with U.S. national interest considerations], and a 'moralistic illusion,' allegedly adhered to by Thomas Jefferson and his supporters [preoccupied with international legal norms and promotion of democracy and other ideological beliefs]."[15]

One can see that, from the start, the United States was faced with hard choices and dilemmas of having to choose between principle and pragmatism, with having to reconcile high ideals with the more mundane practice of statesmanship. Not surprisingly, a host of contradictions in American foreign policy arose immediately. Thomas Bailey notes that, even though Jefferson may have been more caught up with idealism than Hamilton or Washington, he ultimately "never betrayed the *interests* of the United States [italics mine]."[16] And Washington, while remembered in his Farewell Address for his egoistic call to limit intercourse with other countries, also spoke at length about observing "good faith and justice toward all nations. Cultivate peace and harmony with all. Religion and morality enjoin this conduct. . . . It will be worthy of a great nation to give to mankind the . . . example of a people always guided by an exalted justice and benevolence. Who can doubt that in the course of time the fruits of such a plan would richly repay any temporary advantage which might be lost by a steady adherence to it? Can it be that Providence has not connected the permanent felicity of a nation with its virtue?"[17]

One can debate whether early U.S. foreign policy is best described as "isolationist" (i.e., characterized by withdrawal from international affairs) or "unilateralist" (i.e., characterized by international involvement but avoiding major commitments), but certainly it was not multilateralist. David Lake and some other scholars have questioned the conventional characterization of the first hundred or so years of American foreign policy as "splendid isolationism," calling it a "myth."[18] As both Hoffmann and Osgood noted above, while U.S. isolation was never complete, the United States had the luxury of being able to avoid entanglements to a greater extent than the European states, owing to its peculiar geographical position. George Washington said as much in his Farewell Address, when he remarked, "Our detached and distant situation invites and enables us to pursue a different course."[19] Later on, following the extension of "fortress America" from coast to coast through nineteenth century continental expansion, the French ambassador to the United States put it more plainly, observing that America is "blessed among the nations. On the north, she had a weak neighbor; on the south, another weak neighbor; on the east, fish, and the west, fish."[20] As late as 1939, former President Herbert Hoover, also alluding to the country's "liquid assets," argued that the United States was protected by "a moat of three thousand miles of ocean on the east, and six thousand miles on the west."[21] Although the attack on Pearl Harbor in 1941 and, even more so, the attack on New York City on September 11, 2001, eventually rendered any notions of America's geographic invulnerability passé, such notions were to persist from colonial to modern times.

It was not just geography that shaped U.S. foreign policy early in its history but also the fact that the relative military weakness of the young republic argued for staying out of great-power competition as much as possible. Domestic politics played a role as well. Indeed, the first two political parties, the Federalists led by Hamilton and the Democratic-Republicans led by Jefferson, were organized in part around foreign policy differences. Here is one description of the partisan lines that formed in response to the country's first foreign policy "crisis": "The Jeffersonian Republicans, who were generally sympathetic with the French, found themselves arrayed in a hostile camp against the Federalists, who were branded 'British bootlickers.' Political passions, aroused by both domestic and foreign affairs, ran incredibly high. In every walk of life . . . men were divided into Federalist and Republican groups, some of whom drank in separate taverns."[22] According to one account, even Washington's Farewell Address was inspired by Hamilton and was "a partisan campaign document intended to promote a Federalist victory in the next presidential election."[23]

The passions aroused over whether America should tilt toward the French or the British or should remain neutral were unusual, in that the American people during much of the country's first hundred years were mostly indifferent to foreign affairs, the public exhibiting an insularity and belief in "the primacy of domestic affairs"[24] that was to distinguish Americans from many other peoples long into the twentieth century. The nineteenth century, after all, was taken up with the task of fulfilling the country's **manifest destiny** to stretch its borders from "sea to shining sea." Americans generally did not see this as empire-building or imperialism but rather the natural settlement of its frontier. Although there would be the need to dispose of a few obstacles on the continent posed by native American Indian tribes, Mexican property owners, and other claimants to the land—and although slavery would underwrite the southern economic system—the new nation saw itself behaving in a nobler fashion than the already established states. America could both pose as a model of restraint, above the fray and aloof from the competition for colonies conducted by the Europeans, at the same time that its own energetic expansionism and "race for empire"[25] got underway.

True, there would be no empire in any formal, traditional sense, and virtually no overseas land-grabs other than the acquisition of the Philippines and a handful of islands in the late nineteenth century, but there were the beginnings of empire nonetheless. Even Jefferson could not restrain his expansive vision of the country's future, foreseeing an "empire of liberty" (however oxymoronic the phrase), and remarking that "Old Europe will have to lean on our shoulders, and to hobble along by our side, under the monkish trammels of priests and kings, as she can. What a colossus shall we be."[26] Where Jefferson in the Declaration of Independence had urged "a decent respect to the opinions of mankind," as time wore on, the new nation seemed less and less sensitive to and interested in those opinions.

Thomas Jefferson, of course, more than anyone else, was the agent behind the largest single westward expansion in U.S. history, when he negotiated the Louisiana Purchase in 1803, paying France the sum of $15 million for almost half a continent. Actually, it was his emissary, James Monroe, who negotiated the transaction. Having changed his view of the French, and fearing French control of the port city of New Orleans, Jefferson instructed Monroe to try to buy that city and an area east of the Mississippi River for $10 million. Monroe decided to exceed his instructions when the cash-starved French ruler, Napoleon, threw in thousands of western acreage for a few dollars more. As Bailey notes, "the realist [in Jefferson] triumphed over the theorist," as he sought to counter French power and reduce the threat to U.S. security and commerce.[27]

One could see the realist in Jefferson, also, in his handling of the Barbary Coast pirates, precursors of modern-day outlaw terrorists. Based in Algiers, Tripoli, and Tunis, the brigands had long terrorized American vessels, seizing ships and imprisoning American sailors, even after Presidents Washington and Adams had attempted to pay protection money ("tribute") to the Pasha of Tripoli and other rulers in an effort to stop the interference with shipping. Despite his pacifist inclinations, Jefferson saw the failure of the dovish approach and opted for a more hawkish response, sending warships into the Mediterranean and ultimately forcing the Barbary states to cease their piracy. Jefferson, along with his successor in the White House, James Madison, was faced with another crisis involving freedom of the seas, when the British navy began interfering with American commercial vessels bound for Europe during the Napoleonic Wars, despite American neutrality in the conflict. When U.S. economic pressures in the form of an embargo failed to reverse British policy, Madison had Congress declare war against Great Britain, with the United States eventually emerging victorious in the War of 1812 despite the British burning of the nation's capital. American leaders throughout U.S. history would be faced time and again with having to choose between carrot or stick approaches to international bargaining and between economic and military levers of influence, with no assurance which tactic would prove most effective.

Madison's successor, James Monroe, became famous for the doctrine that bears his name—the first such foreign policy "doctrine" in U.S. history. What became known several years later as the **Monroe Doctrine** was delivered as part of the president's annual message to Congress in 1823, aimed at the Holy Alliance of European powers:

> We . . . declare that we should consider any attempt on their part to extend their [monarchical] system to any portion of this hemisphere as dangerous to our peace and safety. With the existing colonies or dependencies of any European power we have not interfered and shall not interfere. But with the Govern-

Photo 3.1 The Monroe Doctrine—The first "doctrine" at the White House. Credit: U.S. Library of Congress

ments . . . whose independence we have, on just principles, acknowledged, we could not view any interposition for the purpose of oppressing them . . . by any European power in any other light than as the manifestation of an unfriendly disposition toward the United States.

In other words, in return for the United States staying out of European affairs—a "hollow act of self-denial,"[28] given the military weakness of the United States and, also, given the nonintervention policy already established in Washington's Farewell Address—the United States expected Europe to stay out of the Americas. Here, too, one could see the juxtaposition of principle (the protection of Latin American states fighting for their independence from European colonial rule) and pragmatism (the desire to open up former Spanish and other foreign possessions to American commerce and the desire to carve out its own "sphere of influence" to rival the Europeans, and the care taken to limit the doctrine to a mere pronouncement rather than entering into a formal alliance with its neighbors, as Colombia and other Latin countries had hoped, that would commit the United States more firmly to their defense). American unilateralism and self-interest coincided with a genuine desire to promote self-determination and democracy, but any tension that might arise between these impulses would be resolved by the former trumping the latter. America became the self-appointed guardian of the hemisphere—a "Big Brother," one-sided relationship that was to color the view from the south throughout the nineteenth century and thereafter.

Following Monroe in the White House, John Quincy Adams was content to concentrate on internal matters. In words that have been invoked recently by critics of
contemporary U.S. foreign policy, Adams said that America "has abstained from interference in the concerns of others" and "goes not abroad in search of monsters to
destroy." Less frequently cited is Adams's characterization of the United States as
"destined by God and nature to be the most populous and powerful people ever
combined under one social compact."[29] Toward that end, American restraint did not
apply to the "near abroad," that is, to places like Mexico.

The Mexican War (1846–1848) was largely provoked by Presidents Tyler and Polk,
who coveted California and other territory that was under Mexican control, although
Mexico itself was not blameless. Once Texas was annexed to the United States in 1845,
following its independence from Mexico ten years earlier, a boundary dispute erupted
in which the United States, over Mexican objections, claimed the Rio Grande River as
its southernmost border. The situation was aggravated not only by Mexican cessation
of diplomatic relations but also by debt-ridden Mexico's refusal to pay full financial
compensation to American citizens for loss of life and property resulting from anarchic, revolutionary conditions in that country. Polk approached Mexico with a diplomatic proposal: in return for the United States canceling its monetary claims against
Mexico, Polk would accept instead the offer of land, namely recognition of the Rio
Grande border, plus, for several million dollars to be paid to Mexico, the incorpora-
tion of California and New Mexico into the United States. When Mexico refused, and
when an incident then occurred in which a dozen U.S. soldiers were killed by Mexican
cavalry that had crossed the Rio Grande, Polk asked for and received a formal declaration of war from Congress. While it could be said that the United States did not seize
California and New Mexico outright, first offering to buy those territories only to be
turned down, it did ultimately gain title by conquest, making Mexico an offer it could
not refuse, through a war whose *casus belli* seemed questionable. One U.S. senator remarked in the immediate aftermath of the war, failing to anticipate the Civil War that
was to preoccupy the country at mid-century, but envisioning the further addition of
the Oregon Territory and Alaska that was to follow shortly, "A more perfect Union,
embracing the whole of the North American continent."[30]

Within fifty years of adding California as its Pacific outpost, the United States was
to extend its reach overseas, outside its continental boundaries, gaining control of the
Philippines, Guam, Puerto Rico, and Hawaii in 1898. While resisting the label of colonial ruler, the United States by the turn of the century had obtained dependencies,
bases, and considerable prestige as a growing—if seemingly reluctant—world power.

US FOREIGN POLICY BETWEEN 1898 AND 1945:
THE TRANSITION TO A WORLD POWER

The Spanish-American War in 1898 is widely considered a watershed moment in the
life of the United States, the time in which the country began to come of age as a
global power, even if it remained less than globalist in its outlook, still wary of get-

ting "sucked into the vortex of power politics."[31] Just as the declaration of war against Mexico in the Mexican War proceeded from a dubious *casus belli* and resulted in significant spoils of victory, the same could be said about the declaration of war against Spain in the Spanish-American War.

The causes of the Spanish-American War have been much debated. Bailey offers a glimpse into the roots of war and the combination of ideas, ideals, and interests that gave rise to the war decision: "The roots of the budding spirit of imperialism are to be found in many places. The Darwinian theory . . . helped to prepare the American mind for the comfortable belief that the world belonged to the nations that were strong and fit. . . . Captain A. T. Mahan, the high priest of navalism, began to preach the gospel that naval power and world power are Siamese twins. . . . The demand for more and bigger battleships had its counterpart in the growing agitation for an Isthmian canal to increase the mobility of the navy to protect both coasts. A man-made waterway also meant that outlying islands like Cuba, the Danish West Indies, and Hawaii, would have to be annexed to guard its approaches. . . . By 1890, post–Civil War reconstruction had virtually been completed" and "everywhere in the United States there were evidences of a growing national consciousness. American history was introduced into the lower schools and respect for the flag was taught in the classrooms. . . . All signs indicated that America was turning her eyes outward. She was restless, eager for new thrills—and a stage commensurate with her bursting power."[32]

One could add to these causal factors others as well, such as the "white man's burden" to bring civilization to people of color, along with the color of money and the pursuit of wealth. What was said about Hawaii when it was annexed by the United States in July of 1898—that it was "a consummation of the work of American missionaries, traders, whalers, sugar planters, big navyites, and imperialists"[33]—could also be said about the American involvement in the Spanish-American War, although Hawaii itself was annexed while the war was going on and was not part of the Spanish cession of territories.

If strategic, economic, jingoistic, and humanitarian impulses were the background causes of the Spanish-American War, the immediate cause centered on the status of the island of Cuba, which was "the spark that set off the powder magazine."[34] The mass media in the United States, led by the sensationalist "yellow journalism" of the Hearst-owned *New York Journal*, fanned the fires of American intervention in Cuba by portraying Spanish rule over the island as tyrannical, as fostering conditions of revolution and anarchy that threatened the Cuban people along with American investments there, and as a source of growing hostilities between Washington and Madrid. When the battleship USS *Maine* mysteriously was sunk by an explosion in the Bay of Havana in February 1898, killing 260 American seamen, the newspapers took up the chant "Remember the *Maine*, To hell with Spain!" President McKinley, anticipating a difficult re-election campaign in 1900 and goaded on by members of his own party (Theodore Roosevelt accusing him of "having no more backbone than a chocolate éclair"), did little to stop Congress from declaring war on Spain in April, even though Spanish involvement in the *Maine* incident was never proven, and the Spanish government had offered to negotiate over the future of Cuba. The war was over by December, with Spain no match for American power and compelled to surrender control over the Philippines, Guam, Puerto Rico, and Cuba.

"Dollars, duty, and destiny"[35] commingled, as the United States took direct ownership of Guam and Puerto Rico, flirted with annexing Cuba before granting the island independence in 1901, and halfheartedly administered the Philippines as a colonial possession before ultimately transferring sovereignty to the Filipino people after World War II. The Cuban and Philippine cases illustrated well the competing pulls of empire and empathy in American foreign policy. In the case of Cuba, the Teller Amendment to the declaration of war against Spain had pledged that the United States would never annex Cuba, so any such action would have violated a clear promise. At the same time, the Platt Amendment (to the army appropriations bill of 1901) contained a number of provisions that Cuba was pressured to accept in a treaty as the price for securing its sovereignty, notably that the United States would have the right to intervene to maintain order and maintain Cuban independence from foreign powers and would have the right to buy or lease land for naval and coaling stations (which led to American control over Guantanamo Bay).

Whatever temptation might have existed to annex Cuba was lessened by the American experience in the Philippines. At first, there was popular sentiment in the United States to grant the Philippines independence, based on long-standing isolationist and anti-colonialist feelings. However, two factors argued against this. First, there was the potential strategic and economic value of the archipelago. As Senator Mark Hanna remarked, "If it is commercialism to want the possession of a strategic point giving the American people an opportunity to maintain a foothold in the markets of that great Eastern country [China], for God's sake let us have commercialism."[36] Second, there was a more benign motivation, a sense of "moral obligation" to provide a degree of stewardship over a desperately impoverished society which, if left to its own devices, might well descend into chaos and revert to rule by Spain or another colonial power. Unfortunately, the Filipinos did not see it that way, mounting an insurrection against American rule in 1899 that was quelled only by the dispatch of some seventy thousand troops, an experience that gave the United States an early taste of guerrilla, asymmetrical warfare and left a bitter taste of the fruits of colonialism that foreordained eventual Filipino independence in 1946.

Robert Osgood refers to the Spanish-American War as America's "first crusade," evidencing the distinctive dualism between realism and idealism running through American foreign policy.[37] He gives particular attention to the role of specific individuals and idiosyncratic factors contributing to U.S. foreign policy behavior in the late nineteenth century. In Captain Mahan, then president of the naval war college in Annapolis, he cites personal qualities that resemble those that some associate with modern day neoconservatives such as George W. Bush:

> Mahan deserves the reputation of a realist . . . and has earned the reputation of an extreme national egoist because he preached the doctrine of imperialism with a force and candor unequaled by most Americans who shared his views. But he . . . understood the power of ideals as well as self-interest. And his appeal

to his contemporaries would certainly have been insignificant had he failed to combine idealism with egoïsm, for that was a popular blend which proved irresistibly intoxicating to the conscience-bound Americans during their imperialist adventure. . . . Mahan's writings resounded with the tones of a crusade. His language was Biblical; the righteous quality of his expression arose from intense spiritual beliefs and a profound knowledge of the Scriptures. Nations, he was accustomed to saying, like religions, decay if they neglect their missionary enterprises. . . . He was confident that the extension of American influence in the world would enlighten backward races and confer upon them the blessings of Christianity and Anglo-Saxon political genius.[38]

Like Mahan, Theodore Roosevelt, as U.S. Assistant Secretary of the Navy in 1897, also "reasoned that, although the United States had thus far escaped the toils of world politics, the geographical basis of her relative immunity would disappear with the extension of her political and economic commitments and with the rapid spread of technological advancements in transportation and communication."[39] Roosevelt thought war would be "good for the Navy,"[40] not only because it would provide a valuable experience and test of American sea power but also because a victory could promote public support for the "Great White Fleet" he hoped to build. It also would comport with his own personality traits:

In his private correspondence just before the outbreak of war he gave humanitarian and broad idealistic considerations about equal weight with arguments for the national self-interest, which called for avenging American honor and establishing American bases in the Caribbean; but by the time he was on the ship off Florida that would carry him and his Rough Riders to high adventure in Cuba, he was urging [American diplomats] to prevent any talk of peace until the United States got Manila, Hawaii, Puerto Rico, and the Philippines. . . . Roosevelt made himself a living example of the virile, fighting qualities, the martial virtues, the strenuous life. And as he despised "mollycoddles," so he abhorred timidity in nations. A nation, like an individual, he believed, must always deal squarely and champion righteousness; but, above all . . . just as an honorable man must on occasion resort to fisticuffs, so an honorable nation must go to war.[41]

Roosevelt became vice president in McKinley's second term and assumed the presidency when McKinley was assassinated in 1901. One year earlier, U.S. Secretary of State John Hay issued his famous "Open Door Notes," urging all foreign powers with leaseholds and port deals in China to resist carving up "that great Eastern country" into their own separate spheres of influence and demanding they maintain China's territorial integrity and, most importantly, keep it open to the United States or any other country wishing to do business there. U.S.-China policy was "materialism with strong overtones of evangelism."[42] Suddenly, the American foreign policy establishment had become aware of the Far East, getting there fairly late in the game and wanting to insure American access to commercial opportunities in the region. (It was not until 1831 that China was even mentioned in a public presidential statement despite China, at the time, accounting for one-third of the world economy; and it was not until 1852 that reference was made to Japan, a year after which Commodore Matthew Perry's expedition sailed into the Bay of Tokyo, the first attempt at "prying open the portals of Japan."[43])

In the 1880s, America had a smaller navy than the Swedish. The challenge that Mahan and Roosevelt faced in seeking to develop a premier distant-water navy capable of projecting American power over faraway sea lanes is captured by David Lake: "In 1883, the United States Navy consisted of 90 ships, 48 of which were capable of firing a gun, and 38 of which were made of wood—all at a time when the British Navy numbered 367 modern warships. At the end of that decade, America's navy was rated twelfth in the world, behind that of Turkey, China, and Austria-Hungary. . . . By 1890, construction plans were underway for a new fleet of 15 cruisers and 6 battleships, which were expected to put the United States on a par with Germany. The navy's fortunes improved further when Theodore Roosevelt ascended to the presidency in 1901. . . . By the time he left office eight years later, Roosevelt could boast that he had doubled the size of the navy."[44] Roosevelt showcased his new deep-water navy by sending the fleet of 22 battleships on an around-the-world tour in 1907–1908.

Roosevelt also started construction of the Panama Canal in 1904, after helping Panama declare its independence from Colombia in exchange for American control of the Canal Zone, thereby supporting U.S. military and commercial interests by connecting the Atlantic and Pacific oceans. American domination of Latin America took another turn when Venezuela and the Dominican Republic, plagued by corrupt governments and weak economies, defaulted on their foreign loan obligations to British and other European investors, creating fears in Washington that the European powers might try to forcibly collect debts and even take over those governments. The American response was the so-called Roosevelt Corollary to the Monroe Doctrine, whereby the United States asserted the right to play the role of "international police power" and to intervene where necessary in Western Hemisphere countries for the purpose of restoring order and financial stability, insuring debt repayment to foreign creditors, and preventing outside interference in the region. Reminding the Europeans that the Caribbean was "an American lake," the United States warned them that it would not tolerate any military intervention by them and pledged, in return for their cooperation, that it would take paternalistic responsibility for helping the "less civilized" nations of the hemisphere manage their governmental affairs in a more efficient manner. Yet again, moral responsibility mixed uneasily with material interest.[45]

It was Woodrow Wilson who, upon becoming president in 1912, took these contradictions to a new level, becoming the embodiment of American self-righteousness that invited charges of hypocrisy. On the one hand, Wilson is considered the prime exemplar of the idealist school of international relations, forever associated with his failed utopian vision of a League of Nations that would make the world "safe for democracy," "end war," and replace the balance of power with a "community of power." Wilson once remarked that "it is a very perilous thing to determine the foreign policy of a nation in the terms of material interest."[46] He pledged that "the United States will never again seek one additional foot of territory by conquest," and also condemned the "dollar diplomacy" practiced by his predecessor, William Taft, who had played up the government's role in expanding American corporate influence and investments abroad.

On the other hand, it was Wilson's very messianic tendencies, grounded in "a Presbyterian conscience,"[47] that led the United States to display an arrogance of power not unlike that witnessed in recent times. Here was someone who had earlier been an outspoken opponent of imperialism yet "became the greatest military interventionist in U.S. history," ordering "troops into Russia and half a dozen Latin American upheavals."[48] Wilson essentially saw the United States as engaging in "humanitarian intervention" in Haiti in 1915 when he attempted to replace a ruthless, brutal dictatorship and internal chaos with an American protectorate, only to find the locals preferring "their own disorder to order imposed by Yankee soldiers,"[49] especially since it was apparent that a major impetus for the intervention was, as in the past, fear of the Europeans offering themselves as policemen in lieu of Washington. The same scene was played out everywhere the United States intervened, good intentions blending with ulterior motives, almost always producing more resentment than gratitude. This included Mexico, where Wilson refused to recognize the repressive Huerta government and eventually helped to overthrow it, hoping to liberate the Mexican masses but ending up saddling them with another dictator and leaving critics at home wondering, "What legal or moral right has a President of the United States to say who shall or shall not be President of Mexico?"[50] In Niall Ferguson's words, "the paradox of dictating democracy" has long been a "characteristic feature of American foreign policy."[51]

Wilson tried hard to keep the United States out of World War I. The war "nobody wanted," caused mostly by mutual misperceptions, started in August 1914. Tensions had been escalating between the Triple Entente (Britain, France, and Russia) and the Triple Alliance (Germany, Austria, and Italy) over arms races and related issues that caused growing paranoia, with the final trigger provided by the assassination of Archduke Ferdinand of Austria in July by Serbian nationalists. Germany backed Austria while Russia backed its Slavic Serbian allies, setting in motion a chain reaction of troop mobilizations and declarations of war.[52] Although the German leader, Kaiser Wilhelm, promised that it would be a short war and that "the boys would be home before the leaves fell," the Great War lasted five autumns and took more than twenty million deaths before it finally ended in 1918. Honoring its isolationist and neutralist past, the United States did not enter the conflict until April of 1917, pressured to come in as a result of a series of incidents, including the sinking of the British passenger liner *Lusitania* (with 128 Americans on board) and several American ships by German U-boats, as well as the Zimmermann Telegram episode that exposed Germany's secret efforts to encourage Mexico to join an alliance against the United States in the event of war; the latter especially aroused public opinion in support of war, overcoming both general indifference toward the fate of Europe as well as the opposition of German-Americans and other domestic groups toward war involvement. Even when the United States did enter the war, "faithful to the hoary no-alliance tradition, at Wilson's insistence, [it] did not become allied with the Allies, merely 'associated,'"[53] and "refused to amalgamate its forces with those of Britain and France."[54]

Osgood calls World War I America's "second crusade."[55] In January 1918, Wilson issued his famous **Fourteen Points** in a speech before a joint session of Congress, offering a rationale for American war participation and a blueprint containing his vision for a new postwar order. Among his pleadings, he called for an end to secret diplomacy and treaties, an end to economic nationalism and trade protection, a reduction in armaments, the promotion of self-determination for colonized peoples, and the creation of a world organization that could "secure mutual guarantees of political independence and territorial integrity to great and small states alike." Once hostilities ceased and a peace conference convened in Paris in 1919, Wilson's "missionary diplomacy," complete with its contradictions between altruism and egoism, was very much on display. Despite his calling in the Fourteen Points for "open covenants, openly arrived at," Wilson, according to one commentator, "went on to organize the most closed and conspiratorial peace conference in history" as he "closeted himself with the British, French, and Italian leaders," locking out the press and marginalizing the participation of the defeated powers and smaller states.[56]

Notwithstanding Wilson's call for "equality among nations," he colluded in reducing the initial assemblage of twenty-seven states (the members of the victorious coalition) to a more workable, elite Council of Four that dominated decision making. In fairness to Wilson, his attempts to promote more lofty goals, such as promoting decolonialization and a just peace treaty that did not excessively punish or humiliate Germany, fell on deaf ears in Britain and France. Many of his dreams and aspirations also fell on deaf ears at home in the United States, particularly regarding the **League of Nations Covenant**, which he hoped would be the centerpiece of a new world order. Made chairman of the drafting commission, Wilson worked hard to design a new global institution and to push for the document's ratification by the U.S. Senate, thinking it "inconceivable that the people of the United States should play no role in that great enterprise."[57] However, he ultimately failed to gain American participation, a victim of his own personal leadership style, partisan bickering (Wilson was a Democrat confronted with a Republican majority in the Senate), and the country's general desire to "return to normalcy" in avoiding foreign entanglements.

According to Osgood, "no president was ever in more complete control of the conduct of the nation's foreign affairs than Woodrow Wilson."[58] Largely for that reason, Osgood and other scholars have focused considerable attention on Wilson's peculiar personal attributes. Osgood contends that Wilson "was remarkably independent of his advisors" and, "partly because of his innate stubbornness," was "quite tenacious" about holding to his opinions once formed.[59] It has been suggested that "his independence and unwillingness to compromise" were "consequences of childhood competition with his father," leading him to "brook no interference" and to "bristle at the slightest challenge to his authority."[60] Whatever the source of his inflexibility and abrasiveness, these traits served him poorly in his dealings with the senators whose support he needed for ratification of the Treaty of Versailles. Wilson

PRESIDENT WILSON: "Now come along and enjoy yourself
with the other children. I promised that you'd be the
life and soul of the party."
London Punch, 1919

CARTOON 3.1 U.S. Rejection of Membership in the League of Nations: The triumph of isolationism and unilateralism over globalism and multilateralism. CREDIT: LONDON PUNCH, 1919.
REPRODUCED WITH PERMISSION OF BRITISH LIBRARY

was particularly intransigent about not compromising on Article X of the Covenant, which introduced the concept of **collective security**, obligating all League members to come to the assistance of any member state that had been the object of aggression. Wilson drove himself to exhaustion campaigning throughout the United States to obtain public support for League membership until he suffered a stroke after a speech in Pueblo, Colorado, in September 1919 that left him paralyzed and unable to function for the rest of his presidency.

Although the failure of the Senate to approve the treaty could be blamed at least partially on idiosyncratic factors ranging from the "intense personal hatred"[61] between Wilson and Senate leader Henry Cabot Lodge to Wilson's physical collapse that prevented his further mobilization of public opinion, it was more the conflu-ence of domestic and international politics that conspired against the United States assuming a global leadership role. As one anti-League advertisement read:

Shall We Bind Ourselves to the War Breeding Covenant?
It Impairs American Sovereignty!
Surrenders the Monroe Doctrine!
Flouts Washington's Warning!
Entangles Us in European and Asiatic Intrigues!
Sends Our Boys to Fight Throughout the World by Order of a League![62]

While the final vote against ratification of the Treaty of Versailles tended to follow party lines, the country as a whole was tired of war, disillusioned by its aftermath, fearful of becoming overcommitted to the defense of other countries in the future, and feeling no urge to assume a global leadership burden once hostilities had ended and when there was still the belief that the nation's homeland was protected from the vagaries of the international system by a huge "moat." In short, "normalcy was what the voters wanted."[63]

The Interwar Period between the two world wars (1919–1939) was one that ap-proached the sort of "apolarity" that Niall Ferguson has written about,[64] that is, no state stepped forward to invest energy and resources to provide "hegemonic stability," to help provide a modicum of world order. The Pax Britannica that had helped pre-vent major systemic war in the century between 1815 and 1914 had died in World War I, and there was no successor international regime to replace it. As Charles Kin-dleberger has said about the failed search for interwar leadership, "the United King-dom could not" lead, given its declining power, and "the United States _would_ not [italics mine]."[65] By the early twentieth century, the United States had all the trappings of a hegemonic, lead state; according to one analysis, "we were the number two white nation in population, still trying to catch up to the Russians. We had bounded into first place in total manufacturing, including top rank in iron and steel—the standard indices of military potential. In addition, we held either first or second place in rail-roads, telegraphs, telephones, merchant marine, and in the production of cattle, coal, gold, copper, lead, petroleum, cotton, corn, wheat, and rye."[66] Yet, reflected in the American absence from the League of Nations, what was lacking was the will to lead.

Osgood states bluntly that "in the history of American foreign relations the [1920s and] 1930s stands out as the period in which isolationism reached its zenith."[67] Lake prefers characterizing U.S. foreign policy behavior during this period as unilateralist, noting that "unilateralism remained the touchstone of American policy"[68] no matter whether the Democrats or Republicans were in control in Washington. Typical was the token American commitment to the Pact of Paris (the Kellogg-Briand Pact). Signed by the United States and more than a dozen other states in 1928 and ratified by the U.S. Senate by a vote of eighty-five to one in 1929, the treaty contained a pious, empty de-nunciation of war, with neither the United States nor any other party obligated to do anything if the treaty were violated. One senator called it the equivalent of an "international kiss,"[69] and most observers came to view it as perhaps the single most naïve, ide-alistic document ever produced in international affairs. When the Japanese invaded Manchuria in 1931, providing "the first big challenge of the post–1919 system," the United States "preached but did nothing,"[70] along with the British, the French, and the rest of the League of Nations. It was the same when Italy invaded Ethiopia in 1935. Meanwhile, the Great Depression was taking hold worldwide. Rather than speaking out against economic nationalism and trade wars, Washington aggravated problems by instituting the Smoot-Hawley tariff in 1930—the most protectionist tariff legislation in American history—taken mainly in response to concerns of American farmers about the flood of food imports from Europe, thereby provoking retaliatory tariffs from other countries and adding to global unemployment.

As World War II approached, the leadership vacuum persisted. A 1937 poll showed that two-thirds of Americans felt that U.S. participation in World War I had been a mistake.[71] Hence, when Nazi Germany under Adolph Hitler invaded and annexed Austria in 1938, followed by Hitler, at his meeting with British Prime Minister Neville Chamberlain in Munich, demanding the annexation of Czechoslovakia as a quid pro quo for agreeing to cease further aggression, it was not surprising that the United States remained on the sidelines. Once World War II started, with Germany's invasion of Poland in September 1939 triggering declarations of war by Britain and France, the United States remained officially neutral. At no time "before Pearl Harbor did the Gallup poll find more than 24 percent" of Americans "in favor of a shooting war."[72] It is true that President Franklin Roosevelt met with Prime Minister Winston Churchill of Great Britain in August 1941 to issue the Atlantic Charter, a joint statement of their postwar vision that echoed many of Woodrow Wilson's Fourteen Points, but the United States at the time was not at war.

The forces that were gradually inching the United States toward involvement in World War II were as complex as those driving the war decision in other wars. However, it is possible that the United States might never have joined the Allies (led by Britain under Churchill, and the Soviet Union under Josef Stalin, following Germany's invasion of Russia in June 1941) in their fight against the Axis Powers (Germany, Japan, and Italy) had it not been for the jolt provided by the Japanese attack on the U.S. naval base at Pearl Harbor, Hawaii, on December 7, 1941. Groupthink and other factors have been offered as explanations for why American leaders were totally caught off guard by the surprise attack by the Japanese,[73] despite awareness of growing Japanese hostility over American efforts to limit Japanese oil supplies as punishment for Tokyo's aggression in East Asia. In any event, the nation quickly declared war on Japan, followed by Germany declaring war on the United States.

Roosevelt has been portrayed as a president who "in some ways was a spiritual descendant of Woodrow Wilson. There can be no doubt that he was deeply impressed with America's moral responsibility for promoting peace, democracy, and a better way of living throughout the world." However, "there was also a streak of pragmatism in Roosevelt that saved him from Wilson's extravagant moral expectations" and "allowed him to accept the half-loaf." He had a "respect for the imperatives of power which Wilson never attained or sought." He "encountered the works of Mahan at the

PHOTO 3.2 The Japanese Attack on Pearl Harbor, Hawaii, on December 7, 1941. The USS *Arizona* sunk and burning. CREDIT: U.S. NAVY PHOTO/NATIONAL ARCHIVES (80-G-19942)

age of fourteen. When he declared that America's isolation had passed forever, as he frequently did, he was thinking in terms of the dependence of American security upon foreign naval bases and upon the vital sea lanes into the Atlantic and not merely in terms of the spiritual interdependence of peoples." And his "view of the realities of international relations" enabled him to grasp the threat to U.S. security posed by "the domination of either Europe or Asia by a hostile and aggressive power."[74] Roosevelt died during the war, in April 1945, but not before meeting with Churchill and Stalin at Yalta two months earlier to plan the future shape of the post–World War II system as victory seemed near. None of the leaders could have fully imagined the revolutionary turn in American foreign policy that was about to occur.

US FOREIGN POLICY DURING THE COLD WAR: THE SHIFT TO GLOBALISM

When America dropped two atomic bombs on Hiroshima and Nagasaki in August 1945, forcing Japan to surrender, it ended World War II and ushered in not only the atomic age but a new American role in a new world order. The Allies had referred to themselves during wartime as "the United Nations," and were already contemplating as early as 1942, while war was raging in Europe and the Pacific, what the successor organization to the League of Nations might look like once peace arrived. The U.S. State Department quietly, behind the scenes, took the lead in drafting the UN Charter.[75] In 1944, a meeting was held at Dumbarton Oaks in Washington, DC, that brought together the Big Five members of the allied coalition (the United States, the Soviet Union, Britain, France, and China) to discuss the draft provisions for a Security Council, a General Assembly, and other organs. In addition, also in 1944, a conference was held in Bretton Woods, New Hampshire, to discuss plans for a new postwar economic order that led eventually to the creation of the World Bank and the International Monetary Fund as specialized agencies of the UN, while another conference was held in Chicago that paved the way for the International Civil Aviation Organization, a UN specialized agency that would be charged with regulating international aviation. It was at Yalta that Roosevelt extracted a commitment from the Soviet Union to participate in the United Nations as long as Stalin could be assured that Russia, along with the United States and the other Big Five members, would each have a veto power over any decisions reached by the council of great powers that would lead the UN. The point is that by the time the San Francisco Conference was convened in April 1945 for the purpose of finalizing the UN Charter and opening it up for signature among the fifty countries present, much of the drafting and bargaining had already been completed. Following the signing ceremony on June 26, the UN Charter, over the next several months, was ratified by fifty-one states, with the organization officially born on October 24, 1945.

　　Suddenly, the United States had abandoned its isolationist, unilateralist history and committed itself to *multilateralism* on a global scale beyond anything that the Founding Fathers had envisioned. Just as the League of Nations had been the brainchild of Woodrow Wilson, the United Nations was the brainchild of Franklin Roosevelt. However, whereas the United States had refused to join the League, it did accept a leadership role in the UN. Indeed, the United States was among the first three countries to ratify the treaty, the U.S. Senate approving the Charter by a vote of eighty-nine to two. What accounted for the dramatic shift in American foreign policy was not merely Roosevelt's personal political skills—unlike Wilson, Roosevelt had carefully consulted with senators throughout the war about his UN vision—but also the changed international environment. If Pearl Harbor had sensitized the American public and elites to the vulnerability of their homeland to foreign developments, the so-called "lessons of Munich"—that is, the need to confront rather than appease aggressors—had created an understanding that countries with the largest stake in international order could not stand idly by when that order was threatened with disruption.

　　President Roosevelt died just two weeks before the San Francisco Conference. He had planned to attend the meeting and had already prepared his opening remarks. Reflecting on the more than sixty million people killed in World War II, his speech included these words: "The work, my friends, is peace; more than an end of this war—an end to the beginning of all wars; . . . as we go forward toward the greatest contribution that any generation of human beings can make in this world—the contribution of lasting peace—I ask you to keep up your faith."[76] Harry Truman, succeeding Roosevelt as president, addressed the fifty assembled delegations in his stead, expressing the hope that they were about to create "machinery which will make future peace not only possible, but certain."[77] Truman shared Roosevelt's vision, having carried in his wallet since his boyhood days in Missouri a copy of Alfred, Lord Tennyson's poem "Locksley Hall" that urged the establishment of a "Parliament of Man, the Federation of the World."[78]

The United Nations was the product of a quintessential American mix of realism and idealism. There was no mistaking the element of *Realpolitik* in the form of the "Perm Five" veto power on the Security Council, which effectively meant that the collective security principle inherited from the League Covenant and incorporated in Chapter VII of the UN Charter could never be used against any of the self-appointed guardians of world order should they be the aggressors. Yet, there was also a strong idealist ethos at work, reflected in Truman's deep-seated belief in global organization and the genuine desire of the World War II generation to avoid another such catastrophe. It could be seen in Fareed Zakaria's reminder that in 1945, "when America was even more powerful than it is today—by some measures it had fifty percent of the world output—it put into place a series of measures designed to rebuild its adversaries, institutionalize international cooperation on dozens of global issues, and alleviate poverty. No other nation would have done this."[79] It could be seen, also, in the comment of a member of the U.S. delegation to the San Francisco Conference, who, in a fit of frustration over small-power criticism of the Big Five veto, expressed a sentiment that was both condescending and indicative of how far Washington was departing from business as usual: "These little countries are going to bellyache and raise hell no matter what you do about it. We're doing all this for them. We could make an alliance with Great Britain and Russia and be done with it."[80] On the growth of global institutions in the twentieth century, John Ruggie, a well-known constructivist theorist, has said, "while numerous descriptions of this 'move to institutions' exist, I know of no good explanation in the literature of why states should have wanted to complicate their lives in this manner." He attributes the phenomenon to the dominance of the United States and its liberal worldview in the postwar period, that is, to a distinctive brand of "*American* hegemony" rather than typical hegemonic behavior or "instrumental rationality" (pure self-interest).[81]

Although the Security Council veto privilege helped to protect United States sovereignty from the majority rule of the UN General Assembly, the United States nonetheless allowed itself to become enmeshed in a host of IGOs and international regimes in a variety of issue-areas, as Washington recognized the need to "pool" sovereignty in economics, health, and other fields, even if in the process of multilateral decision-making its autonomy might be somewhat reduced. For example, the United States led the way in promoting free trade through the newly created General Agreement on Tariffs and Trade (GATT), a UN body designed to facilitate tariff reductions so as to avoid the "beggar thy neighbor" economic nationalism of the Interwar Period that had produced a worldwide depression. Some scholars have argued that it

PHOTO 3.3 The United Nations General Assembly Hall: The United States was among the first countries to ratify the UN Charter. CREDIT: UN PHOTO/ERIC KANALSTEIN

was the collective memory of the Interwar Period and the sheer power of the idea of free trade as a corrective for the problems of that era, more so than narrow national interests or even narrower domestic interest groups, that motivated the United States to champion free trade after World War II.[82] Although it was in the interest of the lead economy, with its competitive advantage, to promote an open world economic order, this entailed some short-term sacrifice for Americans; the United States agreed to provide a "public good" in permitting other states to engage in "free rider" behavior, as Washington gave foreign producers increased access to the American market while tolerating import quotas and other restrictive practices by its trading partners toward American products.[83]

One reason the United States accepted potential trade imbalances, aside from its support for free trade norms, was the stake it had in reviving the economies of those countries considered vital to American security. The shift toward multilateralism and the willingness to tolerate "free riders" was manifested not only by U.S. participation in global economic regimes but also by the substantial military alliance network that Washington organized in response to what was perceived as the Soviet Union's attempt to spread communism after World War II. The origins of the Cold War have been traced to Yalta, where Roosevelt, Churchill, and Stalin agreed to divide Europe into various zones of occupation for purposes of postwar administration. In the late 1940s, as the "iron curtain" descended over Europe, separating the East from the West, and threatened to expand to other regions as well, the United States for the first time in its history entered into a series of peacetime alliances, assuming the defense burden of "the free world." Bailey, referring to the creation of the North Atlantic Treaty Organization (NATO), the Southeast Asia Treaty Organization (SEATO), and alliances with Japan, South Korea, and other states, described the "end of the age of ostrichism" as follows: "The policy of no-entangling alliances has been spectacularly reversed, in response to outside dangers, to the point where the United States is involved in more than forty entangling alliances."[84]

Stephen Ambrose summed up America's "rise to globalism" that was to occur during the course of the Cold War:

> In 1939, on the eve of World War II, the United States had an Army of 185,000 men with an annual budget of less than $500 million. America had no military alliances and no American troops were stationed in any foreign country. . . . Forty-five years later the United States had a huge standing Army, Air Force, and Navy. The budget of the Department of Defense was over $300 billion. The United States had military alliances with fifty nations, 1.5 million soldiers, airmen, and sailors stationed in 117 countries, and an offensive capability sufficient to destroy the world many times over.[85]

Niall Ferguson says "this has justly been called an empire by invitation. But what is striking is that the United States accepted so many of the invitations it received."[86] It should be added that the United States did not always wait for "invitations" during the Cold War, engaging in more than one hundred armed interventions between 1945 and 1990, some of which were aimed at toppling existing governments.[87]

All of this was based primarily on the felt need to contain the Soviet Union, an overriding objective that was to drive much of American foreign policy behavior throughout the latter half of the twentieth century. The **containment** policy owed not to a single decision but a series of decisions, some of which were of the "macro" variety but others of which were taken on the heels of a crisis. To the extent it had an author, the containment theme is generally attributed to George Kennan, the U.S. ambassador to Moscow, whose 1946 "long telegram" to his superiors in Washington, "coupled with an article published the following year in *Foreign Affairs* under the pseudonym 'X,' laid the foundation for a new U.S. grand strategy."[88] In the 1947 article, Kennan warned that "the main element of any United States policy toward the Soviet Union must be that of a long-term, patient but vigilant containment of Russian expansive tendencies . . . designed to confront the Russians with unalterable counter-force at every point where they show signs of encroaching upon the interest of a peaceful and stable world." What Kennan had in mind was not so much a military struggle requiring American toughness in the use of armed force but rather a political and economic struggle aimed at outlasting an ideology that he argued "bears within it the seeds of its own decay" and would eventually lead to the internal

Photo 3.4 Roosevelt, Stalin, and Churchill at Yalta, 1945: Prelude to the Cold War. Credit:
U.S. Department of Defense photo/National Archives (111-SC-260486)

collapse of the Soviet system.[89] Along with the special trade concessions given to
American allies, Kennan inspired the **Marshall Plan** aid program aimed at helping
war-ravaged European democracies recover economically in order to resist communist takeover.

Shortly before the unveiling of the Marshall Plan by Secretary of State George C.
Marshall in the spring of 1947, President Truman in an address to Congress issued the
Truman Doctrine, urging economic assistance to combat political instability in
Greece and Turkey on the grounds that "it must be the policy of the United States to
support free peoples who are resisting attempted subjugation by armed minorities or
by outside pressures." With the communist coup against a democratically elected government in Czechoslovakia occurring in 1948, and with other parts of eastern Europe
becoming Soviet satellite states as well, suddenly military cooperation seemed at least
as important as economic cooperation, triggering the birth of NATO in 1949 as a deterrent against further Soviet aggression in Europe. The NATO treaty committed the
United States firmly to the defense of Western Europe in that the sixteen member
states agreed that "an armed attack against one or more of them in Europe or North
America shall be considered an attack against them all." By 1950, in the wake of the

Truman administration's growing concerns over Soviet expansionism beyond Europe, the fall of China to Mao Zedong's Communist Party, and the outbreak of the Korean War following Communist North Korea's attack on South Korea, Kennan's version of containment was replaced by another, more militarily aggressive version, credited to Paul Nitze, Kennan's successor as director of the State Department's Policy Planning Staff, and embodied in a document known as NSC–68. **NSC–68** called for a major "build-up of the military capabilities of the United States and the free world" as "a precondition . . . to the protection of the United States against disaster," setting in motion the growth of an enormous military-industrial establishment undergirding a global alliance system.

Basing American involvement in Korea on the same **domino theory** that was to be used as a justification for the Vietnam War a decade later, NSC–68 cautioned that "loss of any one of the countries [in southeast Asia] to the enemy would almost certainly result in the loss of all the other countries."[90] The Korean War ended in stalemate in 1952, with North and South Korea remaining divided. The conflict presaged similar conflicts the United States would experience in the future: there had been no formal declaration of war issued by Congress; the conflict had elements of both civil war (among the Korean people) and interstate war (including the involvement of neighboring China); there was substantial loss of American lives (some fifty thousand battle deaths) despite the "limited" nature of the war (given the reluctance to use the full American arsenal, including atomic weapons); and there was much handwringing that it was "the wrong war at the wrong time in the wrong place against the wrong enemy."[91]

There is wide agreement that while "there may have been important misperceptions and overreactions on both sides of the Cold War, and that ideas, personalities, and domestic politics matter as well, . . . the political competition between the United States and Soviet Union was rooted in bipolarity," that is, was largely the result of systemic structures and forces.[92] Indeed, no matter the idiosyncracies of the president or the identity of the party (Democratic or Republican) controlling the White House or Congress, successive American administrations over the next several decades, with only slight variations, were all preoccupied with the same paramount problem of countering the Soviet threat. As David Lake notes, "one of the most remarkable features of American foreign policy during the Cold War was its essential continuity."[93]

When Dwight Eisenhower replaced Truman in the oval office in 1952, he, along with his secretary of state John Foster Dulles, proceeded to behave as a Cold Warrior no less than Truman. In fact, Dulles urged not merely containing communism but rolling it back, "liberating" the "enslaved" peoples of eastern Europe and other societies that had come under the Marxist-Leninist yoke. However, once the Soviet Union acquired the hydrogen bomb, developing the weapon in 1953 shortly after the United States, American decision makers' actions had to be more guarded than their rhetoric, reflected in the unwillingness of the United States to come to the assistance of Hungarian revolutionaries when they attempted to oust Hungary's Soviet-backed communist regime in 1956. The Hungarian Revolution occurred at the same moment as the Suez crisis, which received far more attention from Washington given the larger interests at stake. The crisis, which involved British, French, and Israeli attacks on Egypt following the latter's seizure of the Suez Canal, was defused only when the United States joined the Soviet Union in coaxing American allies to cease hostilities and allow a United Nations peacekeeping mission to arrive as a buffer force. The episode exemplified the kind of pragmatism that was to characterize American foreign policy behavior alongside its anticommunist ideological crusade throughout the Cold War. In particular, because of mutual fears about thermonuclear war, the two superpowers developed certain "rules of the road" to guide their competition, notably a tacit understanding that direct confrontation between American and Soviet forces was to be avoided.

The Suez episode, which was precipitated by nationalist resentment in Egypt over Western control of a strategic waterway within its boundaries, also illustrated the vexing problems the United States was to experience in the third world in general and the Middle East in particular. The United States had taken the lead after World War II in pushing for decolonialization, partly as a moral imperative but also because the United States had few colonies to lose compared to the Europeans and saw an opportunity to gain access to overseas markets in newly independent states. It was in these newly emerging, less developed countries of Asia, Africa, and "the South" that the East-West conflict was most heatedly played out. Eisenhower and Dulles wanted further allies in America's efforts to curtail Soviet expansion. However, third world leaders, such as Gamal Nasser of Egypt and Jawaharlal Nehru of India, viewed colonial rule and economic backwardness as greater problems than communism. Hence, U.S. appeals for alliance were resisted in much of the third world, where nonalignment and the North-South conflict attracted more interest.

What followed was the aforementioned string of interventions. The object of the superpower intervention "game" in the third world was not to acquire territory but to gain influence over the foreign policies of third world states, entailing at times interference in their internal affairs to determine the makeup of their governments. The regimes that one side tried to topple, the other side generally tried to prop up. In addition to direct military intervention (as in U.S. excursions to Lebanon in 1958, the Dominican Republic in 1965, Southeast Asia in the 1960s and 1970s, and Grenada in 1983, and Soviet involvements in Hungary in 1956, Czechoslovakia in 1968, Ethiopia in 1977, and Afghanistan in 1979), the two superpowers frequently relied on more subtle forms of intervention, including supplying arms to local forces, transmitting propaganda, and plotting rebellions or assassinations (as, for example, in CIA "covert action" to overthrow leftist-leaning leaders in Guatemala in 1954, Iran in 1953, and Chile in 1973, and in numerous uses of "proxies" by the Soviet Union to unseat pro-western regimes). The so-called **Eisenhower Doctrine**, articulated in a message before Congress in 1957, essentially was an extension of the Truman Doctrine, offering military assistance upon the request of any country fearing aggression from the Soviet Union or its clients, and was the basis for the Lebanon intervention of 1958.

Nothing reflected U.S. frustrations in the third world more than the Vietnam War. John Kennedy had assumed the presidency in 1961, his Inaugural Address containing memorable, stirring words that were at once a call to containment and a call to fulfill some larger purposes, not unlike presidents before him:

> The same revolutionary beliefs for which our forebears fought are still at issue around the globe—the belief that the rights of man come not from the generosity of the state, but from the hand of God. . . . Let the word go forth from this time and place, to friend and foe alike, that the torch has been passed to a new generation of Americans . . . unwilling to witness or permit the slow undoing of those human rights to which this Nation has always been committed, and to which we are committed today at home and around the world. Let every nation know, whether it wishes us well or ill, that we shall pay any price, bear any burden, meet any hardship, support any friend, oppose any foe, in order to assure the survival and the success of liberty. This much we pledge—and more. . . . Now the trumpet summons us again . . . to bear the burden of a long twilight struggle . . . against the common enemies of man: tyranny, poverty, disease, and war itself.[94]

Presidents after Vietnam would also at times invoke a Supreme Being; but, chastened by the American defeat in the jungles of Southeast Asia, there would never again be quite the same display of machismo, of supreme confidence in the American mission and the seemingly unbounded will to expend American blood and treasure on behalf of others.

As Woodrow Wilson and other American leaders had discovered in their own interventionist experiences long before the Cold War, the choices facing the United States were usually more complicated than merely whether to support "good" regimes or "bad" regimes. Having decided to play the intervention game, since opting out of it would leave the field to the Soviets, Cold War presidents, Kennedy included, tended to support right-wing factions when the only alternative often seemed to be left-wing dictatorships along the lines of Fidel Castro's Cuba. The Bay of Pigs and the Cuban missile crisis, discussed in Chapter 2, were both consistent with the logic of Cold War politics, as Kennedy, in the first instance, tried to overthrow the Castro regime and, in the second instance, having failed to eliminate the Marxist government, tried to limit the Soviet presence on the island. Where non-Marxist governments were under siege, Kennedy's advisors conceived a "nation-building" doctrine that called for development of third world economies to win peasants' loyalty to pro-Western leaders while keeping communist insurgents at bay with U.S. Green Berets and other special counterinsurgency forces. Theories about nation-building were tested in the laboratory of Vietnam, where the United States attempted to assist a pro-American government in the south in fighting a communist guerrilla army based in the north, and were found wanting. As journalist I. F. Stone put it, it proved difficult to win a war in a "peasant society on the side of the landlords."[95] What was at first a modest American counterinsurgency force would become an army of five hundred thousand by the mid-1960s after Lyndon Johnson succeeded Kennedy following the latter's assassination. President Johnson, like President Richard Nixon after him, struggled for "the hearts and minds" of the Vietnamese people; but the bombings and search-and-destroy missions failed to win America's longest war against a regime that enjoyed great nationalist support.

The Vietnam War was attributed to various causes, most prominently the concern over "falling dominos" that threatened America's geopolitical situation in the superpower rivalry, as well as the growing military-industrial complex that some argued was moving the United States toward a permanent war footing, a capitalist-driven quest for profits that the radical Left had always viewed as dictating U.S. foreign policy, as well as Kennedy's own personal demons, particularly the felt need of a young president to demonstrate his backbone and resolve in combating communism after failing to impress Soviet leader Nikita Khrushchev at their 1961 Vienna summit meeting.[96] Whatever the determinants, the Vietnam debacle, which was to cost the lives of fifty thousand American soldiers before it ended in 1972, was to reverberate through American foreign policymaking circles over the next two decades. Among the lingering questions were: When, and at what cost, might U.S. military intervention be warranted or prudent in world troublespots, especially in protracted conflicts where the goals seemed unclear as were the "rules of engagement" and the amount of force the American military could utilize? And what was the proper relationship between the executive and legislative branches in the conduct of U.S. foreign policy? (Following the war, Congress passed the War Powers Act, trying to reclaim its constitutional war-making power from the president—in Korea and Vietnam the president had initiated hostilities without asking the House and Senate for a formal declaration of war, but only muddied the waters as to which branch was entitled to exercise primacy in foreign policy.[97])

The Vietnam War's immediate lessons caused President Nixon and Secretary of State Kissinger, who had brokered the peace treaty, to rethink American military strategy in the early 1970s. Public opinion, which had almost nothing to do with the initial war decision but ultimately dictated the decision to terminate the war (when evening TV newscasts showed more and more body bags of dead American servicemen returning home), seemed less tolerant of casualties, leading to the end of the draft and its replacement by an all-volunteer army. The mission of maintaining U.S. influence in distant regions remained the same, but the techniques were modified with the **Nixon Doctrine**, which stressed self-help by pro-American regional powers in the third world. Washington would supply the weapons and advice to enable friendly governments, such as the regime of Shah Reza Pahlavi in Iran, to resist revolutionaries and preserve regional stability, especially in areas where vital resources were at stake, such as the Middle East. Ultimately, this approach also was found wanting, for example when the Shah and his well-equipped army were unable to suppress a popular domestic revolution fueled by anti-American resentment that brought a militant Islamic fundamentalist regime under Ayatollah Khomeini to power in Tehran in 1979.

Kissinger, known as an exemplar of the realist school of international politics in his earlier academic career, sought to forge a "structure for peace" through a less moralistic, more practical-minded foreign policy. The result was a relaxation in American-Soviet tensions that came to be known as *détente*, based on the recognition that the

Soviets had achieved true nuclear parity with the United States and that both sides had a vested interest in world stability. One result was a series of arms control agreements, both bilateral (e.g., the Strategic Arms Limitation Agreement of 1972, which placed ceilings on the number of ICBMs and other offensive strategic nuclear delivery vehicles each superpower could add to its arsenal) and multilateral (e.g., the Nuclear Non-Proliferation Treaty of 1970, worked on also by the previous administration, which allowed the United States and the Soviet Union to keep their nuclear weapons but obligated nonnuclear-armed parties to forego nuclear weapons development). In addition, as a rift emerged between Russia and Communist China, throwing into question American assumptions about a monolithic communist adversary, President Nixon went to China to meet with Chairman Mao Zedong in 1971, attempting to build bridges on the realist premise that "the enemy of my enemy is my friend."

When Jimmy Carter became president in 1977, he attempted to revise the cardinal tenets of postwar U.S. foreign policy, playing down the obsession with the Soviet Union and the priority of containment that had necessitated interventionism and support for authoritarian leaders, instead making the centerpiece of American policy a commitment to **human rights**. In his speech at Notre Dame University's commencement ceremony in June 1977, Carter said: "I believe we can have a foreign policy that is democratic, that is based on fundamental values, and that uses power and influence . . . for humane purposes. . . . Being confident of our own future, we are now free of that inordinate fear of communism which once led us to embrace any dictator who joined us." In other words, he argued that the United States should be prepared to criticize not just left-wing despots but also right-wing despots, even if the latter were friends like the Shah. He stressed, "We have reaffirmed America's commitment to human rights as a fundamental tenet of our foreign policy." Moreover, he called for "constructive proposals for . . . North-South problems of poverty, development, and global well-being." Unfortunately, Carter's vision, which was compared to the idealism of Wilson, came up against the realities of renewed Soviet interventionism in Africa, Asia, and Latin America, the willingness of European governments and firms to do business with right-wing regimes that American companies were forced by Washington to boycott (thereby making martyrs of American business), and the emboldening of left-wing regimes to expropriate Western property as part of their demand for a "new international economic order." Even Carter's greatest achievement—the Camp David Accords that made peace between Egypt and Israel—proved to be bittersweet, as President Anwar Sadat of Egypt was soon to be assassinated by Islamic militants who were unhappy with the agreement.

The 1980 presidential election pitted Jimmy Carter, running for a second term, against Ronald Reagan. It was partly a referendum on the future of American foreign policy, that is, whether the American public believed the United States should revert to a policy of containment of communism as the centerpiece of its international affairs or should adopt Carter's more liberal orientation. The failure in Vietnam had shattered the post–World War II consensus behind the containment policy, and opened up a debate between, on the one hand, a dovish internationalist school, represented by Carter, that stressed a more cooperative, less confrontational, other-directed approach toward the outside world, and, on the other hand, a hawkish internationalist school, represented by "Rambo" Reagan, that stressed a more hardline approach. The former camp was supportive of the United Nations and working through global organizations, increasing spending on foreign aid aimed at combating poverty in the third world, promoting arms control and reining in the CIA, and prioritizing human rights. The latter camp was associated with the opposite: it was skeptical of using multilateral organizations to promote American interests; it urged poor countries to develop on their own through reforming, especially privatizing, their economic systems; it presumed that the Soviets would only respond to American strength in the form of a further arms buildup and would view arms control as weakness; and it considered intervention, at times in support of authoritarian regimes, as a necessary counterweight to Soviet hegemonic aspirations. There was also an isolationist camp that was opposed to both expanded spending on the United Nations and foreign aid as well as increased defense spending, although the real debate occurred between the doves and hawks. (As discussed below, there are parallels between these competing foreign policy visions of 1980 and the multilateralist, unilateralist, and isolationist debates that were to be heard later on in the post–Cold War era.)

Following Reagan's electoral victory, the United States saw a return to the containment policy and a level of shrill Cold War rhetoric that had not been heard for some time, as the Soviet Union—now referred to as "the evil empire"—was accused of sponsoring terrorism, of involvement in Central America and Africa, and of seeking nuclear superiority in the arms race. Engineering a multibillion dollar defense budget increase, the Reagan administration sought to reassert American military might, which had been maligned since Vietnam. President Reagan enunciated the **Reagan Doctrine**, an interventionist strategy that aimed, through covert action and in some cases direct armed force, at undermining third world Soviet clients, such as Angola, Afghanistan, Grenada, and Nicaragua. Despite some successes, the continued limits of American power could be seen in the ill-fated U.S. intervention in the Lebanese civil war in 1983, as 241 marines were killed in their barracks by a terrorist truck bomb.

With the memory of the Vietnam War still fresh, along with the fallout from the Lebanese humiliation, Secretary of Defense Caspar Weinberger issued the **Weinberger Doctrine** in a speech before the National Press Club in 1984, entitled "The Uses of Military Power." He maintained that in the future the United States should not put troops into battle unless certain conditions were met: (1) vital American national interests had to be at stake; (2) there should be a wholehearted commitment to use overwhelming force, with the clear intention of winning rather than fighting a limited, protracted war of attrition; (3) the level of troops should be matched to clearly defined political and military objectives; and (4) there should be "reasonable assurance" of the support of the American public and Congress. This would be restated in the form of the **Powell Doctrine** in the next administration, named after General Colin Powell, the chairman of the Joint Chiefs of Staff, who added two other provisions: that there be an exit strategy to avoid a quagmire situation and that there be broad international support for American action.

The Reagan administration was criticized by American allies and foes alike for a cowboy mentality that was aggravating Cold War tensions and for engaging in "global unilateralism," flouting international law and refusing to take seriously the United Nations and multilateral institutions; at one point, responding to the suggestion that either the United States should get out of the UN or the UN should get out of the United States, the deputy U.S. ambassador to the organization commented about the latter prospect that "the members of the U.S. mission will be down at the dockside waving you a fond farewell as you sail off into the sunset."[98] Reagan, a former Hollywood actor and host of the TV western series *Death Valley Days*, personally was ridiculed as "an amiable dunce" with a "seven-minute attention span," who simplistically viewed world politics as a morality play between white hats (the capitalist democracies) and black hats (the communist command economies).[99] However, moral sensibilities did not stop the administration from supporting Iraq in its war of aggression against Iran during the 1980s and supplying it with chemical weapons that were used against Iran, since Saddam Hussein was viewed as the preferable villain compared to Ayatollah Khomeini. More importantly, toward the end of his term, Reagan entered into a dialogue with "the evil empire" and its new reformist-minded Soviet leader, Mikhail Gorbachev, who was seeking to move Russian society away from strict Marxist precepts in order to remedy economic and technological problems besetting the communist state. A series of cordial summit meetings was held between the two leaders, resulting in important arms reduction initiatives in the areas of long-range and intermediate-range nuclear weapons.

Against this backdrop, startling events in eastern Europe unfolded as the Cold War drew to a close in the late 1980s, with Poland, Hungary, and other Soviet satellites abandoning Marxist ideology and gravitating toward the West, all of which culminated in the fall of the Berlin wall (that had divided the eastern and western halves of the city of Berlin in communist East Germany for more than twenty-five years) in 1989. The Cold War was over, prompting hopes of a "peace dividend" and even "end of history" prognostications about the final triumph of liberal democracy worldwide. But there was much history left to be made and written, and not as much peace as had been contemplated.

US FOREIGN POLICY IN THE POST–COLD WAR ERA: DÉJÀ VU ALL OVER AGAIN?

When Reagan's successor, George H. W. Bush, was faced with the "first post–Cold War crisis"—Iraq's invasion of Kuwait in 1990, leading to the UN-authorized mobilization of Desert Storm to reverse Saddam's aggression—Bush proclaimed that "what is at stake is more than one small country, it is a big idea—a new world order."[100] He went on to say that in the new post–Cold War era, "our objective must be to exploit the unparalleled opportunity presented by the Cold War's end to work toward transforming this new world into a new world order, one of governments that are democratic, tolerant and economically free at home and committed abroad to settling differences peacefully."[101] Once the Soviet Union itself disintegrated in 1991 into the Russian Federation and a dozen smaller states, thereby eliminating America's superpower rival, Washington had a difficult time making sense of and adjusting to the new international environment. Other than the vague "new world order" phrase, there was no watchword to replace "containment" as the guiding light behind American foreign policy.

However, there remained the familiar tugging between idealist and realist principles. Notwithstanding the Wilsonian overtones of Bush's "new world order" rhetoric and his greater acceptance of multilateralism than Reagan, the United States continued to be preoccupied with maintaining American primacy. This became apparent when the *New York Times* reported in 1992 a leaked version of a Pentagon planning document that put all countries on notice, including American allies, that Washington would not tolerate challenges to U.S. hegemony: "[The United States] must sufficiently account for the interests of the advanced industrial nations to discourage them from challenging our leadership or seeking to overturn the established political and economic order. . . . Our first objective is to prevent the re-emergence of a new rival, either on the territory of the former Soviet Union or elsewhere, that poses a threat. . . . Our strategy must now refocus on precluding the emergence of any future global competitor."[102] The aim of assuring the preponderance of American power extended into both the administration of Bill Clinton after his 1992 election (Clinton vowing to ensure "that U.S. forces continue to have unchallenged superiority in the twenty-first century") and George W. Bush after his 2000 election (Bush urging that the U.S. military be "strong enough to dissuade potential adversaries from pursuing a military build-up in hopes of surpassing, or equaling, the power of the United States").[103]

Stephen Walt argues that, even though George H. W. Bush, Bill Clinton, and George W. Bush all shared a commitment to American primacy,

> critical differences exist between the approaches undertaken by the first two and the third. In general, both the main goals of U.S. foreign policy and the strategies used to achieve these goals did not change fundamentally under the first Bush administration and the Clinton administration. Each sought to preserve or increase U.S. power and influence, to prevent the spread of weapons of mass destruction, to further liberalize the world economy, and to promote the core U.S. values of democracy and human rights. Both administrations pursued these goals by working within the preexisting Cold War order—and especially the multilateral institutions created since 1945—while seeking to maximize U.S. influence within these arrangements. By contrast, President George W. Bush's approach to foreign policy marked a clear departure from the policies of his predecessors. . . . [His] administration was more skeptical of existing international institutions—including America's Cold War alliances—and far more willing to "go it alone" in foreign affairs.[104]

Walt notes that American allies and others were especially critical of the second Bush administration for refusing to commit the United States to a number of multilateral

CARTOON 3.2 President George H. W. Bush helped lead a global coalition during the Gulf War that turned back Iraq's invasion of Kuwait in 1991, ending "the first post–Cold War crisis" and proclaiming the birth of the "New World Order." (The fine print on the poster contains a reference to Japan's Sony corporation having recently purchased Columbia Pictures.) CREDIT: J. VINTON LAWRENCE

treaties, leading *The Economist* to ask, "Has George Bush ever met a treaty that he liked? . . . It is hard to avoid the suspicion that it is the very idea of multilateral cooperation that Mr. Bush objects to."[105] It was this perception that led to rising anti-Americanism in the Bush years and the view of the United States as a "schoolyard bully" and "rogue state."

However, U.S. foreign policy behavior under George W. Bush, while more unilateralist, was not as clear a departure from his two predecessors as Walt suggests. The fact is that, ever since Ronald Reagan, the United States had gotten into the habit of resisting the ratification of many multilateral treaties, including the 1982 Law of the Sea Treaty (establishing rules governing the width of territorial waters, sea-bed mining, and other uses of the oceans), the 1989 Convention on the Rights of the Child (regulating the minimum age of military recruits), the 1992 Biodiversity Treaty (promoting protection of tropical rainforests and other important ecological systems), the 1996 Comprehensive Nuclear Test Ban Treaty (banning the testing of nuclear weapons underground or anywhere else), the 1997 Kyoto Protocol (regulating carbon emissions causing global warming), the 1998 Ottawa Landmine Treaty (banning the deployment of anti-personnel landmines), the 1998 Rome Statute (creating the International Criminal Court for trying war crimes, genocide, and crimes against humanity), and other such pacts. Bush senior found several of these treaties flawed. Despite his administration being associated with "assertive multilateralism,"[106] Clinton, too, for reasons having to do partly with American national security (e.g., the need to keep landmines on the Korean peninsula to prevent a North Korean attack on South Korea) and partly with domestic political opposition (e.g., his unwillingness to challenge a Republican-controlled Congress), either refused to sign these agreements or, when he did sign, refused to expend much political capital to get the U.S. Senate to ratify them, although he was successful in a few other cases, notably the 1993 Chemical Weapons Convention (banning the production of chemical weapons), the 1994 Marrakesh Treaty (creating the World Trade Organization), and the extension of the Nuclear Non-Proliferation Treaty in 1995.[107]

Moreover, U.S. interventionist behavior throughout the post–Cold War era fell into a familiar pattern, even if the purposes were no longer containment-oriented. As Robert Kagan notes, "between 1989 and 2003, a period spanning three different presidencies, the United States deployed large numbers of combat troops or engaged in extended campaigns of aerial bombing and missile attacks on nine different occasions: in Panama (1989), Somalia (1992), Haiti (1994), Bosnia (1995–1996), Kosovo (1999), Afghanistan (2001), and Iraq (1991, 1998, and 2003). That is an average of one significant military intervention every 19 months—a greater frequency than at any time in our history."[108] Under the two Bushes and Clinton, the United States attempted to obtain the United Nations' imprimatur for intervention where possible (for example, in Somalia, Haiti, and Afghanistan), but proceeded to act on its own when UN approval by the Security Council was not forthcoming (as in Kosovo and Iraq).

Where Bush's father had been faced with the not insignificant challenge of managing the transition from the Cold War to post–Cold War era, which he handled well, Bill Clinton had the good fortune of not having to deal with any great foreign policy challenge or crisis at the outset. Indeed, he had campaigned on the theme of focusing on domestic economic problems, such as the growing federal budget deficit. In the international realm, then, there seemed no urgency to give new definition to American foreign policy and to identify a new concept, in lieu of containment, that could capture America's purpose in the world. Still, Clinton was pressured to explain where he was taking the country in its external relations. In Chapter 2, I noted that Clinton attempted to respond to the criticism "Is There a Doctrine in the House?" with the idea that his administration aimed at the "enlargement" of the number of free-market democracies in the world. His National Security Advisor Anthony Lake stated in September 1993 that "the successor to a doctrine of containment must be a strategy of enlargement, the enlargement of the world's free community of market democracies."[109] Clinton's Secretary of State Warren Christopher noted that in the new age of globalization, with the Cold War threats having evaporated, "economic security" had become the main priority of foreign policy.[110]

However, Clinton went further in his democracy promotion effort, asserting the right of the United States to intervene in foreign countries in the name of humanitarian intervention when a government was engaged in atrocities against its own people. What became known as the **Clinton Doctrine** was the principle that the president hoped would be observed by all states—"not just by the United States, not just by NATO, but also by the leading countries of the world, through the United Nations. And that is while there may well be a great deal of ethnic and religious conflict in the world . . . if the world community has the power to stop it, we ought to stop genocide and ethnic cleansing."[111] Animated largely by noble, Wilsonian intentions, "the interventions of the 1990s had, on the whole, selfless rather than self-interested motives. The United States sent troops not to defend its interests, as great powers had done from time immemorial, but to vindicate its values. . . . The United States intervened in those places, which had no relevance to its strategic or economic interests, in order to relieve the palpable suffering of the people who lived in them."[112]

The Clinton Doctrine was applied inconsistently. Where the challenge seemed too daunting, as in the global call in the mid–1990s to stop genocide in Rwanda at a time when the United States had just experienced a disastrous humanitarian intervention in Somalia, Clinton deferred to realist instincts and stayed out of the conflict. Clinton, after Somalia, also deferred to domestic American politics, as "the unspoken Clinton Doctrine" was that "the United States should not engage in any military interventions that might endanger the lives of American service personnel," based on the assumption that "presidents who presided over wars in which American soldiers died did not get reelected."[113] (The so-called CNN effect was credited by some with both getting the United States into Somalia and getting the United States out, in that pictures of starving Somalians pressured Clinton to send troops to deliver aid, while pictures of a murdered GI's body being dragged in the sand in Mogadishu, recounted in the film *Black Hawk Down*, pressured the administration to quit the operation.[114]) In Kosovo, Clinton accepted the challenge, intervening militarily even in the absence of clear national interests at stake and without United Nations approval (when a Russian veto prevented UN Security Council authorization of the use of armed force to stop ethnic cleansing by Serbian dictator Slobodan Milosevic), although no American lives were lost in a low-risk aerial bombing campaign and postwar reconstruction effort. Hence, under Clinton, the United States, at times, again found itself engaged in nation-building on the premise that "disintegrating societies and failed states with their civil conflicts and destabilizing refugee flows have emerged as the greatest menace to global stability."[115]

As noted in the Iraq War case study in the previous chapter, George W. Bush began his presidency with an anti-interventionist mindset. Given the mixed results of interventions in Somalia, Haiti, Bosnia, and Kosovo, Bush campaigned in 2000 on the theme of a cautious American foreign policy, rejecting nation-building and humanitarian intervention as generally beyond U.S. interests and capabilities. In his presidential debate against Al Gore, Bush said, "I'm not sure the role of the United States is to go around the world and say this is the way it's got to be. . . . If we're an arrogant nation, they'll resent us. If we're a humble nation, but strong, they'll respect us."[116] He suggested the United States might be better off remaining out of the ethnopolitical squabbles in the Balkans, the Israeli-Palestinian quarrel, and other conflicts, leading some observers to criticize Bush as not merely unilateralist but isolationist and disengaged altogether. Charles Kupchan points out that the Bush administration dropped "from the State Department's roster more than one-third of the fifty-five special envoys that the Clinton administration had appointed to deal with trouble spots around the world. The *Washington Post* summed up [the early Bush policy] . . . in its headline, 'Bush Retreats from U.S. Role as Peace Broker.'"[117]

The terrorist attacks on September 11, 2001, altered the course of the Bush presidency. As one journalist wrote, "almost instantly, everything changed," as Bush vowed that "the United States would go after not only terrorists but countries that harbored them as well."[118] As another commentator put it at the time, "Isolationism is dead."[119] It remained to be seen whether Bush would become a unilateralist internationalist or a multilateralist internationalist, with the options presented reminiscent of the divergent choices posed by Reagan and Carter in the 1980 presidential campaign.

At first, Bush seemed to pursue the multilateralist route, successfully appealing to NATO allies to consider the 9/11 attack on America as an attack on all alliance members under Article 5 of the treaty, and then successfully appealing to the UN Security Council to authorize a global war on terror under the collective security provisions of Chapter VII of the UN Charter, resulting in several resolutions obligating the entire membership to submit annual reports to a new Committee on Counter-Terrorism charged with monitoring international cooperation in the fight against terrorism. However, as Kupchan notes, "despite its inclusive rhetoric," the Bush administration "was not as avowedly multilateralist as it appeared on the surface. The U.S. certainly wanted as wide a coalition as possible, affording American forces access to bases in the Middle East and providing international legitimacy to the retaliatory attack on Afghanistan. But Washington did not welcome the constraints on its room for maneuver that would have accompanied coalition warfare. The Bush administration preferred 'à la carte multilateralism.'"[120]

The Bush foreign policy was labeled **neoconservative** in that it seemed to combine elements of Wilsonian idealism with "clear-eyed realism,"[121] calling for the muscular use of American military power, unilaterally invoked when necessary, in the service of "the ideology of expanding the American core values worldwide."[122] Charles Krauthammer, a well-known neocon, called it "democratic realism"—"an American foreign policy for a unipolar world."[123] Max Boot called it "hard Wilsonianism," to distinguish it from the "soft Wilsonianism" preferred by multilateralists.[124]

Although Bush's particular idiosyncracies, including his born-again religious experience, no doubt helped to shape his conversion to neoconservatism, the policy was but the latest incarnation of "American exceptionalism," resembling somewhat the worldview of Ronald Reagan, and having a still longer foreign policy pedigree going back centuries. Seeming to echo John Kennedy, Bush said, "There is a value system that cannot be compromised—God-given values. These aren't United States–created values. These are values of freedom and the human condition."[125] He added:

> We are led, by events and common sense, to one conclusion: The survival of liberty in our land increasingly depends on the success of liberty in other lands. . . . Across the generations we have proclaimed the imperative of self-government. . . . Now it is the urgent requirement of our nation's security, and the calling of our time. . . . It is the policy of the United States to seek and support the growth of democratic movements and institutions in every nation and culture, and with the ultimate goal of ending tyranny in the world.[126]

While George Bush could claim he was simply merging Bill Clinton's altruistic concern about humanitarian intervention with the U.S. national interest in addressing the root causes of terrorism by promoting regime change, critics at home and abroad did not see it that way, especially after Bush's "axis of evil" speech in January 2002, which appeared excessively provocative toward Iraq, North Korea, and Iran, followed by his issuing the *National Security Strategy of the United States* document in September of that year, in which he unveiled the **Bush Doctrine** of preemptive war. The document stated that "the gravest danger our nation faces lies at the crossroads of radicalism and technology. Our enemies have openly declared that they are seeking weapons of mass destruction. . . . As a matter of common sense and self-defense, America will act against such emerging threats before they are fully formed. . . . [There is the need for] anticipatory action to defend ourselves, even if uncertainty remained as to the time and the place of the enemy's attack."[127]

Following the invasion of Iraq in 2003, critics maintained that, rather than neoconservatism being just a contemporary version of the classic American blend of idealism and realism, it represented an unprecedented break with the past, in terms of its seemingly reckless warmongering and replacement of a posture of deterrence with aggression, its extreme unilateralist contempt for the opinions of allies no less than adversaries, and its unusually abrasive style of diplomacy.[128] A president who had been criticized when he first arrived in Washington for reaching back to America's isolationist beginnings was subsequently criticized for imperial overreach.

Toward the end of the Bush administration, after a crushing defeat of the Republican Party in the 2006 midterm congressional elections signaled a public desire for change, the president fired Secretary of Defense Rumsfeld and began to rethink the Iraq War and his neocon philosophy. A BBC News headline stated "Bush Brings in Policy 'Realists,'"[129] the implication being that the president was embarking on a policy that was less messianic and more pragmatic, including a willingness to talk to the leaders of axis of evil states. But would talking produce any more results than saber-rattling? President Bush, like his predecessors, continued to struggle with the question of what works in international relations, the carrot or stick, or some measure of both. He was also left having to struggle with the proper role of morality in international relations. If it was misguided to view world politics as a morality play, as many Bush critics contended, then what weight, if any, was one to give moral obligations in making foreign policy decisions? Many of the same liberal critics who ridiculed Bush's black-and-white "moral clarity" were themselves inclined to view foreign policy as "social work,"[130] wanting the United States to intervene in the Sudan to stop genocide in Darfur, to expand American foreign aid in fighting poverty and the AIDS epidemic in Africa and elsewhere, and doing other good deeds. Recalling Robert Osgood's point about "the expediency of idealism," what was the optimal blend of *Realpolitik* and moralism in foreign policy? And, as always, to what extent should one act alone, or together with others, in the world?

We have seen how presidents from George Washington to George Bush have pondered these puzzles, their choices constrained by various domestic and external factors. These dilemmas are not new, but in some respects they are more challenging than ever, given the complexities of the contemporary international system outlined earlier in the book. In the next chapter, the contemporary foreign policy debate and the various schools of opinion as to how the United States might cope with Gulliver's travails will be examined in greater detail.

DISCUSSION QUESTIONS

1. Has U.S. foreign policy during the course of American history been marked mainly by continuity or by change? To the extent there have been persistent patterns and threads running through American foreign policy historically, what have they been?

2. Who were the early architects of U.S. foreign policy? What similarities and differences existed among them in their view of American foreign policy? Aside from "individual" factors, what other factors shaped American foreign policy in its first one hundred years? Was isolationism an accurate description of American foreign policy in its first century?

3. Discuss the Monroe Doctrine and the Roosevelt Corollary. Were these examples of American realist or idealist impulses?

4. Are there comparisons you can make between American interventionist behavior in Vietnam and Iraq in recent times and American intervention in Mexico, Cuba, and the Philippines in earlier times?

5. The idealist strand of American foreign policy has often been most closely associated with the presidency of Woodrow Wilson, who failed in his attempt to get America to join the League of Nations, a global organization that Wilson hoped would end war. Which American presidents since Wilson would you label the most idealist, and which would you label the most realist?

6. What accounts for the United States "returning to normalcy" and withdrawing somewhat from world politics in the Interwar Period after World War I, yet adopting more of a global view after World War II, joining the

United Nations, building several peacetime alliances, and becoming "the leader of the free world"? What was the role played by idiosyncratic characteristics of leaders, domestic politics, and systemic factors?

7. During the Cold War, virtually every U.S. administration was guided, to some extent, by an overarching strategic concern of "containing" the Soviet Union and the expansion of communism. Trace the history of successive administrations during the Cold War and identify any differences that existed in their approach toward containment.

8. What were the Truman, Eisenhower, Reagan, Powell, and Clinton doctrines?

9. Critics of current American foreign policy argue that after World War II, the United States adopted a highly multilateralist orientation—working to build not only strong alliances in Europe and elsewhere, such as NATO, but also major global institutions, such as the United Nations, the International Monetary Fund, and the World Bank—whereas under the Bush administration the United States tended to pursue a much more unilateralist orientation. Discuss. Compare the most recent U.S. presidents—Ronald Reagan, George H. W. Bush, Bill Clinton, and George W. Bush—as to their degree of multilateralism exhibited in the conduct of American foreign policy.

4

US Foreign Policy in the Twenty-First Century

The Contemporary Debate

Life is a sum of all your choices.

—Albert Camus

Unlike the last forty years, the task before us is . . . more complex, and it is more nuanced. It has become less susceptible to the giant gesture, the single solution, or the overarching doctrine.

—Secretary of State James Baker, 1989

If you come to a fork in the road, take it.

—Yogi Berra

Chapter 1 introduced the "Gulliver" problematique facing American foreign policy-makers, describing the many problems the United States is experiencing today as the world's only superpower struggles to adapt to a strange environment that is the contemporary international system. Laying the groundwork for further analysis, Chapter 2 provided some theoretical perspective and tools for conceptualizing foreign policy as a field of study, while Chapter 3 offered an historical perspective on American foreign policy. In Chapter 4, we are now ready to engage in prescriptive analysis, weighing the merits of various foreign policy ideas that have been the subject of much current debate over how to improve America's standing in the world along with its security and well-being. We will examine different schools of thought that are represented by leading scholars and practitioners who have offered critiques of recent American policy.

This chapter considers the menu of foreign policy choices open to the United States today. We are interested here not in micro-decisions but in the really big, meaty decisions. What general path might American foreign policy take in terms of unilateralism versus multilateralism and other broad orientations previous administrations have had to choose between? What are the larger lessons to be drawn from the American experience in the Iraq War? What basic guidelines should be followed in implementing policy—for example, is the Weinberger, or Powell, Doctrine still a useful template for deciding on military intervention? And is there any new buzzword that can perform the function "containment" served during the Cold War in providing an overarching, integrating rationale for American foreign policy in the

"Gentlemen, the fact that all my horses and all my men couldn't put Humpty together again simply proves to me that I must have more horses and more men."

CARTOON 4.1 Performing Policy Evaluation: Drawing "lessons" from the Iraq War and other policy failures. © THE NEW YORKER COLLECTION 1978 DANA FRADON FROM CARTOONBANK.COM. ALL RIGHTS RESERVED.

post–Cold War era? Or is each foreign policy problem on Washington's plate separate and *sui generis* (*à la carte*, to use the Bush administration's phraseology)—how does the United States deal, say, with North Korea, as opposed to Iran? In other words, given the constraints and opportunities found in the contemporary international system, and taking into account the domestic political milieu within the United States, what options are available to U.S. decisionmakers, and which ones make the most sense (keeping in mind the evaluative criteria employed earlier, namely morality, legality, and practicality)?

The options tend to arrange themselves around three schools: (1) **neoconservative**, (2) **liberal internationalist**, and (3) **realist**. Before examining the foreign policy ideas of each school, let us first consider the general dilemmas to which all three will have to provide answers.

BEYOND CONTAINMENT

At the outset of the book, I invoked the imagery of the United States ship of state in the new millennium being adrift without a sextant. In this same vein, Richard Haass, who served as director of the State Department Policy Planning Staff under President George W. Bush, has said:

> Containment, which survived some four decades of Soviet challenge, could not, however, survive its own success. What is needed as a result is a foreign policy doctrine for both a post–11/9 [November 9, 1989, marking the fall of the Berlin wall and end of the Cold War] and a post–9/11 world. . . . That a guiding principle is needed cannot be doubted. An intellectual framework furnishes policymakers with a compass to determine priorities, which in turn help shape decisions affecting long-term investments involving military force, assistance programs, and both intelligence and diplomatic assets. A doctrine also helps prepare the public for what may be required—and sends signals to other governments, groups, and individuals (friend and foe alike) about what the country is striving to seek or prevent in the world.[1]

Haass notes that "none of the three post–Cold War presidencies successfully articulated a comprehensive foreign policy or national security doctrine"—the Bush Doctrine, for example, being "less a coherent policy than a mix of counterterrorism, democracy promotion, preemption, and unilateralism."[2] The same question was asked of Bush that was asked of Bill Clinton: "Is There A Doctrine in the House?"[3] What prescription would a doctor recommend for what ails the patient in the case of American foreign relations?

The standard cures that are usually mentioned today are the same ones that have been contemplated by American foreign policy practitioners for more than two hundred years—isolationism, unilateralism, and multilateralism.[4] However, these age-old approaches seem inadequate to modern times. When former Secretary of State

Henry Kissinger said that the major challenge facing the United States in the post–Cold War era was to define a role for itself in a world that "for the first time in her history" she could neither "dominate" nor "withdraw" from, he was framing the correct diagnosis, even if not providing any remedy other than implying the need to work harder at developing more constructive relations with the rest of the planet and trying to live in better "equilibrium" with others.[5] If this means that both isolationism and unilateralism are now ruled out, then what exactly does multilateralism entail? Niall Ferguson rightly has warned against "splendid multilateralism,"[6] a posture as equally tempting as "splendid isolationism" once was and equally devoid of real meaning.

In formulating a vision of where the United States should want to go in the world, we are reminded by Robert Osgood of the many smaller, harder, and at times incompatible, choices that have to be made along the way:

> A nation's adjustment to its international environment and a nation's ability to achieve its ends in international society depend not only upon reconciling its self-interest with its ideals but also upon reconciling one self-interested end with another, and one ideal end with another. Contradictions among ends in the latter sphere are as inevitable—and, hence, compromises are as necessary— as between ideals and national self-interest; for just as national survival may not always permit the maintenance of peace, so a rash attempt to vindicate the national honor may jeopardize the nation's security, and the principle of nonintervention in other nations' affairs may preclude the defense of international decency and humanitarianism. At the root of this situation is the fact that man is entangled in such a complex environment that he cannot possibly achieve all his goals simultaneously. . . . Because of the greater complexity of international relations, the contradictions among national ends are correspondingly numerous and perplexing.[7]

Unfortunately, then, not all good things go together in life or in foreign policy. Most decisions involve tradeoffs. The perfect is the enemy of the good, in that searching for the 100 percent solution will usually yield nondecisions and, hence, is a recipe for paralysis. All one can hope to do is make the best decision that maximizes benefits and minimizes costs while trying to be true to the legal-moral principles one claims to observe. Should the United States decide to be more multilateralist, the debate does not end but only begins.

The United States as "Sheriff of the Posse"

As just one example of the kinds of dilemmas the United States faces in pursuing greater multilateralism in the peace and security field, let us examine for a moment the **sheriff of the posse** role that both Richard Haass and Joseph Nye have urged the United States to adopt.[8] Haass and Nye believe, as Kissinger suggests, that the United

States often is limited in what it can achieve alone and that it needs to act in concert with others in promoting world order, even if coordinated action somewhat limits U.S. autonomy. What former Secretary of State Madeleine Albright called "the indispensable nation"[9] can be, and indeed frequently must be, the leader (the sheriff), but it needs help (a posse). However, what if the posse is too scared to act, or for some other reason is reluctant to join Washington in addressing some problem? Does the United States then do nothing, refraining from acting entirely, as happened with the failure to stop the genocide in Rwanda in the 1990s? Alternatively, does the United States act alone, perhaps at best mustering a smaller "coalition of the willing," as happened subsequently in the Kosovo and Iraq interventions, neither of which was authorized by the United Nations, even if such actions then make the United States look less like a sheriff than an outlaw or vigilante?

Robert Kagan offers an interesting analogy drawn from the classic American Wild West film *High Noon.* In the movie, a sheriff, played by Gary Cooper, learns that several vicious outlaws are about to arrive on the next train and attempts to organize a posse to greet the gang, only to find that the townspeople are too frightened to fight and, instead, prefer he leave town in the hope of avoiding bloodshed. The sheriff ends up staying and heroically defeating the villains by himself. Kagan compares the United States, in trying to mobilize a coalition to eliminate Saddam Hussein, to Gary Cooper, the marshal, while comparing the behavior of France, Germany, and other American allies, in resisting American calls for help, to the saloonkeepers in the film, who hope the outlaws will settle for a few drinks and then go away.[10] From the European perspective, this is an unfair and inaccurate analogy since France and others believed Saddam was not as much a threat as the United States portrayed him to be, that armed force should be resorted to only as a last resort, and that other alternatives had not been fully exhausted. From the American perspective, there had already been too much willingness to accommodate Saddam's noncompliance with UN resolutions and too little willingness to defend the international community from someone with a record of tyranny and aggression. The United States does not have the luxury of riding off into the sunset as the hero does in the last frame of the movie; the United States cannot leave the town, in this case the planet, but rather must decide if certain fights are worth picking when no posse is available and when unilateral action risks one's losing the confrontation or, even if one wins, being branded as a bully. Only in Hollywood are good guys neatly distinguishable from bad guys and does the good guy always win whether the odds favor him or not.

This also raises the following question: What if the United States needs to rely on some unsavory recruits as part of the posse? Franklin Roosevelt's secretary of state famously once said about American ties to the dictatorial regime in Nicaragua, "Somoza might be a son of a bitch, but at least he is our son of a bitch."[11] Throughout U.S. history, Washington has opted to associate itself with allies whose values seemed antithetical to American values. Witness the alliance with the Soviet Union under Stalin during the World War II, the backing of the Shah of Iran and numerous other authoritarian rulers against left-leaning factions during the Cold War, the support for Saddam Hussein himself during the Iraq-Iran war in the 1980s,[12] and support for

Osama bin Laden and his Islamic fundamentalist comrades against the Red Army during the Afghan conflict in the 1980s. Critics condemned such alliances as not only undermining U.S. moral authority but also being inimical to American interests, as the Soviet Union became America's main Cold War rival after World War II, the Shah and other clients inflamed resentful publics and gave rise to Ayatollah Khomeini and other successor dictators who became American adversaries, Saddam went on to invade Kuwait and become a member of the axis of evil, and bin Laden and al-Qaeda went on to perpetrate 9/11. These critics refused to accept the argument that, at the time, Washington, morally speaking, chose "the lesser of two evils" and, practically speaking, arguably made the wise decision, defeating Hitler, blocking Soviet advances in the third world, neutralizing the *mullahs* in Iran, and causing Moscow to suffer a humiliating loss in Afghanistan that contributed to the demise of the Soviet Union and end of the Cold War. This is not to excuse any number of lapses in ethical and practical judgment that American decision makers have been guilty of, but only to acknowledge the reality of how difficult the foreign policy calculus can be. If one wishes to find complete moral and logical consistency in foreign policy, it admittedly is hard to do so in the American case, although one would probably search in vain for it in the case of any country.

The United States as Team Player

If multilateralism means the forging of global coalitions in addressing common problems facing humanity, this is becoming harder and harder to do, in light of broad structural changes in the international system and their implications for global institution-building. Even supporters of multilateralism have expressed concerns about the practicality of relying on global forums for problem-solving, given the increasingly unwieldy size and diversity of the contemporary international system.[13] An intriguing puzzle in the current era is that the need for coordinated problem-solving on a global scale in economic, ecological, and other areas is arguably greater than ever before, due to technology-driven interdependence, at the same time that "central guidance" mechanisms seem less feasible in some respects than in previous historical periods. One might be forgiven for believing that if comprehensive approaches to world order such as the League of Nations and the United Nations have failed or worked only marginally in the past, they are even less likely to succeed in the present environment. Compared with 1945, when, in President Truman's words, "there were many who doubted that agreement could ever be reached by these fifty countries differing so much in race and religion, in language and culture,"[14] the challenge of global institution-building appears all the more formidable today, with more than 190 states crowding around the global bargaining table. These include many mini-states and weak states lacking the capacity (technical and financial resources) to participate fully in global deliberations commensurate with the formal voting power they enjoy in the UN General Assembly and other venues as the sovereign equals of the United States and other participating states (for example, after Tajikistan became a UN member in

1993 following the breakup of the Soviet Union, its resources were so scarce that its UN ambassador had to serve as a one-man diplomatic corps and had to cook his own state dinners).[15] For these reasons, it has been suggested that the United States may find "minilateralism"—working with a smaller group of like-minded states, perhaps a "club of democratic countries"—preferable to full-blown multilateralism.[16]

Notwithstanding the challenges associated with trying to improve "global governance," some problems almost by definition are global in scope and cannot be managed without global regimes. If multilateralism means being more of a global team player in terms of ratifying more worldwide multilateral treaties (e.g., the 1982 Law of the Sea Treaty and the 1997 Kyoto Protocol on Climate Change, both of which have been endorsed by more than 150 countries), there is some question as to how the United States can do this without sacrificing in some instances its national interests and even its national sovereignty. Nation-states are under no obligation to join any treaty; in their sovereign capacity, they can agree to become a party or refrain from joining, with the former usually signified by a two-step process of signature (by the chief executive or head of state, in the U.S. case, the president) and ratification (by the duly authorized constitutional body, in the U.S. case, the Senate).[17] I noted earlier that U.S. presidents in the last several administrations often have refused to bind the United States to multilateral treaties, either withholding their signature or signing but not working hard to gain legislative ratification. I also noted that the reason in some cases was a determination that the treaty threatened American national interests, while in other cases the explanation owed more to domestic political opposition.

It is important to reiterate here the role played by domestic politics in constraining foreign policy choices. If anything, the link between the international and domestic environment has become more complex in the contemporary era, rendering the conventional billiard ball model increasingly inadequate to understanding the dynamics of world politics. In the United States as well as in other industrialized democracies and political systems, as welfare issues increasingly compete with security issues for attention on foreign policy agendas, the number of actors claiming membership in a state's foreign policy establishment is expanding accordingly, as is the potential for internal cleavages to affect policy. Executive branch agencies along with legislative committees dealing with agricultural, energy, transportation, environmental, and other concerns—bodies that previously had little or no connection to the foreign policy arena—now frequently find themselves involved in the foreign policy process. These entities are pressured, usually, to promote the interests of particular subnational constituencies having the most direct stake in a given sector, reconciling the latter demands with the demands of the external environment, rather than necessarily pursuing the national interests broadly defined. Rather than "politics stopping at the water's edge," one increasingly finds representatives of the farm lobby, the chemical industry, the oil industry, the environmentalist camp, and other "special interests" participating in U.S. delegations at diplomatic conferences.[18]

Robert Putnam has argued that when national leaders get together, "the politics of many international negotiations can usefully be conceived as a two-level game," one pitched at the international level and the other at the domestic level. He says that "each national political leader appears at both game boards. Across the international table sits his foreign counterparts, and at his elbows sit diplomats and other international advisors. Around the domestic table behind him sit party and parliamentary figures, spokespersons for domestic agencies, representatives of key interest groups, and the leader's own political advisors."[19] Putnam quotes Robert Strauss, the chief U.S. official at the Tokyo Round GATT trade negotiations in the 1970s, as saying that "during my tenure as Special Trade Representative, I spent as much time negotiating with domestic constituents [both industry and labor] and members of the U.S. Congress as I did negotiating with our foreign trading partners."[20] Furthermore, if one takes into account the presence of NGOs and multinational corporations at international conferences, then diplomacy can be seen as a "three-level game" in which not only subnational and state actors are involved but also transnational actors.[21]

The politics of the 1998 Ottawa Landmine Treaty and the 1996 Comprehensive Nuclear Test Ban Treaty were primarily of the "high politics" variety, as the United States rejected the treaties mainly on national security grounds, in the first instance insisting on the need to maintain landmines on the Korean peninsula to prevent a possible attack by North Korea against South Korea, and in the second instance insisting on the need to continue to test nuclear weapons both for purposes of insuring the reliability of existing arsenals and developing more advanced technology in the future. In contrast, the politics of the 1989 Convention on the Rights of the Child seemed more of the "low politics" variety, as the United States rejected the treaty at least partly due to opposition from conservative pro-family groups who objected to anti-corporal punishment provisions that they saw as excessive state infringement of parental prerogatives. In the case of the 1997 Kyoto Protocol on Climate Change (requiring the United States to reduce its carbon dioxide emissions by 7 percent below its 1990 level by 2012), the 1998 Rome Statute (creating the International Criminal Court, a permanent Nuremburg Trials–type tribunal that could try soldiers and officials of the United States and other countries for war crimes and other alleged atrocities), the 1982 Law of the Sea Treaty (creating a new UN International Seabed Authority to license deep seabed mining), and a number of other treaties rejected by the United States, there was a mix of high and low politics at work, ranging from fear of relinquishing sovereignty to unelected foreign prosecutors and judges in The Hague, Netherlands (the home of the ICC) or to supranational mining regulators in Kingston, Jamaica (the headquarters of the ISA), to fear of damaging the American economy and the automobile, oil, and mining industries in particular, to alienating many segments of the American public.

Politics aside, there may well have been good reasons for rejecting individual treaties (for example, Kyoto's exempting major greenhouse gas emitters in the developing world, such as China and India, from any reduction obligations, thereby likely rendering the treaty ineffective for combating global warming). However, the *pattern* of growing American isolation from much of the international community in global regime-making—perhaps most embarrassingly reflected in the fact that only the United States and Somalia as of 2007 were nonparties to the Convention on the Rights of the Child—has produced a public relations disaster for the United States. Clyde Prestowitz has called the United States a "rogue nation,"[22] given its refusal to become a party to many major international agreements that have broad support. Prestowitz and others lament the unilateralist turn that American foreign policy has taken in recent years, compared to the leadership Washington provided after World War II in helping to create such global institutions as the United Nations, the World Bank, and the General Agreement on Tariffs and Trade. Although the United States has always marched to its own drummer—for example, even refusing for fifty years to become a party to the 1925 Geneva Gas Protocol (banning the use of chemical weapons in warfare) until finally ratifying the treaty in 1974, and refusing to endorse the 1948 Convention on Genocide for forty years, ratifying in 1988—there has seemed an especially negative drumbeat toward global commitments of late. Multilateralism is not easy, but it would generally seem to be in America's national interest to be seen as cooperative rather than cantankerous.

This will take leadership from the president in playing the kinds of two-level games Putnam describes—both (1) more effectively working with foreign governments at diplomatic conferences in negotiating at least "half-loaf" compromises that satisfy core American security and other concerns while enabling the United States to don the mantle of good citizenship as a constructive member of the community of nations and (2) overcoming domestic political resistance and fractiousness within the American political system so as to gain ratification of those instruments.

The United States as Empathizer and Conciliator

In the search for compromise, especially in reaching out to and dialoguing with one's worst adversaries, how far should one go? Lyndon Johnson is reputed to have said that "it is better to have your enemies inside the tent pissing out than outside the tent pissing in." Adopting this "big tent" notion, what would it take, for example, to get an adversary such as al-Qaeda and the Islamic fundamentalist movement to move inside the tent with the United States? Would the United States have to shift its energy use away from oil so as to lessen the need for a large military presence in the Middle East? Would the United States have to shift its support away from Israel, the only democracy in the Middle East, founded as a refuge for Holocaust survivors? Would the United States have to stop discussing women's rights issues at global human rights conferences since many Muslims consider that a form of cultural imperialism? Would the United States also have to agree to stop promoting freedom of religion at such conferences? And would the United States have to limit freedom of speech and press at home (so as to avoid the kinds of protests sparked by the 2005 publication of cartoons in a Danish newspaper negatively depicting the prophet Mohammed that resulted in violent demonstrations throughout the Middle East)? Even if Washington took all these steps, which would require a significant shift in its traditionally defined interests and values, there would be no assurance that a peaceful relationship would ensue between the United States and the Islamic world.

Much has been made of George W. Bush's reluctance to talk to the leadership of axis of evil states, such as Kim Jong Il of North Korea or Mahmoud Ahmadinejad of Iran. In deflecting criticism of the United Nations as a mere "talk shop," Winston

Churchill once argued persuasively that "to jaw-jaw is better than to war-war." Yet, there are also rather naïve expectations that sometimes attend diplomatic endeavors, reflected in the response of William Borah, an anti-war U.S. senator, upon hearing of Nazi Germany's 1939 invasion of Poland that started World War II. Forgetting the failed effort at appeasement made by British prime minister Chamberlain at Munich in 1938, Borah commented: "Lord, if only I could have talked with Hitler, all this might have been avoided."[23] In formulating what posture to assume toward one's adversaries, one must try to be cognizant of both the possibilities and the limitations of diplomacy. Although President Bush eventually did resume negotiations with North Korea that seemed to bear fruit in 2007, with an agreement whereby North Korea pledged to shut down its nuclear facilities in exchange for tons of fuel oil, one could not be certain the agreement meant complete abandonment of Pyongyang's nuclear weapons program, given that country's past record of cheating.[24]

Avoiding "America-Firster" and "America-Worster" Tendencies

It should be obvious that as the United States attempts to chart a course in the post–Cold War world the choices facing the country are not black and white. Yet many observers persist in seeing the world in those terms. There is a tendency in engaging in normative and prescriptive analysis of American foreign policy, particularly on the part of Americans themselves, to adopt either of two extreme positions. Those in power who are responsible for the conduct of American foreign policy tend to adopt an "America-Firster" attitude, substituting flag-waving and boosterism for analysis, as they often fail to see the United States engaging in wrongdoing or wrongheaded behavior. So, also, do many average Americans, instilled with a spirit of patriotism, overlook negative aspects of U.S. behavior. The inclination is to assume that not only is the *other* side at fault, but, in addition, the latter knows it. At the other extreme are "America-Worsters"—intellectual elites and others who tend to substitute a deeply entrenched cynicism for analysis as they often are prepared to attribute the worst motives to U.S. behavior and rarely, if ever, see the goodness or wisdom of Washington's foreign policy decisions. This is the reverse image of America-Firsters, the inclination being to assume that American foreign policy is nothing more than the latest conspiracy theory waiting to be validated. The reader should beware of both traps that many observers fall into. Each nation, of course, has its own patriotic narrative and counternarrative, but one would hope that the world's "indispensable nation" would have a more mature public debate about foreign policy.

In the following discussion of competing foreign policy schools, I will compare neoconservative, liberal internationalist, and realist viewpoints, each of which has its own take on multilateralism. I will draw on the work of many different writers, some of whom are more critical of the United States than others, but all of whom are generally viewed as serious commentators whose ideas are at the center of the contemporary American foreign policy debate. There are Marxist, feminist, and other critiques of

U.S. foreign policy that provide some useful insights as well, but they are not discussed in this chapter since they tend to fall outside the mainstream policymaking circles.[25]

NEOCONSERVATISM

To the extent that the administration of George W. Bush has had a guiding philosophy in foreign policy, it has been labeled neoconservatism. As represented by such public intellectuals and practitioners as Paul Wolfowitz, Richard Perle, William Kristol, and Charles Krauthammer, what exactly is neoconservatism?[26] Perhaps the best, most succinct definition is the one supplied by Max Boot and cited earlier, that is, "hard Wilsonianism." In other words, neoconservatism combines a peculiar blend of Woodrow Wilson's brand of idealism—in particular, a highly moralistic, almost messianic zeal for promoting democracy—with an extreme hard-nosed realism—one grounded in the assertive, egoistic use of American power, including military might, in the service of what are considered not only American values but also U.S. national interests. Like Wilson, neocons see world politics as a Manichean struggle between the forces of light and darkness, reflected in Bush's speech on the fifth anniversary of 9/11, when (playing on Samuel Huntington's words) he said, "This struggle has been called a clash of civilizations. In truth, it is a struggle for civilization."[27] Unlike Wilson, neocon optimism rests on the aggressive use of hard power and application of pressure to defeat the enemy rather than on preachy efforts at global institution-building. Neocons are prepared to act with or without a posse.

The idealist side of neoconservatism sees "the end of tyranny" as a realistic goal, but the realist side sees it as achievable mainly through policies that lean toward unilateralism more than multilateralism and toward confrontation more than accommodation. Neocons remain very skeptical of the utility of international organizations like the United Nations and the reliability of treaties like those regulating WMDs. Their aversion to international organization and law owes partly to the traditional realist belief in the inherent limits of cooperation in an anarchic international system lacking any central authoritative institutions for enforcing rules and partly to their fear that, should such institutions develop, they would undermine U.S. sovereignty or at least constrain U.S. autonomy in world affairs. As Krauthammer puts it, the more one tries to work through broad multilateral institutions such as the UN, the more one risks "submerging American will in a mush of collective decision-making—you have sentenced yourself to reacting to events or passing the buck to multilingual committees with fancy acronyms."[28] Neocons point to the farcical election of Libya, long under the dictatorial yoke of Muammar Gaddafi, to chair the fifty-three-member UN Human Rights Commission in 2003 as an example of the problems encountered in trying to operate within global institutions absent a real community of shared values and interests. This does not mean that neocons are wholly against U.S. participation in global forums. As evidenced by Paul Wolfowitz leaving the U.S. Defense Department in 2005 to assume the presidency of the World Bank, neocons are willing to give multilateralism a chance, especially where American interests are protected by a veto power or weighted voting arrangements (as in the case of the Bank), but they do not have the same faith in multilateralism as liberal internationalists have.

Despite its blend of idealism and realism, neoconservatism in the Bush years managed to incur the wrath of *both* liberal internationalists and realists, both at home and abroad. As Joseph Nye states, "The trumpeting of American primacy violated Teddy Roosevelt's advice about speaking softly when you carry a big stick. . . . The neo-Wilsonian promises to promote democracy and freedom struck some traditional realists as dangerously unbounded. The statements about cooperation and coalitions [antagonized liberal internationalists since they] were not followed up by equal discussion of institutions."[29]

At the end of the previous chapter, it was noted that neoconservatism had come under such withering criticism by 2006 that President Bush himself was said to have been reconsidering the philosophy and "bringing in policy realists" to add fresh thinking on the Iraq War and other issues.[30] Some neocons, such as Richard Perle and William Kristol, broke ranks with the president, taking the position that it was not the neocon philosophy that was at fault but rather the inept manner in which Bush had implemented it, especially in Iraq; the simple lesson they drew from the Iraq War was that if you are going to engage in military intervention, make sure you have enough troops and enough planning prior to the invasion.[31] Other neocons, such as Francis Fukyama, practically abandoned the neocon banner altogether, arguing that neoconservatism—at least as interpreted by the Bush administration—had been too optimistic about the possibilities for "social engineering" of democracy in the Middle East and too presumptuous about foreign acceptance of American leadership as "benevolent hegemony."[32]

American hegemony is at the center of the neoconservative worldview. The following passage vividly captures the aforementioned comparisons numerous observers have made between the United States today and the Roman Empire:

> At the beginning of the twenty-first century, a term came into use to refer to the American role in the world that conjured up images of Roman legions with helmets, metal breastplates, and sharp lances keeping order in the ancient world, bearded Hapsburg grandees riding on horseback along cobblestone streets in Central Europe, and British colonial officials in pith helmets presiding over tropical kingdoms. The term was "empire."[33]

Whether or not in reality the United States is the equal of Rome or Britain in their heyday, such images have elicited reactions ranging from highly critical Marxist depictions of a U.S. imperium bent on global domination[34] to the neoconservative portrayal of America as a Gary Cooper–like heroic figure single-handedly attempting to keep law and order in the name of hegemonic stability.[35] Outside the United States, there is at best ambivalence, at worst hostility, toward America's self-appointed role of town marshal and its seeming inability or unwillingness to recruit a posse large enough to help police the international system. Among neocons, American hegemony is unequivocally an empirical fact and a normative plus.

The neocon view is expressed by Robert Kagan, who, recalling Jefferson's "empire of liberty" statement, acknowledges the imperial aspirations that America had from its very beginning:

> These days, we are having a national debate over the direction of foreign policy. Beyond the obvious difficulties in Iraq and Afghanistan, there is a broader sense that our nation has gone astray. We have become too militaristic, too idealistic, too arrogant; we have become an "empire." Much of the world views us as dangerous. In response, many call for the United States to return to its foreign policy traditions, as if that would provide an answer. . . . But that self-image, with its yearning for some imagined lost innocence, is based on myth. . . . The impulse to involve ourselves in the affairs of others is neither a modern phenomenon nor a deviation from the American spirit. It is embedded in the American DNA.
>
> . . . In addition to the common human tendency to seek greater power and influence over one's surroundings, Americans have been driven outward into the world by something else: the potent, revolutionary ideology of liberalism [democracy] that they adopted at the nation's birth. . . . [This] inevitably produced a new kind of foreign policy.[36]

In neocon fashion, he sees little wrong with such American foreign policy behavior, noting that "the result has been some accomplishments of great historical importance—the defeat of German Nazism, Japanese imperialism, and Soviet communism," granted there have also been "some notable failures and disappointments," which he tends to play down.[37]

The early twentieth century writer Walter Lippmann once said about the political culture of American exceptionalism that "we continue to think of ourselves as a kind of great, peaceful Switzerland, whereas we are in fact a great, expanding world power. . . . Our imperialism is more or less unconscious."[38] While neocons concede American imperial ambition, they contend that America is an empire unlike any other. Krauthammer puts it this way: "First, we do not have the imperial culture of Rome. We are an Athenian republic. . . . Second . . . *we do not hunger for territory*. The use of the word 'empire' in the American context is ridiculous. It is absurd to apply the word to a people whose first instinct upon arriving on anyone's soil is to demand an exit strategy."[39]

There is something to Krauthammer's point, along with Colin Powell's statement that "we have gone forth from our shores repeatedly over the last hundred years" and "put wonderful young men and women at risk, many of whom have lost their lives, and we have asked for nothing except enough ground to bury them in, and otherwise we have returned home."[40] Even some non-neocons have confessed that the American empire seems an "empire-lite."[41]

However, critics would point out, first, that for the past fifty years or so, virtually no countries—and certainly no great powers—have engaged in territorial annexation through conquest, since the latter has been widely discredited as a goal of foreign policy, making the United States hardly exceptional in its territorial self-abnegation[42];

and, second, that U.S. troops have not always returned home after being deployed abroad, remaining stationed in dozens of countries, albeit usually by "invitation." It is the matter of invitation that seems to be the rub in the contemporary debate over American hegemony. I noted earlier the observation made by Michael Mandelbaum and others that, contrary to realist theory, American hegemony has not led America's chief rivals to form a counteralliance to block American power precisely because, unlike hegemons in the past, the United States is not feared as a predator state. Moreover, Mandelbaum and others go further, arguing that not only is America not feared but, indeed, is welcomed as a provider of "public goods" that nobody else is positioned to supply. It is worth examining this argument through a discussion of the writings of Niall Ferguson and Mandelbaum himself, neither of whom are self-described neocons but whose views have some similarities with neoconservative thought.

In *Colossus: The Price of America's Empire*[43] and other works, Niall Ferguson worries not about an American imperium but the opposite—a power outage in the international system that he calls "apolarity." He and others have noted that historical periods in which there is no hegemon (no single large state) able or willing to maintain a semblance of world order are characterized by global instability in terms of both war and economic volatility.[44] Ferguson warns, "Anyone who dislikes U.S. hegemony should bear in mind that rather than a multipolar world of competing great powers, a world with no hegemon at all may be the real alternative to U.S. primacy." The "alternative to a single superpower is not a multilateral utopia" but "could turn out to mean an anarchic new Dark Age: an era of . . . religious fanaticism; of endemic plunder and pillage in the world's forgotten regions; of economic stagnation and civilization's retreat into a few fortified enclaves."[45] He claims there is growing acceptance of the view that neo-imperialism may be the only way to address the problems spawned by "failed states" such as Afghanistan.[46] He goes so far as to say, "I believe that empire is more necessary in the twenty-first century than ever before."[47]

To many, Ferguson's defense of "a liberal empire" as a good thing invites derision as the latest spin on the "white man's burden" theme that had provided a major rationale for colonialism in centuries past. Ferguson explains that, by liberal empire, he is referring to "one that not only underwrites the free international exchange of commodities, labor and capital but also creates and upholds the conditions without which markets cannot function—peace and order, the rule of law, noncorrupt administration, stable fiscal and monetary policies—as well as provides public goods, such as transport infrastructure, hospitals and schools."[48] Hence, he calls for not only American stewardship in international institution-building but also American engagement in nation-building, not unlike the British civil administrations of yesteryear in India and other faraway places. However, he is not sure that Washington is up to the challenge.

Ferguson laments the fact that the United States, despite "awesome strengths," has been "a surprisingly inept empire-builder" over the years and is especially ill-suited to play that role today because of various "debilitating weaknesses" having to do mostly with the nature of the American political system, which is characterized by a constitutional fragmentation of power among the three branches of government and an electoral politics that seeks instant results.[49] He notes only four cases of successful American military intervention and occupation since 1945, where the United States presence eventuated in the emergence of relatively stable, democratic societies; these are the ones referred to earlier—Germany, Japan, Panama, and Grenada. In the case of Japan, formal occupation did not end until 1952, seven years after World War II, while the occupation of West Germany lasted another three years; and to this day the United States still maintains forty thousand and seventy thousand troops respectively in those countries.[50] He questions the willingness of Washington to maintain that level of long-term commitments of military and economic resources in Iraq, Afghanistan, and other locales that would be needed to produce similar successes. Why? Because "the American electorate is averse" to such commitments and lacks "the imperial cast of mind. . . . They would rather consume than conquer. They would rather build shopping malls than nations." The "threat to America's empire does not come from embryonic rival empires to the west or to the east" but from "within."[51] Unlike their British counterparts during the days of the British Empire, "few, if any, of the graduates of Harvard, Stanford, Yale, or Princeton aspire to spend their lives trying to turn a sun-scorched sandpit like Iraq into the prosperous capitalist democracy of Paul Wolfowitz's imaginings. America's brightest and best aspire not to govern Mesopotamia but to manage MTV; not to rule the Hejaz but to run a hedge fund."[52]

If what Ferguson is saying is true, that neither the public nor elites in the United States has the appetite for empire, then it is unlikely America can play that role. The American political system was already growing weary of the Iraq War three years into the conflict, with polls showing two-thirds of the American people opposing the war and wanting to find a way out of it[53] and 72 percent of eighteen- to twenty-four-year-olds feeling the United States should not take the lead in solving global crises.[54] In addition to this "attention deficit" problem that Ferguson sees as endemic in the American political culture, he points to the budget deficit and other current structural factors in the domestic economy impinging on U.S. foreign policymaking. In particular, "the true feet of clay of the American Colossus are the impending fiscal crises of the systems of Medicare and Social Security," which he envisions competing for scarce resources and greatly constraining the foreign policy choices of future administrations.[55]

By 2007, due to a combination of tax cuts and increased spending on homeland security and the Iraq War, the annual federal budget deficit had climbed to roughly $500 billion. Washington was borrowing increasing amounts of money to cover revenue shortfalls, with almost half of the total $5 trillion public debt owed to foreigners, especially Asian central banks—a level of "external indebtedness more commonly associated with emerging markets than empires."[56] This dependency could prove to be the main Achilles heel of American hegemony, since "the willingness of Japan, China, and other Asian countries to hold dollar obligations, while demonstrably large [since it keeps their own currencies from appreciating so much as to harm their export trade with the United States], was presumably not infinite."[57] With an aging population demanding greater social security and health benefits while resisting tax increases to pay for them, increasingly difficult policy decisions will have to be made in Washington regarding the funding of **guns versus butter**.

Ferguson ends up comparing the United States to a "sedentary colossus," a "kind of strategic couch potato," whose citizens "will not tolerate a prolonged exposure of U.S. troops to the unglamorous hazards of 'low-intensity conflict,'" that is, "suicide bombers at checkpoints, snipers down back streets, rocket-propelled grenades fired at patrols and convoys."[58] He comes close to adopting the "sheriff of the posse" metaphor when he writes that "the obvious solution, short of a substantial expansion of the U.S. Army, is to continue the now well-established practice of sharing the burdens of peacekeeping with other United Nations members—in particular, America's European allies";[59] but he holds out little hope that such cooperation will be forthcoming to the degree necessary to provide order.

In *The Case for Goliath: How America Acts As the World's Government in the 21st Century*, Michael Mandelbaum shares Ferguson's view of the United States as a relatively benign hegemon, but is less comfortable with the word empire and with the exclusive American calling to engage in nation-building. Rather than a predator, the United States is seen as an eco-friendly member of its habitat: "It is not the lion of the international system, terrorizing and preying on smaller, weaker animals in order to survive itself. It is, rather, the elephant which supports a wide variety of other creatures—smaller mammals, birds, and insects—by generating nourishment for them as it goes about the business of feeding itself."[60] Mandelbaum insists this is not merely America's self-image but one grudgingly accepted by most members of the anarchic jungle that is the state system, the proof being that, following the demise of the other superpower, they "did not pool their resources to confront the enormous power of the United States because, unlike the supremely powerful countries of the past, the United States did not threaten them."[61]

Mandelbaum elaborates: "Mark Twain once said of the weather that everybody talks about it but nobody does anything. So it [is] with the rest of the world and the United States. Heated and widespread complaints about its international role [are] combined with an almost complete absence of concrete, effective measures to change or restrict it."[62] About the criticism, Fouad Ajami has written, "It is the fate of great powers that provide order to do so against the background of a world that takes the protection while it bemoans the heavy hand of the protector."[63] Mandelbaum speculates that if "a global plebiscite on the role of the United States in the world were held by secret ballot many, perhaps most, of the foreign policy officials in other countries would vote in favor of continuing it."[64] Why the tacit acceptance of American hegemony? "Because . . . its ultimate purpose was to promote values widely shared in the international system, and because many of its specific features in fact met with the approval of those with a direct stake in them, the American role as the world's government commanded wider international acceptance than the chorus of criticism and the visible anti-American sentiment that marked the early years of the twenty-first century suggested."[65]

The values that Mandelbaum is referring to are peace, democracy, and free markets, the latter one having become, in his judgment, "perhaps the most widely accepted cultural institution in all of human history."[66] Fred Bergsten, endorsing the theory of hegemonic stability, observes that "history shows that an effective international system [in support of such values] requires a custodian which is willing to internalize systemic costs," that is, tolerate free riders in subsidizing **public goods** that benefit not only the hegemon but others as well, whether in the form of security (e.g., the nuclear defense umbrella that the United States provided for Western Europe and Japan during the Cold War) or free trade (e.g., the widened access to the American market the United States provided in order to promote GATT norms after World War II).[67] Although there is no world government, Mandelbaum sees Washington as the functional equivalent, "as it furnishes services to other countries, the same services, as it happens, that governments provide within sovereign states to the people they govern."[68]

Just as Kagan invokes the film *High Noon* as a parable supporting America's role as town marshal, Mandelbaum invokes another classic American film, *It's A Wonderful Life*, as an apology for American hegemony. In the movie, a self-doubting bank clerk in a small town—George Bailey, played by Jimmy Stewart—eventually realizes how instrumental he has been in improving his neighbors' lives. Mandelbaum argues that the United States also has made a difference, in that without the United States' role as the world's government, "the world very likely would have been in the past, and would become in the future, a less secure and prosperous place."[69] Mandelbaum describes the kinds of governmental services the United States has provided to the international system: "The most basic of all public goods is personal safety. . . . American forces remained in Europe and East Asia because the countries located in these two regions wanted them there" since "the American presence offered the assurance that these regions would remain free of war and, in the case of Europe, free of the costly preparations for war."[70] In addition to the physical security function, a government performs various "economic tasks." One is "the enforcement of contracts and the protection of property. . . . America's international military deployments have these effects on transactions across borders. Governments also supply the power and water. . . . Similarly, the United States helps to assure global access to the economically indispensable mineral, oil. Governments supply the money used in economic transactions: The American dollar serves as the world's money."[71]

One should not overdraw the comparison of America with George Bailey or any other hero of American cinema. Still, Robert Samuelson makes a compelling case that, notwithstanding frequent American failures in Vietnam, Iraq, and elsewhere, the United States can claim a record of accomplishment since World War II that perhaps is not fully appreciated:

> By objective measures, the Pax Americana's legacy is enormous. . . . In World War II an estimated 60 million people died. Only four subsequent conflicts have had more than a million deaths (the Congo civil war, 3 million; Vietnam, 1.9 million; Korea, 1.3 million; China's civil war, 1.2 million). . . . Under the U.S. military umbrella, democracy flourished in Western Europe and Japan. It later spread to South Korea, Eastern Europe and elsewhere. In 1977 there were 89 autocratic regimes in the world and only 35 democracies. In 2005 there were 29

autocracies and 88 democracies. Prosperity has been unprecedented. . . . [From] 1950 to 1998 the world economy expanded by a factor of six. Global trade increased twentyfold. . . . Since 1950 average incomes have multiplied about 16 times in South Korea, 11 times in Japan, and six times in Spain . . . and three in the United States.[72]

Although America alone is not responsible for this progress, it has come during America's "watch." Samuelson worries, as Ferguson does, about bidding "farewell to Pax Americana" if Gulliver cannot get his act together. Mandelbaum, also, frets about growing U.S. weakness as well as what seems to be growing American parochialism and unwillingness to provide public goods as generously as in the past. Whereas Ferguson believes empire is more necessary than ever, Mandelbaum believes that "the world has a greater need for *governance* in the twenty-first century than ever before [italics mine]."[73] However, "whether, and for how long, the United States will remain the world's government is an open question, the answer to which will depend on the willingness of the American public, the ultimate arbiter of American foreign policy, to sustain the costs of this role."[74] Citing the estimated $45–$75 trillion in future "unfunded mandates" associated with spiraling health care and social security expenditures, Mandelbaum warns that "the entitlements explosion" will produce "a new political climate in the United States" in which "the international services that the country came to provide during and after the Cold War are not necessarily destined to flourish."[75] He echoes Ferguson's skepticism over whether the Europeans or others are willing to fill the breach and engage in burden-sharing: "Rather than being home alone," the United States is "abroad alone. Insofar as American foreign policy is unilateral, this is by default as well as by choice."[76] He concludes by making the following prediction about American hegemony: other countries "will not pay for it; they will continue to criticize it; and they will miss it when it is gone."[77]

Mandelbaum is a bridge to the liberal internationalist school insofar as he argues that the choice the United States has made of late, veering toward greater unilateralism, has been a mistake. He strongly feels it is in the interest of the United States to continue to promote global governance and international institution-building that advances the triad of Wilsonian values represented by peace, democracy, and free markets. Granted America's critics are themselves hypocritical, biting the hand that feeds them, he nonetheless finds fault with the Bush administration for not doing more to improve America's image in the world and to earn the respect of other peoples.

We are still left with the question, though, of whether it is possible to mobilize a posse to help Washington lead. The liberal internationalist school seems to think it is doable.

LIBERAL INTERNATIONALISM

Liberal internationalism can be defined as "soft Wilsonianism," in the idealist tradition of international relations. As represented by Woodrow Wilson and Jimmy Carter,

CARTOON 4.2 The Debate over Unilateralism versus Multi-lateralism. CREDIT: ANDREW SOUTHON/ALAMY

liberal internationalists are committed to global multilateralism and the development of international law and institutions such as the United Nations.[78] They argue that, notwithstanding the failures of the UN, "for $1.25 billion a year [the annual regular budget of the organization]—roughly what the Pentagon spends every thirty-two hours—the United Nations is still the best investment that the world can make in stopping AIDS and SARS, feeding the poor, helping refugees, and fighting global crime and the spread of nuclear weapons." All told, total annual expenditures of the UN and its specialized agencies "equal about one-fourth the municipal budget of New York City."[79] Liberals add that, while the United States pays 22 percent of the annual UN budget, this is down from 30 percent in 1945, and amounts to small change—less than the cost of one bomber a year. Liberals cite these figures to underscore that the United Nations is vastly underfunded and that the United States can easily afford to donate more monies to the organization without it straining the federal budget.

Although the practical realities of governing (domestically and internationally) at times made Bill Clinton stray from liberal internationalist precepts, his heart and soul seemed wedded to that school of thought. His own assistant secretary of state for global affairs, Strobe Talbott, went so far as to speak approvingly of the "birth of the global nation."[80] Not only did Clinton see foreign policy as "social work," but in administering America's caseload he was less focused on U.S. primacy and hegemony than on collaboration, and he was more inclined to try to use soft power than hard power where possible. Sounding very much like a liberal internationalist critic of neoconservatism, Clinton expressed his worldview at a Yale University talk in 2006, when he said, "A lot of respectable opinion" argues that America should act like "we're the biggest, most powerful country in the world now. 'We've got the juice, we're going to use it.' . . . But if you believe that we should be trying to create a world with rules and partnerships and habits of behavior that we would like to live in when we are no longer the only military, economic, and political superpower in the world, then you wouldn't do that."[81] As Zbigniew Brzezinski, who served as Jimmy Carter's National Security Advisor, has framed "the choice," the United States should aim for "global leadership," not "global domination."[82]

That Clinton largely failed to build up either U.S. soft power or global governance during his eight years in office shows the difficulty of putting liberal internationalist ideas into practice, and it shows why proponents of this school invite frequent criticism as utopian thinkers who ignore the importance of nationalism. When Clinton flirted with placing American peacekeeping troops in Somalia and other hotspots under a foreign commander appointed by the United Nations and suggested that America no longer had the leverage or resources to act alone—the so-called Tarnoff Doctrine, named after his undersecretary of state for political affairs—adverse reaction from the U.S. Congress and American public opinion over possible loss of U.S. sovereignty forced him to reconsider, with the administration reassuring constituents that "multilateralism is a means, not an end" and that collective action "requires—and cannot replace—American leadership."[83] When a Russian veto on the UN Security Council blocked the international community's approval of humanitarian intervention in Kosovo, he settled for the imprimatur of NATO instead. It was noted in Chapter 3 that Clinton's "assertive multilateralism" was more assertive in rhetoric than action. The United States under Clinton straddled the line between leadership and domination, its foreign policy often amounting to little more than a "courteous form of Bushism" rather than an exercise in genuine consensus-building with allies and others.[84]

Still, liberal internationalists contend that, if only the United States were willing to work harder at forging true partnerships—at playing down the sheriff role and playing up the member-of-the-posse role—then it might be able to mobilize broad coalitions in support of world order. Although many liberals supported American interventions in Kosovo and Iraq as necessary efforts at regime change against human rights violators,[85] they would have much preferred these being sanctioned by the UN rather than by smaller coalitions of the willing, if only because the invasions would have enjoyed greater legitimacy. The lesson they draw from the Iraq War is that American military intervention is more prone to failure when it does not have the benefit of political cover furnished by the international community at large. They trace the Pax Americana to Franklin Roosevelt's Great Design for a postwar United Nations embodied in the Atlantic Charter[86] and Harry Truman's belief in the "Parliament of Man" envisaged in Tennyson's poem, and they regret that these multilateral-ist roots planted after 1945—in "the shift to globalism"—have not branched out but, especially of late, have seemed to retract.

With the passing of the Cold War and its polarizing frictions, liberals see an opportunity to take global institution-building to the next stage. They envision a world "after hegemony"[87] in which nation-states' mutual interests in regulating everything from pollution to the Internet will provide a basis for cooperation more than ever. One variant of liberalism, the **functionalist** school, posits that, as states develop habits of cooperation by collaborating in narrow, low-politics technical fields—such as sharing cancer research data—cooperation will spill over into higher-politics areas, including arms control. Liberals assert that intergovernmental organizations (IGOs) are likely to provide key vehicles in the twenty-first century whereby nation-states can retain their sovereignty while managing to function in a global political space in which human transactions and concerns increasingly transcend borders. In other words, the name of the game of international relations will be "shooting pool" while "pooling sovereignty," that is, the billiard ball paradigm will need to be adapted to changing times.[88] The challenge of pooling sovereignty without sacrificing national interests and autonomy will likely grow as complex interdependence grows, and the challenge will be particularly problematical for great powers such as the United States, which are not used to having their behavior so circumscribed. But it is a challenge, liberal internationalists argue, that can be ignored only at one's peril.

Lawrence Korb, in his critique of the Bush administration's National Security Strategy submitted to Congress in 2006, wrote that it "makes a number of conceptual errors that undermine its relevance for solving or managing many of the complex global problems now confronting the United States." For example, the amount of money in the Bush budget "allocated for offense is approximately 20 times higher than prevention." Although the Bush administration was spending $3.5 billion in trying to help meet the Millennium Development Goals established by the UN in 2000 (for example, to reduce by half, by 2015, the number of people on the planet living on a dollar a day and suffering from hunger), it did not "spend the political capital necessary to prevent the Congress from cutting its foreign aid budget request by 10 percent."[89] Liberals point out that, although the United States may be the world's number one foreign aid donor in absolute dollars spent on assistance (roughly $20 billion annually), it is virtually dead last among the richest twenty countries in terms of its level of charity based on giving as a percentage of national income (roughly one-tenth of one percent of the U.S. GNP).[90]

The conceptual differences between the liberal internationalist and the neoconservative prescriptions for the post–Cold War world can be clearly seen in a brief review of the writings of Joseph Nye and Richard Haass, both of whom have been scholar-practitioners whose careers have engaged them in various modes of inquiry about foreign policy and have led them to arrive at the sheriff-and-the-posse solution to Gulliver's travails.

Nye served in the U.S. Department of State during the Carter administration and is a leading scholar in the neoliberal school of the international relations discipline.

In his essay "U.S. Power and Strategy After Iraq," Nye summarizes the liberal faith in the United Nations: "Rather than engage in futile efforts to ignore the UN or change its architecture, Washington should improve its underlying bilateral diplomacy with the other veto-wielding powers and use the UN in practical ways. In addition to overseeing the UN's development and humanitarian agenda, the Security Council may wind up playing a background role in diffusing the crisis in North Korea; the Committee on Terrorism can help prod states to improve their procedures; and UN peacekeepers can save the United States from having to be the world's lone sheriff."[91] Like Ferguson, Nye sees America as having "a military that is better suited to kick down the door, beat up a dictator, and go home than to stay for the harder work of building a democratic polity." Unlike Ferguson, he sees a more vigorous multilateralism as a solution to the problem; for example, in the case of the Iraq War, a conceivable scenario might be the following: "The United States would entice NATO allies and other countries to help in the policing and reconstruction of Iraq, a UN resolution would bless the force, and an international administrator would help to legitimize decisions."[92] Even if it may be too late for that solution to work in Iraq, it is one that has been used with some success in Bosnia and Kosovo and might serve as a model for future interventions.

However, how practical is it to expect that the United States can get "the other veto-wielding powers" on the UN Security Council, much less the membership at large, to support Washington's foreign policy agenda? Thomas Friedman rightly notes, "Thanks to North Korea's nuclear test [in 2006], we've come to a moment of truth. Yes, we have to make up our minds, but so, too, must Moscow and Beijing. They constantly advocate 'multilateral' solutions. Well, will they sign up for the kind of biting multilateral sanctions that would work vis-à-vis Iran and North Korea and make 'unilateral' U.S. military options unnecessary? If Russia and China want to see the post-Cold War world continue, they can't be free riders anymore—opposing both U.S. unilateralism and effective multilateralism that requires them to do something hard."[93]

As of mid–2007, there were hopeful signs of Moscow and Beijing finally taking up Friedman's challenge in helping the United States change North Korean behavior, although the full dismantling of North Korea's nuclear program was still in doubt, and the status of Iran's nuclear program just as uncertain. Friedman could have added Paris to the list of veto-state capitals that have frustrated American efforts to utilize the United Nations to address U.S. concerns.

In *The Paradox of American Power: Why the World's Only Superpower Can't Go It Alone*, Nye claims to stake out a middle ground[94] between unilateralist internationalists and multilateralist internationalists, but his book tilts strongly toward the latter camp. He says, "Granted multilateralism can be used as a strategy by smaller states to tie the United States down like Gulliver among the Lilliputians. . . . Multilateralism involves costs, but in the larger picture, they are outweighed by the benefits. International rules bind the United States and limit our freedom of action in the short term, but they also serve our interest by binding others as well."[95] He calls for a redefinition of the national interest calculated to enhance American soft power, noting that "failure to pay proper respect to the opinion of others and to incorporate a broad conception of justice into our national interest will eventually come to hurt us."[96]

He does allow that unilateral action should not be ruled out, especially "in cases that involve vital survival interests," or where "multilateral arrangements interfere with our ability to produce stable peace in volatile areas," or when "unilateral tactics sometimes help lead others to compromises that advance multilateral interests," or when "multilateral initiatives are recipes for inaction or are contrary to our values." Having said that, he then articulates "a long list of items," ranging from the spread of infectious diseases to the stability of global financial markets to the control of WMDs and transnational terrorism, "that cannot be achieved except by multilateral means," and concludes that American foreign policy "should have a general preference for multilateralism, but not all multilateralism."[97]

He stops far short of recommending that the United Nations become a world government: "Rather than thinking of a hierarchical world government, we should think of governance crisscrossing and coexisting with a world divided formally into sovereign states."[98] Again, sovereignty is to be pooled, not surrendered. He adds that "hybrid network organizations that combine governmental, intergovernmental, and nongovernmental representatives, such as the World Commission on Dams or Kofi Annan's Global Compact [which has engaged the UN, NGOs, and MNCs such as Microsoft in an effort to reduce the digital divide between developed and less developed countries] are other avenues to explore."[99] However, as lines of accountability for problem-solving become blurred, there is not only the possibility of some erosion of sovereignty but also of a "democratic deficit." He recognizes that "the problem of democratic accountability of multilateral institutions . . . remains a real one." There is the need to "try to design multilateral institutions that preserve as much space as possible for domestic democratic processes to operate."[100]

Nye concludes by commenting that "if the United States plays its cards well and acts not as a soloist but as the leader of a concert of nations," then "the Pax Americana, in terms of its duration, might . . . become more like the Pax Romana than the Pax Brittanica."[101] Of course, if multilateralism were taken as far as many liberal internationalists wish to take it, Pax Americana would be closer to Tennyson's "Federation of the World" than to the Roman Empire. Nye cites statistics reinforcing the view that the American public prefers multilateralism to unilateralism, as "upwards of two-thirds of the public oppose, in principle, the U.S. acting alone overseas without the support of other countries."[102] It bears repeating, though, that this is the same public that raised alarm bells over the thought of the Clinton administration placing American troops under a UN commander or subjecting the United States to the authority of the International Criminal Court. The signals that policymakers receive from their internal environment at times can be as mixed and confusing as those from their external environment.

Overlapping Nye's writing is that of Richard Haass, who, like Nye, has been a public intellectual as well as a policymaker, having served in the State Department during both Bush administrations and having authored numerous articles and books as a member of the Council on Foreign Relations, a well-known independent advisory organization.

On the spectrum between idealism and realism, his ideas place him closer than Nye to the realist school, although he shares some of Nye's views about multilateralism.

In his 1997 book *The Reluctant Sheriff*, Haass introduced such concepts as "à la carte multilateralism," "coalitions of the willing," and other pragmatic, flexible modes of cooperation that were adapted subsequently by the Bush administration.[103] He offered a modest vision of global institution-building, cautioning that "the capacities of the United Nations are unlikely ever to be up to handling most of the challenges sure to arise in the post–Cold War world," and suggested "a scaled down version of multilateralism, one that would still try to develop stronger and more independent international institutions but with limited powers and for narrow purposes."[104] Not nearly as bullish about the UN as Nye, he was emphatic in stating that the "approval of the United Nations is not required to intervene or legitimate any foreign policy."[105] However, by the time he wrote *The Opportunity* in 2005, his views had evolved in tone and substance toward a somewhat more expansive conception of multilateralism. Although the 2005 work borrowed some of the same themes from the earlier volume, the author prescribed a new policy direction he called "integration," which he suggested could be "the natural successor to containment."[106]

In *The Opportunity*, Haass explains:

> This book could just have easily been titled "The Necessity." The principal challenges of this era . . . must be met collectively or they will come to overwhelm the United States. . . . The United States will need to adjust its foreign policy to cooperate more with other countries if we are to avoid a return to classic balance-of-power politics that would drain valuable resources that ought to be devoted elsewhere. . . . That is why the goal of integrating the major powers of the day into international efforts and arrangements designed to combat the dangerous dimensions of globalization is so vital.
>
> Integration cannot be limited to the major powers. . . . It needs to include those medium powers such as Brazil, South Africa, Nigeria, South Korea, Australia, Indonesia, and others. . . . A concerted effort must also be made to integrate those who have largely missed out on the benign aspects of modernity and whose lives are circumscribed by poverty. . . . [The] real foreign policy debate ought to be . . . how to choose wisely among the various forms of [multilateralism], that is, when to turn to the UN as opposed to other standing clusters of states, alliances, regional groupings, or ad hoc coalitions. . . . The guiding principle should be to aim for forms of cooperation that are as broad and formal as possible—and to choose narrow (less inclusive) and informal forms of cooperation only as required.[107]

Even if there is a compelling logic dictating a reformation in U.S. foreign policy and international governance arrangements, the question must be asked, as Stanley Hoffmann once put it, "will the need forge a way?"[108] As an intellectual framework and possible buzzword to replace containment, integration sounds almost too fuzzy and too hortatory to provide guidance for foreign policymakers.

Haass tries to flesh out what he has in mind:

> The United States should be using its power and influence to persuade the major powers of the day, along with as many other countries, organizations, corporations, and individuals as possible, to sign up to and support a set of rules, policies, and institutions that would bring about a world in which armed conflict between and within states is the exception; where terrorists find it difficult to succeed; where the spread of weapons of mass destruction is halted and ultimately reversed; in which markets are open to goods and services and in which societies are free and open to ideas; and where the world's people have a good chance to live out lives of normal span free from violence, extreme poverty, and deadly disease.[109]

On the subject of poverty, Haass believes firmly in the need for the United States to do more to help the downtrodden in developing countries, for "humanitarian, strategic, and economic" reasons, this being both a moral imperative as well as serving American security and economic interests to promote more stable societies and export markets.[110]

Lest he be accused of utopianism, it turns out that integration is mainly premised upon the reality of the long peace and, while sensitive to the concerns of medium and lesser powers and even nonstate actors, is focused on restoring a "concert of great powers" approach to world order along the lines of the nineteenth-century Concert of Europe that inspired the creation of the UN Security Council. Haass says, "At the heart of the opportunity is the fact that we live at a time when the prospect of war between states is less common than has been the case for several centuries and in which the prospect of conflict between this era's major powers is remote. . . . History is largely determined by the degree to which the major powers of the era can agree on rules of the road—and impose them on those who reject them. . . . To have a chance of succeeding, the United States will need to view other major powers less as rivals and more as partners. . . . It will have to make a concerted effort to build international consensus on the principles and rules that ought to govern international relations."[111]

It is easy for Haass to say that "ruled out" as "a national security doctrine is unilateralism" and that "isolationism is no better as an alternative."[112] However, it is not certain that his take on multilateralism would work. First, he papers over the problem of getting consensus among great powers within or outside the UN Security Council. Indeed, he acknowledges that "it is this absence of complete consensus and the Security Council's rules [including the veto power of the permanent members] and composition [the absence of several major players, such as Japan and Germany] that make it and the UN a too brittle and too narrow instrument to be the centerpiece of any attempt at this moment to build a more integrated world. This may change in the future, but we are not there now."[113] He falls back on the possibility of using other great power groupings, such as the **G-8** (the group of seven major industrialized democracies that since the 1970s have held annual economic summits and which recently added Russia to the club), to which might be added China and India. Alternatively, one could "create more specialized groupings consisting of those countries and others that are particularly relevant for a specific challenge" (e.g., the six-power forum working on the North Korean problem or the "quartet" of the United States, Europe, Russia, and the United Nations working on the Israeli-Palestinian problem).[114] How this piecemeal approach squares with the concept of integration is unclear. Second, there remains the problem of power having become increasingly diffused among smaller states and nonstate actors, which, through asymmetrical warfare and other means, are often able to frustrate the will of the lead powers.

Although difficult to implement, a concert of great powers' approach to world order might have merit and might be able to develop widely accepted norms for combating terrorism and related problems if it could overcome the obvious appearance of elitism. One way to build greater legitimacy would be to widen the membership to insure greater coverage of the world's regions and cultures. Already, there is a **G-20** that meets periodically, composed of the finance ministers of the largest developed and developing economies, representing 90 percent of world economic power. Haass suggests that such bodies can contribute importantly to global governance, although the larger the "n," the greater the chances of paralysis.

When one talks of a concert of great powers, one is shading into the realist school, which treats power as a central concept in its analysis of international relations. If Haass is a bridge between liberal internationalist and realist thought, so also is Charles Kupchan. In *The End of the American Era*, Kupchan urges "rebuilding a liberal internationalism that guides America toward multilateral engagement through international institutions," based on "the right mix of realism and idealism."[115] Critical of neoconservatives, he argues "the United States cannot and should not resist the end of the American era" but should be willing to "use its influence to fashion the institutions upon which it will soon have no choice but to rely."[116] The United States "should seek to establish a directorate of major states focused on managing relations among the world's main centers of power. . . . A global directorate should function along the lines of the Concert of Europe. . . . Its founding members should be the United States, the European Union, Russia, China, and Japan. Major states from other regions—Indonesia, India, Egypt, Brazil, and Nigeria would be top candidates—should also have a seat at the table. . . . The directorate would meet on a regular basis and as needed to deal with emergencies. Like the Concert, it would be guided by the goals of promoting cooperation among the world's power centers and managing regional crises. . . . Strong institutions are also needed to manage specific components of international life."[117] Although America "should not sign up to every international institution," when "Washington feels compelled to withhold its participation, it should not just pursue its own course" but "should propose alternatives and compromise with others to fashion a mutually acceptable agreement."[118]

John Kennedy once described himself as "an idealist without illusions."[119] Are the kinds of policies recommended by Haass and Kupchan, not to mention unabashed members of the liberal internationalist school such as Nye, illusory? Or do they represent real options? This leads us to consider, next, the realist school.

REALISM

Realists believe that an "idealist without illusions" is an oxymoron—that, by definition, idealists are out of touch with international reality. Hence, they reject liberal internationalism as a frame of reference. They consider its emphasis on moral-legal principles and its ambitious hopes for cooperation among states as fanciful. Given the anarchic nature of the international system, they see international relations as inherently conflictual; even in situations where bargaining between states has the potential to produce win-win outcomes, "cooperation under anarchy" is difficult, since not only is there no central authority that can be entrusted with enforcing agreements, but also states are more concerned with relative gains than with absolute gains, due to the fact that the former might be converted into military advantage.[120] Realists continue to view world politics as a billiard ball competition between nations played for high stakes, with liberal internationalist models of collaboration relevant only to low-politics, technical fields. The realist world revolves around states, sovereignty, national interests, and national security, not interdependence and institutions.

This does not mean that realists are unconcerned about world order and are necessarily hawkish in the use of armed force, only that they believe, to the extent order is possible, it is based on the enlightened, wise management of power between states rather than a preoccupation with "democracy promotion" within states or the "false promise of international institutions"[121] outside states. Since one's power is limited, one must husband it and employ it judiciously in pursuit of only vital interests. We noted that, just as many liberals undovishly supported the 2003 invasion of Iraq, many realists unhawkishly opposed the war.[122] But, again, realists did so based not on principle but practicality—it made no sense to them. When newspaper headlines reported toward the end of the Bush administration that the president was turning to "policy realists" for advice,[123] the headlines were referring to the likes of Brent Scowcroft, James Baker, Robert Gates, and others who had served in his father's administration and who were viewed as more level-headed than the neocons who had authored the Iraq War (or, for that matter, the liberal internationalists, such as Hillary Clinton, waiting in the wings should the Democrats return to power). Many of these policy veterans had been associated with the formulation of the Weinberger and Powell doctrines and lamented how those cautionary guidelines on the use of force had been ignored in the Iraq intervention.[124]

Realist prognoses tend to be guarded and offer no panaceas for what ails American foreign policy. Many realists are no more sanguine about a concert of great powers approach to world order than they are about the UN, noting that the Concert of Europe eventually collapsed due to balance of power politics as the nineteenth century progressed. Although realists pose as no-nonsense types whose analysis is grounded in experience, history often has proven them wrong; indeed, realists missed out on predicting or explaining two of the most significant developments since World War II, in particular the formation and growth of the European Community and the sudden, quiet end to the Cold War. Regarding the former, which has now matured into a European Union whose member states share a common currency and supranational decision-making machinery amidst a total absence of hostilities, realists had presumed that the centuries-old Franco-German rivalry and other nationalistic animosities would make regional integration impossible. Regarding the latter, realists could not envision a great power such as the Soviet Union going quietly into the night, peaceably accepting its demise.

While the EU recently has stalled, its members having voted down a European Constitution, and while Russia seems to be stirring again as a country with great-power aspirations, world politics has hardly evolved the way classic realism would expect. When the realist John Mearsheimer wrote an essay in 1990 entitled "Why We Will Soon Miss the Cold War," what he foresaw was "the tragedy of great power politics" inevitably being played out, as the end of bipolarity figured to evolve into the return of multipolarity and great-power competition in Europe and elsewhere.[125] As one commentator noted, "Neorealist Cassandras predicted that Japan and Germany (within or without the European Union) would emerge as new poles in the international system [and] countries fearful of American power would balance against the United States."[126] Mearsheimer failed to understand the long peace. Also, since realists are state-centric analysts inclined to ignore the importance of nonstate actors, he failed to anticipate the long war. Realists do not necessarily have a better handle on the complexities of the post–Cold War international system than neocons and liberals have, and in some respects are less intellectually equipped to deal with subnational, transnational, and other messy aspects of the contemporary environment.

Still, realists persist in their basic argument that the only way for the United States to remain on top as a superpower is to be sufficiently attentive to the interests of its chief rivals so as to give the latter no reason to form a counteralliance against Washington. Realists argue that Washington should try to maintain the U.S.-Japan alliance as well as the NATO alliance (through consultations especially with Britain, France, and Germany) and should try, also, to cultivate as amicable relations as possible with Russia and China, or at least not excessively antagonize them, granted there will be unavoidable tensions. Realists dismiss Europe as a chief rival, agreeing with Michael Mandelbaum that "Europe seems destined, in the short term, to be neither a counterweight nor a makeweight but instead a lightweight" since it is not willing to invest in a large military establishment and, more importantly, is not yet able to act in unison.[127] (As Henry Kissinger once derisively asked, "If I want to speak to Europe, what number do I call?"[128]) Realists are even more dismissive of "medium powers"; how Washington should relate to states such as Indonesia and Nigeria is not of much consequence to realists, other than possibly the need to ensure the flow of oil. As for the states on the bottom of the international ladder, namely the most disadvantaged states beset with the worst poverty problems, realists would concern themselves primarily with those countries having the most strategic importance to the United States, either posing a potential threat to America as a haven for terrorists or offering potential promise as an ally in the war on terror. Although realists would not completely ignore humanitarian concerns, these would have the lowest priority in their calculus.

The absence of a moral compass continues to be the most unattractive feature of realism as a foreign policy guidepost. The only vision realists have is tunnel vision, aimed at cold calculation of interests. Realists are not even concerned with matters of national honor or prestige or keeping commitments except insofar as they affect the credibility of one's ability to project power. Realists would counter that their main virtue is humility, in contrast to the self-righteousness of neocons and the conceit of liberals, with their nation-building and save-the-planet social engineering projects.[129]

However, critics see realist prescriptions for a post–Cold War world as bordering on neo-isolationism, inviting the kinds of criticisms George W. Bush faced initially in his presidency, prior to 9/11, when he, too, spoke of humility and against over-involvement in the Balkans, the Middle East, and other conflict zones considered somewhat peripheral to U.S. interests or beyond U.S. capabilities.[130] As one article on "The Realists" comments, "an almost forgotten school of foreign-policy thinkers says that it's time for the United States to make a strategic withdrawal from the Middle East."[131] Rather than America providing public goods, "we can go back to more of the buck passing" and "rely on local actors to uphold the balance of power" in troubled regions.[132] Realists contend that the big mistake Washington made in the Middle East was permanently stationing American troops in Kuwait and Saudi Arabia after the Desert Storm operation in 1991, raising America's profile as a target of terrorism and anger on the Arab street. As Barry Posen, a member of the realist school, says, "The trick should be to make the United States less present in the lives of other countries."[133] To the extent the United States remains active in the Middle East, it should be by returning to its earlier "offshore balancing" role, using force from afar as necessary to ensure "no one country" dominates the region.[134] As for the war on terror, realists argue that instead of trying to turn dictatorships into democracies, there should be a "U.S. diplomatic offensive to engage Middle Eastern regimes in the joint project of combating al-Qaeda and related jihadists," on the assumption that "states share a common interest in controlling nonstate actors."[135] Although realists do not ordinarily use the language of a posse, that seems to be what is being suggested here. Here, too, rounding up a posse may prove difficult, since some states' interests may lie in sponsoring rather than curtailing terrorism; as Henry Kissinger observes, Middle East "leaders are torn between following the principles of the existing international order, on which their economies may depend, and yielding to (if not joining) the transnational movements on which their political survival may depend."[136]

Stephen Walt is an exemplar of realist thought. In *Taming American Power*, he explores what the American response should be to much of the world's seeming desire to gang up on Gulliver. He writes, "The United States may be far stronger than any other country—or even any likely coalition of rival powers—but other states have many ways to thwart, harass, undermine, deter, annoy, and generally interfere with U.S. efforts to promote its own interests."[137] Although it may be true that we have not seen "hard balancing" in the form of a formal counteralliance established against the United States, Walt notes there is a great deal of "soft balancing" and other strategies being employed, aimed at frustrating American hegemony.[138] He is alluding to, for example, Russia's 2001 Friendship Pact with China and its growing "strategic partnership" with Iran,[139] along with the "collective opposition" of France, Germany, and

Russia to the U.S. invasion of Iraq in 2003, which "made it safer for lesser powers such as Cameroon and Mexico to resist U.S. pressure during the critical Security Council debate" and ultimately denied the United States "the legitimacy it had sought."[140]

Walt insists, "Any attempt to devise an effective foreign policy for the United States must take into account the strategies of both friends and foes. Once we understand how other states are trying to tame American power, it becomes easier to devise a foreign policy that will minimize opposition and maximize global support. In particular . . . the United States should return to a more restrained policy of 'offshore balancing' and devote more attention to persuading others that its policies are legitimate and broadly beneficial"[141] or "at least bearable."[142] He wants America to meld a "mailed fist" with a "velvet glove."[143] Implied here is the use of Nye's "soft power," but for much more modest ends than Nye has in mind—not to create a new world order but to return to an earlier order, one in which, in Walt's judgment, America was a "status quo"[144] power that was more realistic in its global reach. He is critical of the Clinton administration not only for its humanitarian intervention adventures but also because, "by declaring itself to be the 'indispensable nation,' the United States ended up taking responsibility for a vast array of global problems" that "proved too difficult and expensive" and "cast doubt on U.S. credibility."[145] As critical as Walt and other realists may be toward liberal internationalist naïvete, they are even more contemptuous of neoconservatives in the Bush administration for having undermined American national interests by engaging in imperial overstretch and arrogant, abrasive behavior that has alienated much of the world. Realists condemn the Bush White House for squandering whatever good will and sympathy the United States enjoyed after 9/11, of the sort evidenced by a *Le Monde* headline a day later that read "We Are All Americans."[146]

Walt gives voice to "the expediency of idealism"[147] that Robert Osgood, another realist, articulated, as he argues that the United States should try to act morally—for example in avoiding double standards[148]—not because it is the right thing to do but insofar as it enhances the legitimacy of American power in the eyes of others. Even if European criticism of the United States may be unfair, that is irrelevant, says Walt, since objective standards of morality and fairness do not apply to international relations. At times, the United States must abandon "do-gooder" intentions. For example, with regard to the Bush administration's efforts to target foreign aid in the Millennium Development Project at countries that were "pursuing policies and building institutions that adhere to the principles of good governance," Walt says the latter "means conforming to a set of pre-specified benchmarks based on U.S. practices" and encouraging "other countries to become more like the United States. These remedies may be wholly desirable from an economic point of view, but they also provide another example of America's seeking to impose its own preferred solutions on others."[149]

However, one might rightly ask, how realistic is realism? Take Walt's key prescription that Washington return to what he calls "America's traditional grand strategy"—"offshore balancing," whereby "the United States deploys its power abroad only when there are direct threats to vital U.S. interests" in a few important regions of the world and there is a need to ensure that these regions "do not fall under the control of a hostile Great Power."[150] When Walt applies this guideline to the one region that is currently the epicenter of geopolitical faultlines in U.S. policy, the Middle East, he produces an odd set of policy recommendations.

First, he says "the United States should use its considerable leverage to bring the Israeli-Palestinian conflict to an end," as if Washington has not tried for decades without success; he puts the onus on Israel, arguing that "Israel should be expected to withdraw from virtually all territories it occupied in June 1967 [during the Six-Day War], in exchange for full peace,"[151] as if Israel has not already conceded 90 percent of that land to a future Palestinian state and as if, even were Israel not to exist at all, "peace" would come to a region where, in the recent past, Arabs have fought Arabs (in the Iraq-Kuwait conflict) and Sunni Muslims have fought Shiite Muslims (in the Iraq-Iran war and in the current Iraq civil war), with almost all viewing America as a common enemy. As one commentator muses, "would the United States, freed of its burdensome ally, suddenly find itself beloved throughout the Muslim world?"[152] Second, to allay Arab and Muslim resentment, Walt advises that the United States reduce its military presence and "footprint" in the Persian Gulf,[153] since there is no threat that a "peer competitor" great-power state will seize control of the region, as if the threats now posed by rogue states (Iran), failed states (Lebanon), and nonstates (al-Qaeda) do not constitute serious challenges to U.S. oil and other interests. Walt is convinced that the United States could reduce the anti-Americanism of Iran and jihadist groups by simply changing its policies that antagonize those actors, by not only distancing itself from Israel and reducing its military presence in the region but also, at least in the case of Iran, signing a "non-aggression pact" and, if Tehran persists in its nuclear ambitions, allowing it to develop nuclear weapons.[154] Walt does not consider this appeasement. Employing the cold, hard logic of realism, he argues that, if both Iran and Israel had nuclear weapons, they would each deter the other and help stabilize the region; never mind that this might trigger further nuclear proliferation in the region, as Egypt and other regional rivals of Iran might feel a need for WMDs, or that this would increase the possibility of WMDs falling into the hands of terrorist groups, or that nuclear weapons "flatten the hierarchy of the international system" and fundamentally alter the balance of power, "turning Lilliputians into Gullivers."[155]

Walt's last word of advice suggests how realism itself may be losing its hard edge: "In most circumstances, the key is not power but persuasion."[156]

WHITHER US FOREIGN POLICY?

The reader may be forgiven if his or her view of what is the best U.S. foreign policy for the twenty-first century has been more muddled than clarified by the survey of foreign policy schools presented in this chapter. Other than engagement with the world, rather than disengagement, there are no obvious, simple paths to follow. Each school of thought offers worthwhile insights, but also suffers from some drawbacks. Perhaps the best of all worlds is to combine some elements of each. As one observer notes, "policy heavyweights from Washington to New York to Boston are grasping for the Next Big Idea, the grand strategy that will guide U.S. foreign policy in a post-Iraq world. . . . So who will be the next George Kennan?"[157] However, as James Baker's statement quoted at the beginning of the chapter suggests, the current situation may not lend itself to "the giant gesture, the single solution, or the overarching doctrine." Instead, given the messiness and complexity of the contemporary international system, American policymakers may find themselves struggling with an array of distinct, disparate, smaller, but nonetheless huge problems. In Chapter 5, the focus will be on five such issues—the war on terror, the Bush Doctrine and self-defense, WMD arms control, humanitarian intervention, and the International Criminal Court—as case studies that illuminate the special dilemmas experienced by the United States today.

DISCUSSION QUESTIONS

1. In your opinion, is there any single buzzword or concept that can perform the function of providing an overall direction and coherence to American foreign policy in the post–Cold War era similar to the function performed by "containment" during the Cold War? If so, what is it? If not, what is it about the current era that does not lend itself to such thinking?

2. Former U.S. Secretary of State Henry Kissinger has said that the challenge for the United States in the post–Cold War era is to define a role for itself in a world that "for the first time in her history" she "cannot dominate, but from which she also cannot simply withdraw." Discuss.

3. Joseph Nye has said that, in promoting world order, the United States cannot be the Lone Ranger, that it must settle for the role of "sheriff of the posse," that is, it can be the sheriff—the leader—but it needs to get others to join with it. However, what if Washington cannot mobilize the UN Security Council and important allies to support its efforts in places such as Iraq and Iran? Should it do nothing, or should it act alone and thereby risk being called a rogue state or a bully?

4. View the classic American western movie *High Noon*, which is about a sheriff in a small town who learns that several vicious outlaws are about to arrive on the next train. He tries to get the townspeople to form a posse to help him but finds the townspeople are scared and want him to leave town instead, and he ends up having to fight the outlaws by himself. Robert Kagan, in *Of Paradise and Power*, has compared the United States to this heroic sheriff, and he has compared the French and other reluctant U.S. allies to the saloonkeepers who want to give the bad guys a few drinks in the hope they will go away. Discuss whether you think this is an accurate portrait of the United States and its reluctant European allies.

5. View the movie *Syriana*, in which the United States is depicted in a negative light as often having to choose between supporting a pro-democratic faction and an anti-democratic faction in developing countries (e.g., between

"the good emir" or "the bad emir" in Middle East states) and tends to back the latter. Discuss whether you think this is an accurate depiction of U.S. foreign policy, or is it the case that the United States often is confronted with poor choices and selects the lesser of two evils (e.g., allying with Stalin against Hitler in World War II, propping up right-wing dictators during the Cold War as an alternative to left-wing dictators, backing Saddam Hussein's Iraq against Ayatollah Khomeini's Iran in 1979, arming al-Qaeda against the Soviet Union in Afghanistan in the 1980s)? Should the United States recruit unsavory regimes as part of a posse?

6. The United States has refused to join many treaties that almost every country in the world, including every western democracy, has ratified, such as the Convention on the Rights of the Child, the Convention on Elimination of All Forms of Discrimination Against Women, and the Law of the Sea Treaty. What explains the U.S. absence from these treaties?

7. President Lyndon Johnson once said that "it was better to have your enemies inside the tent pissing out than outside the tent pissing in," that is, it was wise to offer compromises that would reduce opposition to one's policies if such bargaining would permit the achievement of one's core objectives. What would it take to get, say, al-Qaeda or Iran inside the tent? Has the United States made a sufficient effort to "talk" to its adversaries, or do you think this is futile? What tactic works best in international bargaining—the use of threats (sticks) or promises (carrots)?

8. Are you an "America-Firster," "America-Worster," or somewhere in between?

9. What are the general paths or options open to American foreign policymakers today? In other words, what are the main competing schools of foreign policy? Which do you find most persuasive as a basis for American foreign policy?

10. What are the pros and cons of the "neoconservative" approach to foreign policy? The "liberal internationalist" approach? The "realist" approach?

5

Current US Foreign Policy Dilemmas

Cases

Policymakers generally do not get to choose on the future
of the state system; they confront choices on exchange
rates, trade deficits, arms-control treaties ... terrorist
attacks on airport lobbies and embassy compounds, and
garbage that floats down a river or is transported through
the air.

> —John Ruggie, in James Rosenau and Ernst-Otto Czempiel,
> *Global Changes and Theoretical Challenges*, 1989

It's one damn dilemma after another.

> —Anonymous

Neoconservatism, liberal internationalism, and realism are broad foreign policy orientations and philosophies. We have noted that, in the real world, policymakers rarely have the luxury of contemplating the "Next Big Idea," since they are necessarily faced with making more discrete sorts of decisions of the type John Ruggie refers to above. We have also noted that, even if policymakers were to find the time to indulge in big picture thinking, it is not clear what single foreign policy vision might emerge that would make sense in today's multidimensional world.

In order to demonstrate further the perplexing choices surrounding American foreign policy at this moment in time, I will examine five *specific* sets of problems that U.S. foreign policymakers are attempting to grapple with, each of which presents its own dilemmas. These are by no means exhaustive of the concerns American leaders face. They are a sampler of some of the more difficult challenges. In the course of examining these concerns, we will revisit some of the thorny questions raised in the previous chapter but with a more in-depth analysis that a focus on concrete issues affords. We will start with the war on terror and then proceed to discuss the Bush Doctrine and self-defense, WMD arms control, humanitarian intervention, and the International Criminal Court. Although all five of these concerns are somewhat interconnected and fit into a larger mosaic, each is best viewed as a separate piece of the puzzle that is contemporary American foreign policy.

THE WAR ON TERROR

At the core of America's Gulliver problem is the fact that the traditional levers of influence that have defined and enabled great powers historically—namely, the quantity and quality of one's military arsenal—are no longer as readily usable in a world in which the nature of warfare has been fundamentally altered. Not only have intrastate and extrastate violence displaced great-power interstate war as the central security problem of world politics, but intrastate and extrastate violence tend to be associated with the kind of *asymmetrical warfare* that levels the playing field through weaker actors changing the conventional rules of engagement.[1] Hence, the statistical fact that the United States alone accounts for 40 percent of global military expenditures, outspending the next dozen or so countries combined, has less relevance to the successful exercise of power today than it might have had in the past. It may well be the case that "the United States is unchallenged in several realms of military action, including the military use of outer space, air operations above 15,000 feet in altitude, armored engagements at ranges beyond one or two kilometers, and 'blue water' naval battles";[2] but these assets are less useful in situations of urban guerrilla warfare and other venues in which the American military increasingly finds itself fighting.

I am especially interested here in highlighting the dilemmas posed by *extrastate* violence, committed by al-Qaeda and other terrorist groups who are the object of America's war on terror in the post–9/11 era. If observers are correct in their assessment of the long peace (that is, that "great powers have put warfare behind them, at least in their interactions with one another") and that the most immediate national defense problem facing the United States is the long war (the name the Pentagon has given the war against terrorism),[3] then "many of our central beliefs about state behavior will have to be rethought and adjusted to better describe twenty-first century realities."[4] Not only our theories, but also our policies, will have to catch up to the new conditions.

Dozens of Dilemmas

The 2006 *Quadrennial Defense Review Report* presented to Congress opens with the statement, "The United States is a nation engaged in what will be a long war."[5]

PHOTO 5.1 On September 11, 2001, the World Trade Center in New York City was attacked by terrorists who had skyjacked two airplanes and flew them into the twin towers. This photo shows the south tower on fire and the north tower about to be hit. Some three thousand people were killed. CREDIT: AP IMAGES/ CARMEN TAYLOR

The document, however, fails to come to grips fully with many of the dilemmas posed by this war, such as the following:

1. What are the implications for changing U.S. force structures and revamping the U.S. defense budget—should Washington continue to fund big-ticket weapons systems such as the Joint Strike Fighter and the Army's Future Combat Systems, which are premised on the need to be able to continue to fight conventional wars either regional or global in scope, or should budget priorities shift toward developing "irregular warfare" capabilities, including greater resources invested in special forces, intelligence-gathering, and the like, as well as "mootwa" (military operations other than war), including

training in peacekeeping, civil administration, and nation-building tasks aimed at helping stabilize failed states which are breeding grounds for terrorists? And is there willingness on the part of American taxpayers to provide the necessary support for political institution building and economic development to help the "2 billion people living in 60 states at risk of collapse"?[6]

2. How does the United States develop the capability to fight and win a lengthy war of attrition in which its adversaries "aim to erode U.S. influence, patience, and political will"? "Irregular opponents often take a long-term approach, attempting to impose prohibitive human, material, financial, and political costs on the United States to compel strategic retreat from a key region or course of action."[7] Gruesome suicide bombings in Iraq that have taken the lives of hundreds of American soldiers, along with thousands of Iraqis, are emblematic of the problem. Democracies especially can experience problems fighting such wars when restless public opinion eventually demands victory or withdrawal. The administration can attempt to delay public outcry by controlling press coverage, as when the Bush administration prohibited televised pictures showing the body bags of dead GIs returning from Iraq to the U.S. air base at Dover, Delaware; but such media manipulation only feeds cynicism toward the war.

3. Even more problematic than the threat to freedom of the press is the potential threat to civil liberties posed by the U.S. Patriot Act passed by the Congress (that relaxed prohibitions against government domestic spying), racial profiling at airports, and other measures taken after 9/11 in the name of homeland security. Although it is true that, as the late U.S. Supreme Court Justice Robert Jackson once said, "the U.S. Constitution is not a suicide pact" in which national security has to be compromised in order to sustain civil liberties, profound dilemmas nonetheless arise over how to strike the proper balance between these values.

4. Agonizing dilemmas arise, also, over how far the United States should go in engaging in tit-for-tat behavior with terrorists, if such reciprocity violates international legal norms and throws into question the very moral distinction that the United States seeks to maintain between "us" and "them." For example, as in Iraq, terrorists tend to embed themselves in heavily populated areas, blending in with civilians and not only targeting noncombatants but practically daring their adversary to strike at them in the hope that the adversary will suffer devastating public relations fallout from the resulting collateral damage and the appearance of violating international humanitarian law that prohibits indiscriminate attacks on civilians. When terrorists take refuge in mosques or apartment buildings, anti-terrorist forces such as U.S. Marines frequently are damned if they do use armed force (engendering bitterness on the part of local publics and raising the ire of international human rights groups) and damned if they don't (permitting terrorists to hide and escape retribution).

5. Legal and moral quandaries arise, too, over the issue of treatment of prisoners, as was noted in the evaluative analysis of the Iraq War decision conducted in Chapter 2. Are captured terrorists entitled to the same prisoner of war protections normally granted to soldiers under the 1949 Geneva Convention? The Bush administration has argued that members of al-Qaeda and other terrorist groups are entitled to neither POW protections (since they do not wear uniforms and are not part of a regular chain of command that itself observes Geneva rules) nor the normal due process procedures guaranteed by constitutional democracies in a court of law (since they are not mere criminals but "unlawful enemy combatants"), thus justifying their being imprisoned indefinitely at the U.S. naval base at Guantanamo Bay in Cuba and other sites. However, U.S. judges and international legal scholars have questioned the administration's interpretation of the laws of war. Questions have arisen, too, over how far the administration can go in using interrogation techniques that border on torture, in possible violation of not only the Geneva Convention but the UN Convention on Torture and other international treaties.[8]

Norman Podhoretz has defended the Bush administration, complaining that "you cannot fight a revanchist insurgency and certainly not one that uses terrorist tactics [as in Iraq] without good intelligence . . . and you can only get that kind of intelligence by squeezing it out of prisoners."[9] How does one weigh the tradeoff between, on the one hand, the need to honor treaty commitments (if only to uphold rules that protect American servicemen should they be captured) and, on the other hand, the need to extract vital intelligence data that might protect American soldiers from future ambushes or might prevent a future terrorist attack on the U.S. homeland? Given the high stakes and the tendency to view terrorists as less than human, it is tempting to ignore the usual standards of civilized conduct, even if so doing reduces the United States to the level of the enemy and, as Colin Powell has said, leads the world "to doubt the moral basis of our fight against terrorism."[10]

Getting Agreement on the Definition of Terrorism

Were the United States to leave Iraq, leave the Middle East, and rethink other aspects of its foreign policy, it is possible that it would face fewer dilemmas caused by terrorism. However, as was shown by the 2001 World Trade Center attacks, whose victims represented dozens of different nationalities, terrorists do not respect such distinctions when carrying out their mayhem. Clearly, the terrorism problem is much larger than an American problem. Indeed, before 9/11, many states in Europe, the Middle East, and other regions routinely had experienced terrorist incidents while few such incidents had occurred on American soil, even though Americans had often been targeted abroad. Immediately after the 9/11 attacks, I told a class of students that what was at stake was nothing less than the future of the state system in terms of the capacity of nation-states to function in at least a minimal global order that affords their citizens such basic services as, for example, being able to board an aircraft and expect to arrive safely at one's destination. In my mind, the key question was whether the collective weight of the world's two hundred governments, representing more than six billion people, could prevail over a few thousand thugs. Along these lines, Richard Haass has said, "The goal of American policy" should "be to get wide acceptance of the notion that no form of purposeful killing of innocents is permissible in today's world. Branding terrorism as wrong is important. . . . The world needs to agree to this."[11] Shortly after 9/11, George W. Bush declared that "more and more, civilized nations find ourselves on the same side—united by common dangers of terrorist violence and chaos."[12]

However, even though one might assume that "states share a common interest in controlling nonstate actors" and that the correlation of forces favors an anti-terrorist coalition, the problem is that not all of the world's governments and peoples frame the issue in this fashion.[13] As Haass notes, there is no consensus definition of what exactly constitutes **terrorism**. One study finds that the term had at least 109 different definitions between 1936 and 1981, and many others have appeared since.[14] The search for an authoritative definition has been likened to "the Quest for the Holy Grail."[15] It has been said that one person's terrorist is another's freedom fighter. However, if one accepts this view, then any act of violence can be excused and legitimized, however barbarous, as long as someone invents a justification.

One simple, helpful definition considers terrorism "premeditated, politically motivated violence perpetrated against noncombatant targets by subnational groups or clandestine agents, usually intended to influence an audience."[16] This definition suggests that terrorism entails a combination of at least three elements. First, terrorism ordinarily involves the threat or use of *unconventional violence*—violence that is spectacular, violates accepted social mores, and is designed to *shock* so as to gain publicity and instill fear in the hope of extorting concessions. Terrorists generally observe no "rules" of combat whatsoever. Their tactics can include bombings, hijackings, kidnappings, assassinations, and other acts.

Second, terrorism is characterized by violence that is *politically* motivated. The political context of terrorism distinguishes it from mere criminal behavior such as armed robbery or gangland slayings, which may be every bit as spectacular but are driven primarily by nonpolitical motives. One would not ordinarily call the Mafia, for example, a terrorist organization, even though it is heavily involved in international drug trafficking and other criminal activities, at times in league with terrorist groups, prompting references to "narcoterrorism." Most terrorist groups are more clearly motivated by political goals, ranging from the creation of a national homeland to the elimination of foreign cultural influence in a region to the total political and economic transformation of society.

A third key distinguishing characteristic of terrorism, following from the first two, is the almost incidental nature of the *targets* against whom violence is committed. That is, the immediate targets of terrorism—whether persons or property, civilian or military—usually bear only an indirect relation to the larger aims impelling the terrorist but are exploited for their shock potential. Sometimes the targets are carefully chosen individuals (prominent business leaders or government officials), while on other occasions the targets are faceless, nondescript masses (ordinary men, women, and children randomly slaughtered in airports, department stores, and other public places). What is especially worrisome is the growth in the number of religious-based terrorist groups that seem to prefer a lot of people "dead" to a lot "watching."[17]

The latter phenomenon points up a fourth ingredient of terrorism, having to do with the nature of the *perpetrators* of such violence. As suggested above, terrorism tends to be the work of *nonstate* actors, that is, it is mainly the tactic of "outgroups"— the politically weak and frustrated (for example, al-Qaeda and other Islamic fundamentalists throughout the Middle East and South Asia, the Irish Republican Army in Northern Ireland, Shining Path in Peru, or Basque separatists in Spain), who see terror as the best tool for contesting the sizable armies and police forces of the governments of nation-states. Although certain excessive forms of violence used by government authorities themselves are sometimes referred to as "state terrorism"—in particular the systematic torture and repression a government inflicts on dissidents within its own society, or assassinations and "dirty tricks" committed by secret state agencies abroad—the terrorism label normally does not apply to actions taken by official government bodies. Terrorists generally do not wear uniforms, although some have been at least indirectly supported and sponsored by governments (most notably, Iran and Syria) and may even have representation in a country's government or form militias as part of a country's armed forces (as in the case of Hezbollah in Lebanon).[18]

It is this last dimension of terrorism—the identity of the perpetrators—that has occasioned the most definitional controversy. In the past, some members of the international community have excused the most heinous acts of violence when committed by those engaged in "wars of national liberation" or fighting against "occupation" forces. In 2004, Kofi Annan appointed a study group that attempted to craft a clear definition of terrorism that would establish a universal ban on the slaughter of innocents no matter the context of the conflict. The Report of the Secretary-General's High-Level Panel on Threats, Challenges, and Change defined terrorism as "any action . . . that is intended to cause death or serious bodily harm to civilians or noncombatants, when the purpose of such an act . . . is to intimidate a population, or to compel a government or an international organization to do or to abstain from doing any act."[19] The hoped-for consensus foundered on whether the definition covered the actions of not only nonstate actors but also the governments of states, which might lead some to include the American shock and awe aerial bombardment of Baghdad in 2003 as a terrorist action. Even if there was no evidence that American leaders, upon awakening on March 20, 2003, pondered "how many babies can we kill today?" (as al-Qaeda operatives seemingly do), their decision did result in considerable loss of civilian lives nonetheless. The United States argued that the definition should be confined to the actions of nonstate actors, claiming that rules already existed that govern indiscriminate use of armed force by national armies, such as those contained in the Geneva Conventions, and what was needed were rules explicitly aimed at curbing "irregular" combatants.

The United Nations Charter, when it was drafted in 1945, assumed a world of states in which the primary mission of the UN would be the resolution of interstate conflict, where national armies in formal military attire confronted each other across well-marked fronts. There is now a need to revise the Charter, along with the Geneva Conventions and other international instruments, to take into account the new combatants that are more often than not subnational and transnational groups whose members do not display insignia and are not likely to provide their name, rank, and serial number upon being captured. The 1949 Geneva Conventions attempted to develop international humanitarian law covering both international and noninternational armed conflict (with Common Article 3 stipulating minimal obligations for the protection of civilians, prisoners of war, wounded and sick members of armed forces, and other victims of interstate and civil wars), but these provisions have been erratically observed in instances of intrastate and, especially, extrastate violence, where battlelines have become increasingly murky.[20] There is a need, then, to recodify, or at least clarify, the rules governing who is or is not entitled to POW protection, the limits of acceptable conduct by guerrillas, insurgents, and other "irregular" fighters, and the limits of acceptable conduct by forces engaged in counterinsurgency, as well as other aspects of noninternational armed conflicts as opposed to traditional international armed conflicts. However, such efforts are hampered by both the lack of American leadership and the reluctant followership on the part of others—the fact that other major powers remain somewhat suspicious of the United States while the majority of lesser powers in the UN generally are suspicious of the powerful.

Despite continued obstacles to be overcome in waging the long war, it is possible to point to at least some glimmers of progress. More than a dozen international conventions have been produced as part of a global anti-terrorism regime, including three skyjacking treaties (the Tokyo, Hague, and Montreal Conventions) that generally have been successful in greatly reducing the incidence of aerial hijackings, as well as a flurry of UN Security Council resolutions unanimously approved in the immediate aftermath of 9/11, notably Resolution 1373, which taken under Chapter VII of the Charter binds all members to prevent the financing of terrorism, to deny safe haven to terrorists, to cooperate in intelligence and policing activities in the apprehension of terrorists, and to report annually to the Committee on Counter-Terrorism regarding their compliance. Although compliance has been sporadic, due more to the inadequate technical and financial capacity of many UN members to meet their obligations than to willful violation, the international community is on record as having condemned terrorism beyond previous statements.

Unlike previous wars, the long war will probably have no end, given the virtual impossibility of eliminating the last terrorist. As one U.S. government report stated, "Victory against terrorism will not occur in a single, definable moment. It will not be marked by the likes of a surrender ceremony on the deck of the USS *Missouri* that ended World War II."[21] Instead, victory will consist of the management of terrorism so that what incidents occur are isolated and relatively minor in their lethality and destructiveness. The good news is that much of the top leadership of al-Qaeda has been captured or killed since 9/11, making it more difficult for that group to mount another attack on the scale of 9/11; the bad news is that the organization's resultant decentralization and atomization into local cells has made it that much harder to locate would-be plotters and that there are other groups proliferating that are capable of doing substantial damage to U.S. interests at home and abroad.[22] One can take heart from the pacification in recent years of some terrorist groups (for example, the Irish Republican Army) and the extermination of others (the Red Brigades that terrorized Italy in the 1970s). Further progress in the war on terror may have to await a wider internalization of the norm worldwide that—like dueling, slavery, and colonialism—terrorism is a human institution that deserves to be relegated to the history books. Here again, soft power may prove more important than hard power.

THE BUSH DOCTRINE AND SELF-DEFENSE

In the previous section, the author discussed the need to reconsider the rules governing the conduct of war once a conflict is underway, such as treatment of POWs and the targeting of civilians—the body of international law known as *jus in bellum*. Here, putting the horse back in front of the cart, we need to consider how the changing nature of security threats may be necessitating a reconsideration of the rules governing the resort to armed force in the first place—the body of law known as *jus ad bellum*.

The Ultimate Dilemma

Perhaps the ultimate dilemma the United States encounters in the war on terror relates to the Bush Doctrine and Bush's attempt to redefine the UN Charter proscription against the first use of armed force in a way that stretches the concept of **self-defense** to include **preemption**. Recall that the Bush Doctrine asserts the right of the United States to use armed force against any actor Washington thinks might possibly pose a threat to American security at some point in the future. Recall, also, that the UN Charter specifies that states may legally resort to the use of armed force against another state only under two conditions: (1) in the act of individual or collective *self-defense* if it or an ally is attacked (Article 51) or (2) in the act of *collective security* if another UN member is attacked or if there is a "threat to the peace" as determined by the Security Council (Chapter VII). Any other resort to armed force constitutes aggression and is illegal.[23] In claiming the unilateral right of *anticipatory* self-defense—resorting to the use of armed force against an adversary *prior* to an actual attack by that foe, on the assumption that an attack might be forthcoming—the Bush Doctrine collides with the UN Charter's outlawing of the first use of armed force.

For President Bush, the problem was this: In the post–9/11 era, must a country such as the United States wait and absorb the first shot—which could be a radioactive bomb or anthrax or a nerve gas attack destroying large areas of New York City or Washington, DC—before it can legally respond in self-defense against a terrorist group that plotted the action or a state harboring that group? Or can the United States not act in advance of the actual aggression? (Most analysts agree that, while "deterrence"—the mere *threat* of countering force with force—can work against *states*, which have clearly marked return addresses that an attacked country can target in retaliation and, hence, which would be reluctant themselves to initiate a WMD strike, it is less effective against shadowy, mobile terrorist organizations, whose addresses are less identifiable and which are therefore less vulnerable to a reprisal; in addition, how does one deter a suicide bomber who welcomes death?)

For much of the international community, the problem was viewed differently: Once one accepts the Bush Doctrine, does this not invite and legitimize any state using armed force anytime it wishes on the pretense that somebody might conceivably pose a threat down the road? Would it, for example, provide a rationale for Pakistan initiating a nuclear attack on India as a preemptive strike against India's nuclear arsenal?

Getting Agreement on the Definition of Self-Defense and the Right to Use Armed Force

In order to understand what is at issue here, it is important to distinguish between the American attack on Afghanistan in October 2001 and the American attack on Iraq in March 2003. Regarding Afghanistan, the United States clearly was attacked on September 11, 2001, when airplanes struck the World Trade Center and the Pentagon. The attack was perpetrated not by another state but by a nonstate actor, al-Qaeda, which had been operating out of Afghanistan with the tacit support of its Taliban government, who refused to turn over Osama bin Laden to American authorities. The international legal issue was not simply self-defense but whether State A (the United States) could enter the territory of State B (Afghanistan) to apprehend or kill actors (in this case, bin Laden and his associates) thought to have been responsible for a terrorist attack on State A. Although state practice has been inconsistent, the general rule is that if State B is not clearly sponsoring or harboring the terrorists but merely finds itself used as a refuge, State A cannot intrude upon the latter's sovereignty by engaging in military activity on its soil without its permission. On the other hand, if State B can be shown to be an active sponsor or close collaborator giving succor to the terrorists and has not taken adequate steps to prevent terrorism, then State A is on stronger legal footing in taking military action.[24] In bombing Afghanistan and removing the Taliban government that had refused to surrender bin Laden, the United States invoked the customary right of self-defense codified in Article 51 of the UN Charter, an action generally supported by the international community even if some international lawyers tried to argue that the invasion amounted more to retaliation than self-defense and that the United States had no right to engage in regime change.

The American invasion of Iraq in 2003 was far more controversial. As noted in Chapter 2, Secretary-General Annan said it was illegal since the United States could not invoke the right of self-defense (the United States had not been attacked by Iraq) and could not invoke the "collective security" provisions of the UN Charter (Washington had never received specific authorization from the Security Council to mete out military sanctions against Saddam Hussein's government despite Saddam's repeated violation of Security Council resolutions, due to opposition to war on the part of France, Russia, and China).[25]

The most interesting legal argument advanced by Washington was the right of *preemptive* self-defense embodied in the Bush Doctrine. This was not a completely new idea; in some respects, it seemed little more than basic common sense of the sort Franklin Roosevelt conveyed in a 1941 fireside chat, when he told the American people "when you see a rattlesnake poised to strike, you do not wait until he has struck before you crush him."[26] Such a justification had been relied on by Israel in 1967, when its troops crossed the border and attacked Egyptian forces thought to be massing for an impending invasion of Israel, and in 1981, when its planes destroyed an Iraqi nuclear reactor thought to be a threat to Israeli security. There is a long "**just war**" tradition that provides some support for this position, although the onus is put on the attacker to demonstrate that the resort to force is necessary. As Hugo Grotius, the seventeenth-century jurist considered the father of international law, put it, "Fear with respect to a neighboring power is not a sufficient cause. For . . . self-defense to be lawful it must be necessary; and it is not necessary unless we are certain, not only regarding the power of our neighbor, but also regarding his intention."[27] To the extent there exists a customary right of anticipatory self-defense, the *Caroline* case is often cited as providing the standard definition. In 1837, the *Caroline*, a ship owned by U.S. nationals and docked on the American side of the Niagara River, was attacked by the British navy and sent over Niagara Falls because the British feared that the vessel would be used to support an insurrection by Canadian rebels; U. S. Secretary of State Daniel Webster, in protesting the action, stated that for such action to be legal, it would have to be demonstrated that "the necessity of that self-defense is instant, overwhelming, and leaving no choice of means, and no moment of deliberation."[28]

Critics of the American attack on Iraq argued that it did not meet the *Caroline* test, that it appeared to represent a "preventive war" rather than a "preemptive war"—a war Washington wanted to fight rather than one it needed to fight. They pointed out that no attack by Iraq was imminent, there was no clear evidence it still possessed WMDs, and there was no clear connection between Iraq and the 9/11 terrorists. However, there can be a fine line between a preemptive and preventive war, especially given the inherent uncertainty of intelligence that was noted earlier; it is a line that pundits find easier to operationalize than practitioners responsible for a nation's security.

On the one hand, it perhaps was reasonable for the Bush administration to take the position that, after 9/11, the United States could not afford to be a sitting duck waiting for a state or nonstate actor to initiate a WMD attack on New York City or another American target before retaliating. Yet, on the other hand, the relatively loose definition of self-defense implied in the Bush Doctrine threatened to unravel the entire UN Charter regime that had been developed to control the outbreak of war. It could be argued, with good reason, that Bush's mistake was not so much his contemplating the need occasionally to circumvent the UN's formal rules, but rather his feeling a need to proclaim preemption as a new policy; after all, other presidents before him at times had engaged essentially in the same practice without stirring up criticism by public pronouncement of a new doctrine sharply at odds with the Charter. (For example, President Kennedy's deployment of a naval blockade during the Cuban missile crisis, despite the absence of any attack on the United States, was not accompanied by any doctrinal ballyhoo.)

Even if there is a need to reexamine the rules governing *jus ad bellum*, and not only *jus in bellum*, this cannot be done unilaterally. In 2004, the UN Secretary-General's High-Level Panel on Threats, Challenges and Change attempted to address the problem by calling for legalizing the preventive use of military force (say, to eliminate the potential for horrific terrorist attacks) as long as such use of force was authorized by the UN Security Council. President Bush dismissed such a proposal, commenting during the 2004 presidential debate with Senator John Kerry that "my opponent talks about foreign policy. He proposed America pass a global test. In order to defend ourselves, we'd have to get international approval. . . . We'll continue to build strong coalitions. But I will never turn over our national security decisions to leaders of other countries."[29] Although the president might have been right to be leery about relying on the recommendations of a panel that could not even forge agreement on the definition of terrorism, the continuing flak over the Bush Doctrine is another reminder of the United States shooting itself in the foot in terms of its international reputation as a standard-bearer of world order.

CONTROLLING WEAPONS
OF MASS DESTRUCTION

One area in which the United States has helped to lead the way since World War II is **arms control**. It has been said that "the best way to keep weapons and weapons-material out of the hands of nongovernmental entities is to keep them out of the hands of national governments."[30] In 1998, U.S. Secretary of State Madeleine Albright, "citing the increasing threat to civil aviation posed by shoulder-fired surface-to-air missiles," issued a call for "an international agreement to place tighter controls on the export of such portable, easily concealed weapons."[31] Of even greater concern are concealed weapons in the form of bags of plutonium, vials of Ebola virus, and canisters of nerve gas, along with harder-to-conceal nuclear-tipped ICBMs and other weapons of mass destruction.

In the wake of the WMD intelligence failures of the Iraq War and the difficulty in assessing the nuclear threat presented by Iran and North Korea, there is a concern that a number of the arms-control regimes that have been instituted over the past several decades to prevent WMD proliferation are at risk of breaking down, due to various loopholes in the treaties, inadequate verification technology, and the reluctance of the international community to impose sanctions on violators. The latter has only reinforced the Bush administration's skepticism toward international law in general and arms control in particular, even though arms control treaties have served

American interests very well up until now, providing a legal basis for the United States to retain parts of its arsenal while denying other states that same right and, more importantly, curbing arms races and limiting the amount of deadly firepower on the planet. Before discarding existing treaties, it is worth remembering how much effort the United States and other states have expended in pursuing humanity's ongoing quest to fulfill the biblical prophecy that nations "shall beat their swords into plowshares and their spears into pruning hooks" and "neither shall they learn war anymore" (Isaiah 2:4).

The ABCs of WMD Arms Control: Atomic, Biological, and Chemical Weapons Treaties

The **Geneva Gas Protocol of 1925**, established after World War I, banned the use of poison gas and other lethal chemical agents in warfare, but it did not prohibit their production, stockpiling, and nonwar use. (The United States Senate did not consent to ratification of the agreement until 1974, although the United States joined other nations in honoring the prohibition on use during World War II.[32]) In an effort to outlaw chemical weapons altogether, the **1993 Chemical Weapons Convention** obligated all states party to the treaty "never under any circumstances to develop, produce, otherwise acquire, stockpile or retain chemical weapons, or transfer, directly or indirectly, chemical weapons to anyone" or "to use chemical weapons." Any parties that already had chemical weapons were obligated to destroy those arsenals within ten years following the treaty entering into force. A verification system was established in the form of a new IGO headquartered in The Hague, called the Organization for the Prohibition of Chemical Weapons (OPCW), which, upon the "challenge" of any member state, was allowed to do on-site inspection in any state suspected of violating the treaty. The treaty took effect in 1997, after the sixty-fifth ratification, and by 2007 had more than 180 parties. The CWC is considered a landmark agreement since it is "the first comprehensively verifiable multilateral treaty that completely bans an entire class of weapons, and firmly limits activities that may contribute to the production of those weapons."[33]

However, there are problems surrounding the CWC. Three-fourths of the two dozen states thought to have chemical weapons capabilities have joined the treaty, led by the two with the largest arsenals—the United States and Russia (together accounting for more than 90 percent of total tonnage). Although both have acknowledged the existence of these stockpiles and have committed themselves to destroying these by the end of the current decade, environmental and financial problems have hampered the dismantling efforts. Only 22 percent of the world's declared stockpile of 71,000 metric tonnes of chemical agents have been verifiably destroyed.[34] Moreover, in addition to those countries thought to possess chemical weapons that have not yet ratified the CWC, such as Egypt, Syria, Israel, and North Korea, there are some parties to the treaty that are assumed to be in possession of chemical weapons that have not formally declared them, such as China and Iran. Given the ease with which one can conceal chemical weapons—it is easy to make and store these in a basement or garage, or to hide them in dual-use facilities such as paint factories—concerns have been raised about the transparency of the verification regime and whether cheating can be detected.

Similar problems have plagued the **1972 Biological Weapons Convention**. Now ratified by 155 states, including the United States and Russia, the treaty prohibits any development, production, and stockpiling of toxins and other bacteriological weapons for use in germ warfare. The United States and Russia claim to have terminated their biological weapons programs in the 1970s, although there is still some question whether they and a few other states (the same ones suspected of developing chemical weapons) continue to possess some stockpiles and whether biodefense programs (e.g., the Pentagon's storage of anthrax strains used to test the effectiveness of vaccines) are permitted by the treaty.[35] A major weakness of the treaty is the absence of any verification procedures, so that it is exceedingly difficult to judge how much compliance has actually occurred. An effort in 2001 to produce a Biological Weapons Protocol that would have created a counterpart to the OPCW failed, largely due to U.S. lack of trust in the detection apparatus and concern about inspections possibly harming the American biotech industry. Nonetheless, the regime can be considered a success in that states generally have refrained from using biological weapons against other states.[36]

The centerpiece of the nuclear arms control regime is the **1968 Nuclear Non-Proliferation Treaty** (NPT). The treaty has been endorsed by almost the entire UN membership, the only remaining holdouts being India, Pakistan, and Israel. The NPT has been one of the most remarkably successful arms control treaties in history, insofar as much of the international system has defied realist expectations in agreeing to deny themselves the ultimate badge of national power and prestige. The NPT obligates states that do not have nuclear weapons to refrain from developing them and obligates existing nuclear weapons states to refrain from transferring such weaponry to the nuclear have-nots. A tremendous accomplishment was the agreement, in 1995 (as the NPT was about to expire), to renew the NPT in perpetuity. The nuclear powers had to overcome objections by many states that contended that the United States and other members of the nuclear club had not done enough to build down their own nuclear arsenals and to adopt a comprehensive ban on any future nuclear testing.

Regarding the issue of nuclear testing, the Partial Test Ban Treaty of 1963 prohibited atmospheric testing of nuclear weapons but permitted underground testing, and was followed up in 1996 with a **Comprehensive Nuclear Test Ban Treaty** that was slated to take effect upon ratification by not only the members of the nuclear club but all forty-four countries possessing nuclear energy reactors; this treaty has been called "the longest-sought, hardest-fought prize in the history of arms control,"[37] since a stoppage of all nuclear testing might effectively put the nuclear genie back in the bottle. However, the United States, India, and some other states have yet to sign on, with the United States, in particular, expressing concerns about adequate verification mechanisms as well as adequate alternative technologies for determining whether the existing nuclear arsenals were in working order should they be needed.[38]

PHOTO 5.2 The Second Atomic Bomb Blast at Bikini Atoll, July 24, 1946. CREDIT: JOINT ARMY-NAVY TASK FORCE ONE PHOTO/NATIONAL ARCHIVES (111-SC-259370)

Seven countries currently are official members of the "nuclear club," whose membership includes only those states that have openly detonated a nuclear explosive. The club includes the United States, Russia, Britain, France, and China (all of which were nuclear "haves" by 1968), along with India and Pakistan (NPT non-signatories that officially joined the club in 1998). Israel (the only other non-signatory) is presumed to have nuclear capabilities. Brazil, Argentina, and South Africa had active programs in the 1980s, but have since renounced any intention to build nuclear weapons, as have states such as Japan and Germany that clearly have the technological base and resources to go nuclear if they chose but have thus far abstained. Three former Soviet republics—Belarus, Ukraine, and Kazakhstan—have transferred leftover nuclear weapons on their soil to Russia. Total stockpiles are down from the almost fifty thousand nuclear weapons that existed during the Cold War, thanks to deep cuts in superpower arsenals negotiated by the United States and Russia. However, the world still has some twenty-eight thousand nuclear warheads, containing the explosive power of roughly two hundred thousand Hiroshima bombs, with the United States and Russia accounting for more than 90 percent of the total.[39] Further progress depends not only on actions taken by Washington and Moscow but on decisions taken in other national capitals. At issue is whether the existing nuclear nonproliferation regime is still effective in constraining state behavior or whether the entire edifice is on the brink of collapsing.

NPT Meltdown?: North Korea and Iran

In particular, alarm bells have sounded recently over the fact that two parties to the NPT—North Korea and Iran—have attempted to establish active nuclear weapons programs in violation of their treaty commitments. Under the NPT, states are permitted to pursue peaceful nuclear energy programs for electric power–generation purposes, including engaging in either uranium enrichment or plutonium production from reprocessing spent fuel (both potential bombmaking materials), as long as they report their activities and submit to inspections by the International Atomic Energy Agency (IAEA), the UN agency charged with monitoring NPT compliance. However, parties can legally withdraw from the treaty upon giving three months notice, which they can do after having already acquired much of the technology and fissile material needed to build nuclear weapons.

In 1993, North Korea was found to be in breach of its obligations, due to its engaging in reprocessing without notifying the IAEA. It was also suspected of engaging in uranium enrichment, although it denied doing so. When it tried to take advantage of the NPT loophole to withdraw from the treaty, Pyongyang was persuaded to remain in the NPT and was promised economic inducements by the Clinton administration to end its weapons program, although it continued to pursue its nuclear aspirations. The Bush administration urged that North Korea be punished rather than rewarded for its behavior, hoping a hardline policy would force Pyongyang to cease nuclear weapons development, but was unable to convince China, Russia, Japan, and South Korea to cooperate in backing such a policy. China, whose substantial energy and food assistance to North Korea gave it great potential leverage, was reluctant to support UN Security Council economic sanctions against its neighbor lest that precipitate the latter's economic collapse and cause a massive flow of refugees across the Korean-Chinese border. On October 9, 2006, North Korea conducted a test of a nuclear device of which the explosive force was too low to confirm that a new member had been added to the club but raised further apprehensions in the region, including the United States, whose West Coast cities were practically within target range of Kim Jong Il's missiles. Within days, the nuclear test put pressure on China, along with other Security Council members, to agree to sanctions in the form of restrictions on the export of military and technological equipment, an embargo on luxury goods (such as cognac, caviar, lobster, sushi, and other items known to be favored by Kim and the North Korean leadership), a freezing of the financial assets of businesses connected with the nuclear program, and a travel ban on persons working on the program. The sanctions were not as strong as Washington had hoped but did contribute to a breakthrough in early 2007, when North Korea committed to shutting down various nuclear facilities in exchange for energy assistance. It was too soon to tell whether the agreement would be honored or whether there would be false hopes as the Clinton administration had experienced.[40]

Almost an exact replay of the North Korean standoff has occurred with Iran, which has long harbored nuclear ambitions. By 2002, Iran was also accused of violating its NPT obligations under the guise of "peaceful nuclear energy" development when it was found to be engaging in the early stages of uranium enrichment without properly notifying the IAEA. It was not clear why Iran felt compelled to develop nuclear energy when it possessed the second largest petroleum reserves in the world. France, Germany, and Britain attempted to coax Iran to suspend its nuclear development program in exchange for technology and fuel transfers, along the lines of the inducements offered North Korea, concessions that yielded a similar outcome, as Iran resumed its nuclear program after temporarily cooperating with the IAEA. The election of a hardline Islamic fundamentalist, Mahmoud Ahmadinejad, as Iranian president in 2005 only stiffened Iran's resolve to go forward with its nuclear program, in turn causing the Bush administration to step up its efforts to apply sanctions on Iran, even though Russia, China, and other countries with energy and other economic ties to Tehran were resistant. In December 2006, the UN Security Council did vote unanimously to restrict Iran's trade in sensitive nuclear materials and to freeze the assets of Iranian officials involved in the nuclear program, but did not go nearly as far as Washington had hoped, for example refusing to include a travel ban among the penalties.[41] It was not clear whether the sanctions would work or not.

Several questions linger about both these cases. One question some have raised is: Why is it considered acceptable for the United States and a few other countries to possess nuclear weapons but not North Korea and Iran? Supporters of the U.S. position would respond with at least two arguments. First, unlike the United States, or for that matter the likes of Israel, India, and Pakistan (who never signed the NPT), North Korea and Iran are parties to the treaty who violated their obligations, so that permitting them to escape sanctions and, indeed, to engage in nuclear blackmail by extracting economic benefits for their partial cooperation undermines the effectiveness of the NPT regime and sends the wrong message to other countries who might consider the nuclear option in the future. Second, both North Korea and Iran are hardly the types of countries who inspire confidence as potential custodians of nuclear weapons—North Korea has been called a "kleptocracy," a state run by a tyrannical leadership with a history of engaging in counterfeiting, drug trafficking, and the sale of missile technology to anyone willing to pay hard currency, while Iran is a theocracy that has a history of supporting terrorist groups; even if these governments might themselves be unlikely to use nuclear weapons against the United States, for fear of retaliation, there is no assurance they would not transfer such weapons to criminal or terrorist groups.[42]

A second question that arises relates to a recurring dilemma: What are the merits of using sticks, as opposed to carrots, in encouraging delinquent states to honor their NPT obligations? If Bill Clinton was criticized for his naïvete in negotiating with Pyongyang and expecting the offering of carrots to produce North Korean compliance, George Bush was criticized for failing to engage in bilateral diplomacy alongside multilateral diplomacy and for using neither carrots nor sticks very effectively.[43] Bush considered the toughest action of all, the military option, against both North Korea and Iran; but it was deemed too risky in the case of North Korea because of their formidable million-man army and the thirty-thousand American troops stationed in South Korea whose lives would be endangered, and it was equally unattractive in the Iran case due to likely calamitous consequences in the form of not only huge battlefield casualties but also disruption of Middle East oil production and resultant hikes in worldwide oil prices, the aggravation of anti-American anger in the Muslim world, and the sparking of Iranian nationalism that would override the nascent democratic movement that was gestating among students and others in Iranian society.[44] Perhaps if the United States had been able to get the UN Security Council to authorize military sanctions under Chapter VII and to recruit others to a posse, the threat or use of armed force might have had greater chance for success, but Washington was barely able to get the Security Council to approve even economic sanctions. It is possible that creative use of lesser sticks, such as the aviation travel ban that was mandated by the Security Council against Libya in the 1990s (as punishment for its sponsorship of terrorism) that eventually altered Libya's behavior, might work if given a chance.

Richard Haass has said, "Either the international community will succeed in stopping the spread of nuclear weapons, or we could soon find ourselves in a world of twelve or fifteen or even more nuclear weapons states. Ideally, an international consensus would form around steps that could be taken to cap, or better yet, roll back the North Korean and Iranian programs. In addition, governments would agree to shore up global arrangements designed to see that no state or terrorist organization develops or acquires either nuclear weapons or the nuclear fuel (either enriched uranium or plutonium)."[45] The United States could help mobilize a consensus by taking some measures itself to enhance its soft power on this issue, such as working with the Russians to make even deeper cuts in their nuclear arsenals, working with other nuclear fuel suppliers to guarantee supplies of nuclear fuel to energy-needy countries that would be made available under IAEA supervision at subsidized prices, agreeing to forego any new generations of nuclear weapons and ratifying the Comprehensive Test Ban Treaty, and announcing a policy of "no first use" of nuclear weapons.[46]

Although the NPT and other WMD arms-control regimes are imperfect, with several states refusing to ratify treaties, compliance spotty even among the legally bound parties in some cases, and many issues not covered by any agreements, it is hard to dispute the general proposition that the United States, as well as much of the world, will be safer to the extent that confidence can be restored in the effectiveness of arms control as an approach to world order.

HUMANITARIAN INTERVENTION

For centuries, the core underlying principle of world order has been **sovereignty**, that is, the principle that each state (1) is entitled to exercise control over its own citizens within its own territory and (2) recognizes no higher authority than its own government outside its borders. As one observer says, "the starting point of international relations is the existence of states, of independent political communities."[47] Although, like all principles, sovereignty at times has been violated and unevenly practiced,[48] it is a tenet so sacrosanct that it may be the only value upon which all 192 United Nations members agree. The upshot of sovereignty is that the international system is an inherently decentralized, anarchical polity lacking any hierarchical, overarching world government and that whatever order exists relies on nation-states agreeing to form rules and institutions (regimes) to regulate their interactions.[49] As with all political systems, the power to develop rules is not equally shared by all members of the system. As flimsy a basis for world order as it may seem, sovereignty has provided at least a foundational architecture for human governance, at least up until now.

Sovereignty is now being challenged not only by globalization and the growth of multinational corporations, cyberspace, and other modernizing trends that are blurring national boundaries and identities,[50] but also by the emergence of a new norm that seems directly at odds with the concept of state independence—**humanitarian intervention**. As mentioned previously, this is a contested idea, one that many states are understandably uncomfortable with and that even those states which have invoked the principle, such as the United States under the Clinton and Bush administrations, have subjected to differing interpretations. The concept of humanitarian intervention, while a noble notion intended to address the worst sorts of atrocities committed on the planet, further complicates efforts to clarify the rules governing the use of armed force in international affairs, including both *jus in bellum* and *jus ad bellum*.

The Controversy Over Humanitarian Intervention

The roots of the concept can be traced back to the earliest development of **human rights** after World War II.[51] World War II marked a pivotal moment in the historical effort to extend human rights protection under international law to *all* individuals on the globe. As one writer puts it, "the Second World War marked the ultimate transition of international law from a system dedicated to State sovereignty to one also devoted to the protection of human dignity."[52] Most notably, at the Nuremberg Trials in 1945, leaders of Nazi Germany were charged with having committed, along with other crimes, crimes against humanity. German officials were convicted of having violated the rights of the indigenous Jewish population in Germany and neighboring states by engaging in genocide, killing an estimated six million Jews; as a result, several German leaders were sentenced to life imprisonment or execution. Nuremberg, therefore, was a landmark event in setting an important precedent supporting the proposition that, under international law, individual citizens have rights that even their own government cannot deny them and that individual leaders have obligations that even sovereignty cannot shield them from meeting. Despite the inconsistent application of the Nuremberg principles over the next several decades, they set in motion the development of a human rights regime based on the ratification of more than a dozen multilateral treaties, including conventions dealing with genocide, racial discrimination, discrimination against women, political and civil rights, and economic and social rights.

However, it is one thing to encourage governments to sign onto human rights treaties, which is a well-established practice. It is quite another for members of the international community to claim the right to engage in armed intervention to protect a people from its own government and to unseat that government if necessary for having engaged in ethnic cleansing or other such crimes, as the United States did against Slobodan Milosevic in Serbia and Saddam Hussein in Iraq, and as some human rights advocates wanted to do in Rwanda in the 1990s and in the Sudan more recently. If the post–World War II human rights movement "turned traditional conceptions of sovereignty almost inside out,"[53] the post–Cold War extension of this movement, in the form of humanitarian intervention, threatens to play havoc with sovereignty altogether. It also threatens to add to charges of double standards and hypocrisy that many countries have leveled at the United States, since Washington is not about to welcome the international community sitting in judgment on race relations or other human rights conditions in America, much less tolerate "intervention" of any sort.

What rules apply to humanitarian intervention and regime change? UN Secretary-General Kofi Annan, in his 1999 address to the General Assembly, had remarked that the protection of human rights must "take precedence over concerns of state sovereignty," that sovereignty cannot provide "excuses for the inexcusable," and that the UN Charter "was issued in the name of 'the peoples,' not the governments, of the United Nations."[54] The next day, President Clinton, echoing the Clinton Doctrine, declared that the secretary-general "spoke for all of us . . . when he said that ethnic cleansers and mass murderers can find no refuge in the United Nations."[55] Anne-Marie Slaughter notes that a commission appointed by the Canadian government at the suggestion of Annan endorsed this principle when it "released a report at the end of 2001 that defined a state's membership in the United Nations as including a responsibility to protect the lives and basic liberties of its people" and that posited "if a member state failed in that responsibility, the international community had a right to intervene."[56] However, I noted earlier the traditionalist view that international law grants "no general right unilaterally to charge into another country to save its people from their own leaders."[57] What about *multilateral* intervention, that is, an action taken by the international community at large, authorized by the UN Security Council under Chapter VII?

There is a widely held view that "humanitarian military intervention now must be multilateral to be legitimate,"[58] yet international law is not entirely clear on this point. As William Slomanson observes, "The permissible contours of humanitarian intervention have not been defined in a way that represents a meaningful State consensus. An essential reason is that . . . neither word has been precisely defined."[59] Critics have raised concerns that humanitarian intervention threatens sovereignty-based ordering arrangements and is at odds with the UN Charter, insofar as it contradicts Article 2 (7), which stipulates that "nothing contained in the Charter shall authorize the UN to intervene in matters which are essentially within the domestic jurisdiction of any state." Since Article 2 (7) adds that "this principle shall not prejudice the application of enforcement measures under Chapter VII," many UN members have expressed fears that such language is an invitation for Security Council members to interfere in the domestic affairs of smaller, weaker states even to the point of forcing regime change. As one third-world spokesperson has said, "We do not deny that the United Nations has the right and the duty to help suffering humanity. But we remain extremely sensitive to any undermining of our sovereignty, not only because sovereignty is our last defense against the rules of an unequal world but because we are not taking part in the decision-making process of the Security Council."[60] Of greatest concern, though, is a state or group of states using humanitarian intervention as a pretext to bring about regime change without any UN approval. The 114 members of the Non-Aligned Movement, representing the developing nations, have condemned such intervention, declaring it has "no legal basis under the Charter."[61] The theory and practice of humanitarian intervention remain mired in controversy.

US Policy Dilemmas: To Intervene or Not?

As in other areas of foreign policy, humanitarian intervention presents a number of dilemmas for American policymakers. First, is there enough blood and treasure to intervene militarily everywhere people are oppressed? Freedom House counts forty-five countries as "not free," in which dictatorships of some kind reign.[62] Assuming that one cannot possibly intervene in all of these places, how does one pick and choose where to intervene? Second, how does one choose between competing, at times incompatible, objectives, in particular sorting out national interest concerns from moral concerns?[63] For example, after the First Persian Gulf War in the 1990s, the United States, as part of a UN Security Council mandate, enforced a "no-fly" zone against Iraqi aircraft that had been intimidating Kurdish villages in northern Iraq, thereby providing a safe haven for Kurds that protected them from their own government; at the same time, Washington looked the other way when Turkey, an American ally facing rebellion and calls for self-determination from its own Kurdish population, strafed Kurdish camps inside Iraq's boundaries in retaliation for those camps supporting Kurdish rebels operating within Turkey.[64] Third, even if the United States intervenes on purely moral grounds, as it did with the delivery of food aid and other humanitarian assistance in Somalia in the 1992 Operation Restore Hope mission authorized by the Security Council, it nonetheless may well exacerbate perceptions of the United States as a bully, arrogantly engaging in "cultural imperialism." Many people in the third world felt as an Egyptian newspaper editor did, that, by letting the UN into their country, "the Somali commanders have handed their country over to the Americans on a golden plate."[65] To the extent the United States pushes foreign governments to become more democratic along the American model and to adopt other western notions of human rights, it risks being seen as "injecting alien values in societies"[66] and breeding further resentment.

Should the United States ignore John Quincy Adams's 1821 admonition and go "abroad in search of monsters to destroy," promoting the norm of humanitarian intervention, knowing that "Wilsonian presidents drive [American enemies and friends alike] crazy"?[67] If so, what guidelines should inform military intervention decisions? Aside from applying moral and legal criteria, what seems *smart*?[68]

At least three guidelines would seem to make sense. First, humanitarian intervention should be reserved for only the most egregious cases of human rights violations. There is a lack of global consensus on many human rights dimensions; for example, some countries in Asia contend that "Asian democracy" is a variant of western democracy that blends Confucian and other Oriental cultural traditions with basic democratic values, but in a way that is somewhat more deferential to authority. There is much greater consensus behind the opposition to genocide. Although at times it has been hard to get universal agreement among United Nations members to combat genocide—witness UN inaction in the face of the slaughter of Tutsis by Hutus in Rwanda in the 1990s and the Darfur tragedy in the Sudan in the early twenty-first century—there is likely to be greater support for intervention the wider the scale of atrocities and the louder the global outcry.

Second, related to the first criterion, the United States would generally be wise not to engage in humanitarian intervention without the imprimatur of the United Nations, through Security Council resolutions taken under Chapter VII of the Charter. Even if there may be a moral imperative to act, intervention is more likely to succeed if it can be not only legitimized but also legalized by the rules of the Charter as opposed to being the result of a decision taken unilaterally or outside the Charter framework. The American invasion of Iraq no doubt suffered from the widespread view that it was illegal. This means that intervention decisions may possibly be held hostage to the opposition of Perm Five members Russia and China, who obstructed American proposals for UN action not only in Iraq but also in the greater humanitarian emergencies in Kosovo and the Sudan and who have been much less anxious than western democracies to support the norm of humanitarian intervention. However, that is a price that may have to be paid in order to line up the largest possible posse in support of intervention. This is in keeping with the Powell Doctrine's requirement that Washington not undertake armed intervention without substantial international support.[69]

Third, even if one has morality and legality on one's side, it would seem unwise to intervene unless one has reason to believe that one can, practically speaking, make a difference in the humanitarian conflict, particularly where armed intervention comes up against civil strife fueled by a complex stew of ethnic, racial, religious, and other divisions, as experienced in Somalia and so many other third world locales. In other words, as the Powell Doctrine also urged, don't intervene unless you think you can win. The Clinton administration knew it could not win in Rwanda when it sent a token unit of only two hundred U.S. troops to Kigali airport in 1994 as a belated attempt to salvage American honor after the United States and other UN members had refused to act to stop the carnage there, but it is uncertain whether several thousand more troops would have fared any better in such a volatile conflict.[70]

On the matter of practicality, before venturing into Darfur or some other humanitarian disaster area, one needs to consider the major "nation-building" and "state-building" tasks that would have to be undertaken in order to create a durable peace and, again, whether American taxpayers are prepared to foot the lion's share of the reconstruction bill. Nation-building refers to bringing about national reconciliation among warring factions, while state-building refers to everything from repairing roads and other infrastructure to reestablishing a court and policing system. About Somalia, Madeleine Albright acknowledged at the time that the United States was engaged in "an unprecedented enterprise aimed at nothing less than the restoration of an entire country."[71] Around that same time, in his *Agenda for Peace* proposals presented at the start of the post–Cold War era in 1992, UN Secretary-General Boutros Boutros-Ghali introduced the concept of **peacebuilding** as an important new mission for the UN in failed or devastated states.[72] The 2000 *Report of the Panel on United Nations Peace Operations* (the Brahimi Report) suggested the enormous range of activities that such a mission might entail. Aside from raising the question of whether the United States and other UN members would support the establishment of a UN rapid deployment force that could respond to humanitarian conflicts within thirty to ninety days, the Brahimi Report also noted the special challenges such a force would face:

> These operations face challenges and responsibilities that are unique among United Nations field operations. No other operations must set and enforce the law, establish customs services and regulations, set and collect business and personal taxes, attract foreign investment, adjudicate property disputes and liabilities for war damage, reconstruct and operate all public utilities, create banking systems, run schools, pay teachers and collect the garbage. . . . In addition to such tasks, these missions must also try to rebuild civil society and promote respect for human rights, in places where grievance is widespread and grudges run deep.[73]

This does not even touch upon the still greater challenge of trying to install "democracy at gunpoint" in societies that have never known democratic governance.[74]

In fact, such challenges have been experienced in Kosovo, Afghanistan, Iraq, and other hotspots recently, with at best mixed results. To the extent the United States is involved in such conflicts, it would seem more likely to succeed if there were burden-sharing among the UN membership as a whole. A hopeful model for the future, if it can get "major stakeholders" to collaborate, is the recently created UN Peacebuilding Commission, which "is comprised of 31 members including: seven members of the Security Council (including all P-5); seven members of ECOSOC [the UN Economic and Social Council] with experience in post-conflict reconstruction; five of the top ten financial contributors to the UN budget; five of the top ten troop contributing countries; and seven additional members from the General Assembly to round out the remaining geographical imbalances and ensure representation by those countries with post-conflict rebuilding experience."[75]

When tyrants fall, there is always the "post-conflict" matter of what to do with the deposed leadership. In the past, the latter typically have either fled to another country where they have sought asylum or, if they have not been lucky enough to find sanctuary elsewhere, have been imprisoned or executed with or without a trial. There is often a sense that justice has not been served, other than perhaps "victors' justice." The International Criminal Court, discussed next, is an attempt by the international community to address this problem. Inspired by the example of the Nuremberg Trials, the International Criminal Court has faced its greatest opposition from the same country that was Nuremberg's chief champion, the United States, which finds itself in yet another dilemma.

THE INTERNATIONAL CRIMINAL COURT

Critics of the Bush administration have charged the president with undermining America's soft power through its use of torture tactics and other POW practices in violation of the Geneva Convention, its promulgation of a preemptive war doctrine that is at odds with the United Nations Charter, and its refusal to support several arms control agreements as well as a number of other multilateral pacts having near-universal adherence. However, perhaps nothing has caused a greater public relations problem for the United States than its absence from the International Criminal Court, an institution that human rights advocates consider the foundation of a new democratic order in world affairs.

The Creation of the ICC

The **International Criminal Court (ICC)** was conceived as a permanent Nuremberg Trial judiciary designed to institutionalize punishment for gross human rights violations.[76] The trials that had been organized by the United Nations in the 1990s to prosecute the leadership of the former Yugoslavia and Rwanda—Serb President Slobodan Milosevic was charged with war crimes and crimes against humanity, notably ethnic cleansing of Bosnian civilians in Bosnia-Herzegovina and Albanian civilians in Kosovo, while Rwandan Prime Minister Jean Kambanda was charged with genocide against ethnic Tutsis—were *ad hoc* tribunals established solely to hear those two cases. (Kambanda was sentenced to life in prison, while Milosevic died in jail before final sentencing. Capital punishment was ruled out as a penalty.) Meanwhile, there were other dictators who had escaped punishment for human rights abuses, such as General Augusto Pinochet, the former president of Chile, who a Spanish court attempted in 1998 to prosecute for torture and other human rights violations committed during his tenure in the 1970s and 1980s. Spain had requested Pinochet's arrest and extradition from the United Kingdom, where he was receiving medical treatment at the time. He asserted the traditional legal principle of "head of state immunity" from prosecution in the national courts of another country, which the British authorities rejected, although they ultimately denied the Spanish request, citing that Pinochet's ailing health prevented travel.[77] Along with Spain, Belgium and some other countries in the 1990s invoked "universal jurisdiction" over "crimes against humanity" as a basis for asserting their right to try foreign heads of state in their courts for human rights violations. However, many observers were uneasy with national courts performing this function, since an international court figured to be better able to assure impartiality and speak for the international community.[78]

Hence, many states worked hard to create the ICC as just such a forum, as a Nuremberg-style sitting court that hopefully would serve to deter future atrocities and, if deterrence failed, to punish those individuals responsible. Among the leaders were states such as Australia, Canada, the Netherlands, and Sweden. These efforts culminated in a gathering of almost 150 states in 1998 to finalize the drafting of the Rome Statute establishing the Court in The Hague, the Netherlands. A total of 120 countries voted in favor, twenty abstained, and seven opposed, including the United States, Israel, China, Iraq, and Libya. The ICC officially came into existence in 2002, with more than one hundred countries having ratified the Rome Statute treaty by 2007.

The Statute authorizes prosecution of any individuals (private citizens, military personnel, and former or current public officials—from member or nonmember states) who are accused of any of the following crimes: war crimes (either in a civil war or interstate war), genocide, or crimes against humanity. War crimes are defined as breaches of the 1949 Geneva Conventions. Genocide is defined as any acts intended to destroy a national, ethnic, racial, or religious group. Crimes against humanity are defined as acts intended to inflict widespread, serious harm upon a civilian population. The Statute also lists the "crime of aggression," although leaves the definition unclear. In addition to cases that may be referred by the UN Security Council, proceedings may be initiated by any ICC member state on whose territory the alleged crime occurred or by the state of the nationality of the accused; the state whose national has been charged with a crime is given the first opportunity to try that individual, but must defer to the ICC if it is unwilling or unable to take action.[79]

Although President Clinton was an early ICC supporter, he and others in Washington had misgivings about some final provisions of the Statute, based both on national security considerations raised by the Department of Defense and concerns about how the treaty would play in Peoria and elsewhere in domestic American politics. What little the American public knew about the ICC tended to register negative reactions in opinion surveys, with the public especially unhappy with the prospect of American GIs possibly being prosecuted for war crimes. Clinton reluctantly signed the Statute just before leaving office, declaring it flawed but arguing that he felt compelled to do so since only those states willing to sign by December 31, 2000, would be permitted to participate in the future development of the court's procedures. The United States has not yet ratified the treaty, despite the fact that virtually all European nations and U.S. allies have. In fact, President Bush went so far as to take the unusual step of withdrawing the U.S. signature in 2002, around the same time that Congress passed the American Service Members' Protection Act, which threatened to cut off foreign aid to countries that joined the ICC, prohibited U.S. troops from serving in UN peacekeeping forces unless they were granted immunity from ICC jurisdiction, and authorized the president to use military force to free any U.S. soldiers who might be held by the ICC (leading critics of U.S. policy to call the legislation "The Hague Invasion Act").

As has been noted, the United States has refused to become a party to many multilateral treaties, including some human rights treaties predating the Bush administration. In addition to the 1989 Convention on the Rights of the Child (ratified by 192 states), the United States is noticeably absent from the 1979 Convention on the Elimination of All Forms of Discrimination Against Women (ratified by 185 states) and the 1966 Covenant on Economic, Social, and Cultural Rights (ratified by 155 states). The United States has dragged its feet on endorsing the children's rights treaty due not only to disagreements with the treaty's handling of parental rights but also with the provisions of the treaty governing the minimum age of military recruitment, which is slightly more restrictive than that of the U.S. armed forces; as for the other two treaties, conservative members of the U.S. Senate have viewed them as promoting excessive government regulation, for example by guaranteeing paid leave for women before and after childbirth, and containing language considered stronger than that contained in the Equal Rights Amendment that failed to gain the necessary support to be amended to the U.S. Constitution in the 1980s. Commenting on the spotty American commitment to human rights treaties, Michael Ignatieff echoes Clyde Prestowitz in characterizing the United States as "a nation with a great rights tradition that leads the world in denouncing human rights violations but which behaves like a rogue state in relation to international legal conventions."[80] In the case of the Rome Statute, Washington has not only refused to become a party to the treaty but has given the appearance of trying to actively sabotage and undermine the ICC.

To be fair, one could argue that the reluctance of the United States to join as many human rights treaties as some other countries reflects not so much contempt for international law as respect for the *pacta sunt servanda* principle, that is, Washington's belief that it could not honor treaty provisions at odds with U.S. law and norms, and hence its aversion to becoming an outlaw state even if, as a result, it risked being viewed as a pariah outside the mainstream of human rights thought. Contrast Washington's behavior with that of many parties to the Convention on the Rights of the Child, who have employed more than three hundred thousand child soldiers (as young as eight years of age) in armed conflict; in 2002, UN Secretary-General Kofi Annan reported that twenty-three parties, including Liberia, Burundi, and the Congo, were guilty of treaty violations.[81] Contrast U.S. behavior, also, with many Asian, African, and Middle Eastern countries that, unlike the United States, are parties to the Convention on Discrimination Against Women; although there is still considerable sexism in American society, the United States' record of sexual equality is superior to the likes of Ghana, Kenya, Japan, Malaysia, Myanmar, and Saudi Arabia (where, under strict Islamic tenets, women are not even permitted to drive a car, much less vote). Then, too, there is the example of Russia and Iraq as original members of the Covenant on Civil and Political Rights, having joined in 1976 (long before American ratification), despite never permitting even the semblance of a free press. The Rome Statute itself counts as parties two dozen African and Latin American states with questionable human rights records.

Still, the United States has the dubious distinction of being the only established democracy that remains outside the ICC, and has left the impression that its absence is due at least partly to worry over whether it has fully lived up to the treaties it *has* ratified—the Geneva Conventions and such—and fear that it might be held to account for shock and awe aerial bombardment campaigns, torturing of terrorist suspects, and other possible criminal conduct.[82]

American Objections to the ICC

The main U.S. objections are: (1) not only American soldiers but American leaders might well be prime targets of an ICC investigation, given the relatively heavy involvement of U.S. armed forces in peacekeeping, humanitarian intervention, or other overseas military operations (so that, say, George Bush might conceivably be apprehended while traveling abroad and indicted over alleged Iraq War transgressions); (2) the Statute undermines the primacy of the UN Security Council and, hence, the American veto power that protects the United States from sanctions, by permitting cases to be initiated by any member state or by the ICC Prosecutor; and (3) ICC procedures under the Rome Statute are to be determined by a majority of states party to the treaty, so that, assuming the ultimate goal is to make the treaty universal, the majority of the world's countries that are "not free" or "partly free" (according to Freedom House) might be positioned to dominate the Court over the will of its democratic members.[83]

ICC supporters counter that these scenarios are highly unlikely. However, American concerns are not completely far-fetched, given the resentment that Gulliver tends to breed and the desire of many states to rein America in, the frequency with which American troops find themselves engaged in asymmetrical warfare situations where sticking to the letter of international humanitarian law at times can be difficult, and the track record of Libya having chaired the UN Human Rights Commission and of many dictatorships cynically joining human rights treaties without any intention of taking them seriously. There are also legitimate questions Washington has raised over the transparency of selection of prosecutors and judges and other aspects of the ICC procedures. More than anything, there is the concern that the ICC represents an unprecedented threat to both American power and sovereignty, insofar as it could constrain America's use of armed force and could even be a first step toward a world government in which the United States is just one of two hundred member states.

Despite these concerns, it would seem to behoove the United States to associate itself with an institution that has the potential to provide an important deterrent and punishment mechanism against the worst sorts of evildoers. Here, too, the ICC could provide the United States with an opportunity to demonstrate constructive global leadership if it is willing to invest the effort to engage the international community in further dialogue to see if some compromises can be reached that would alleviate Washington's greatest concerns about the court. Although it is open to question how such a body can function while a major actor such as the United States remains outside its purview, it is also open to question how long the United States can continue to play the Lone Ranger in world politics. The Lone Ranger at least had Tonto, if not a full-fledged posse. Is the United States willing to trade off a degree of autonomy for a degree of help? This would seem to be the central dilemma running through most of the predicaments the United States faces today. Every generation of American leaders from the Founding Fathers onward have been faced with the issue of how far "foreign entanglement" should go, but answering that question today seems especially problematical. In the next chapter, I offer a few concluding thoughts on Gulliver's travails and the future of American foreign policy.

DISCUSSION QUESTIONS

1. The United States experiences many foreign policy dilemmas today. For example, in the war on terror, the United States is up against an enemy that tends to ignore the conventional "rules of engagement" and engages in asymmetrical warfare, including, first, targeting civilians and, second, hiding in densely populated urban centers, daring American forces to attack, thereby leading at times to the deaths of civilians through "collateral damage" caused by U.S. weaponry and inviting international outrage against American violations of international humanitarian law. The United States itself has been called a terrorist state because of its shock and awe aerial bombing campaign against Baghdad in 2003 and other seemingly indiscriminate uses of armed force. What is your view on this, and how can the United States fight a war against terrorism and combat its enemies without resorting to similar tactics as terrorists?

2. Another dilemma surrounds the Bush Doctrine. The latter holds that the United States has the right to engage in the preemptive use of armed force against any country that Washington believes possibly poses a threat to the United States in the future. This is a blatant violation of the UN Charter, which bans the first use of armed force and allows the right of self-defense only if a country has actually been attacked or the attack is imminent, that is, the onus is on the defender to wait to absorb the first blow before responding with armed force. However, can the United States afford to wait if the first blow might be a dirty radioactive bomb that could render New York City or Washington, DC, uninhabitable? Or must the United States try to preempt such an attack if intelligence suggests it might materialize soon? If you were president of the United States, would you be able to distinguish between the "preemptive" (necessary) use of armed force as opposed to the "preventive"(desired) use of armed force? How does one weigh the defense of the United States against the collapse of the UN Charter's proscription against aggression and the Bush Doctrine's legitimizing Pakistan possibly launching a nuclear attack against India or India against Pakistan? Does the Bush Doctrine promote a more secure world or a less secure world?

3. Another dilemma has to do with arms control. Since World War II, there have been a number of relatively successful arms-control regimes that have curbed the proliferation of weapons of mass destruction (WMDs), including the ABC (atomic or nuclear, biological, and chemical) weapons. However, these regimes are at risk of collapsing due to reduced confidence in the ability to verify and enforce compliance, as manifested by the recent violations of the Nuclear Non-Proliferation Treaty by North Korea and Iran. Chemical and biological weapons can now be made and stored in a basement or garage, while the NPT treaty contains a loophole that allows a state to pursue the development of nuclear weapons under the guise of developing "peaceful" nuclear energy. Should the United States give up on WMD arms control or continue to work to support and improve these treaties? What kinds of sanctions should be meted out against countries violating their treaty obligations? What can the United States do to persuade countries to abide by these treaties?

4. Another dilemma has to do with humanitarian intervention. There are some fifty countries in the world that Freedom House labels as "not free." How does one choose which countries are worth intervening in for the purpose of improving the human rights situation and possibly engaging in "regime change"? The United States has been criticized for its "naïvete" and "arrogance" in thinking it could install a democracy in Iraq, yet some of these same critics have urged the United States to go into the Sudan to do something about the atrocities in Darfur. What criteria—decision guidelines—would you use in deciding when the United States should engage in humanitarian intervention and regime change? Must the atrocities have reached the level of genocide? Must there be a clear plan of action and expectation of success, including a commitment to provide billions of dollars in support of "peacebuilding"? Must Washington have the approval of the UN Security Council before acting?

5. The United States has suffered a public relations disaster due to its refusal to join the International Criminal Court, a permanent "Nuremberg Trials" tribunal that virtually every western democracy has joined. Discuss the pros and cons of the ICC.

6

US Foreign Policy and the Future

We cannot know how the new millennium will end,
but we do have the power to determine how it begins,
and, perhaps, what it will remember of us.

—*New York Times* editorial, January 1, 2000

The essence of ultimate decision remains impenetrable to
the observer—often, indeed, to the decider himself. . . .
There will always be the dark and tangled stretches in the
decision-making process—mysterious even to those who
may be most intimately involved.

—John F. Kennedy, cited in Graham Allison, *Essence of Decision*

The original, full title of *Gulliver's Travels* by Jonathan Swift was *Travels into Several Remote Nations of the World*. Today, in an age of instantaneous communication, no nation is truly remote. This was recognized by Václav Havel, the president of the Czech Republic, when, appearing in the United States to give a July Fourth speech shortly after the fall of the Berlin wall, he issued a "declaration of interdependence." Havel stated that we are living at a time when "everything is possible and almost nothing is certain." He went on to say that, while recognizing the counterforces at work, he envisioned eventually a "single interconnected civilization" based on "the miracle of Being, the miracle of the universe."[1] In calling for unity amidst diversity, Havel was an especially suitable messenger. He had personally played a leadership role in the mindboggling—some would say miraculous—events of the late-twentieth century, having helped to bridge the East-West divide by leading Czechoslovakia from communist dictatorship to liberal democracy at the end of the Cold War in 1989, having presided over a nation-state torn by competing nationalisms that resulted in the peaceful "velvet divorce" of the Czech Republic and the Slovak Republic in 1993, and having steered Czech entry into the European Union in 2004. His words in his speech reflected his background as a poet who came belatedly to the job of statesman. The qualities of the poet and the statesman will both be needed in the twenty-first century if we are to blend idealism and realism.

In this chapter, we will peer into the future and contemplate the nature of the world order, or disorder, that American foreign policymakers will need to make sense of in the near term, and how they might attempt to reconcile American national interests with larger global interests. Lots of decisions will have to be made, hopefully good ones.

AMERICA'S ROLE IN
THE POST–COLD WAR WORLD

Henry Luce, the founder and publisher of *Time* magazine, famously declared the twentieth century "the American Century." His fuller statement, uttered during the Interwar Period at a time when isolationism was still in vogue, called upon Americans to "bring forth a vision of America as a world power, which is authentically American. . . . America as the dynamic center of ever-widening spheres of enterprise, America as the training center of the skilled servants of mankind, America as the Good Samaritan, really believing that it is more blessed to give than to receive, and America as the powerhouse of the ideals of Freedom and Justice—out of these elements surely can be fashioned a vision of the Twentieth Century . . . the first great American Century."[2] Luce was reflecting the streak of "American exceptionalism" that could be found throughout the history of American foreign policy, with high-minded principles fitting uneasily with the expansion of national power, and leaders never completely self-conscious as to which of the two were the prime motivation—the "essence of decision"—driving their foreign policy actions. The United States met Luce's challenge with its leadership in defeating fascism and communism and helping to create the United Nations and an array of global institutions, in the process becoming a hegemonic power. If the twentieth century was the "American century," to whom will the twenty-first century belong?

At the beginning of this book, I quoted Charles Kupchan's claim that "America today arguably has greater ability to shape the *future* of world politics than any other power in history [italics mine]."[3] One recent work suggests how far the reach of American power extends:

> The reality of the multidimensional power of the United States today and the immense gap in capabilities between the United States and even the second-

CARTOON 6.1 The Power to Shape the Future. CREDIT: MALCOLM HANCOCK

ranked powers affects the United Nations in profound ways. The UN largely remains an American-controlled organization. . . . Almost everything the UN does or does not do is greatly conditioned by the will, whims, and resources of the United States. . . . As one European diplomat explained, few [peacekeeping] operations are likely to move ahead without financial contributions from Washington, so that even after the U.S. administration approves a mandate, "We must simply sit and wait until Congress decides on the money." . . . "Nothing can be done without the concurrence of the United States," a French diplomat acknowledged. "It reflects the reality of the world."[4]

But does it? Does the United States actually have "greater ability to shape the future of world politics than any other power in history"? Veto power, to block action by the international community at large, perhaps yes. However, does America have the power to make things happen, as opposed to merely preventing action?

Much of this book, in telling the story of Gulliver's travails, has endeavored to point out the wide disconnect between American power and performance, between its seemingly unbounded potential to influence events and its general failure to do so. We have noted how Washington has not only been unable to convert its enemies to its way of thinking but also has not been able to convert its best friends. Going at least as far back to the 1980s' portrayal of Ronald Reagan as "Rambo" and the 1990s' portrayal of the United States in the Clinton years as "a hyper-power" and a "hectoring hegemon," America's European allies have complained and worried about American arrogance and unilateralism.[5] Even an American observer was driven to call Clinton advisor Madeleine Albright "the first Secretary of State in American history whose diplomatic specialty . . . is lecturing other governments, using threatening language and tastelessly bragging of the power and virtue of her country."[6] With George W. Bush, anti-Americanism, or at least the reluctance to follow Washington's lead, reached a new nadir, captured in the statement by London's mayor, Ken Livingstone, that Bush was "the greatest threat to life on this planet that we've most probably ever seen."[7]

By 2007, based on a BBC World Service poll of thousands of people across twenty-five countries, the "world view of the U.S. role" had gone "from bad to worse," as three in four people disapproved of U.S. policy in Iraq and one in two felt the United States was playing a negative role in the world, with the biggest negative rating found among Germans (74 percent).[8] Stephen Walt has pointed out the disparity between America's self-image and the view of America from abroad. On the one hand, notwithstanding growing criticism of George Bush at home, recent public opinion polls show more than 70 percent of U.S. citizens are "very proud" to be Americans, while more than half of all U.S. opinion leaders believe the United States "does a lot of good around the world" and 70 percent believe Washington has taken "the interests of its partners into account" in conducting the war on terrorism and other aspects of its foreign policy. In contrast are the aforementioned polling results from twenty-five countries that are unfavorable to the United States, and a survey of opinion leaders in other states that shows only one-third of them sharing the positive view of American opinion leaders.[9] Walt observes that foreigners are especially wary of American "cultural intrusion in their country."[10] Should one merely accept the neocon rationalization that "resentment comes with the territory" and that "it is the inescapable reality of American power in all its forms"?[11] Or should Americans not be concerned, as liberal internationalists and also some realists are, that such hostility toward America undermines the effective use of American power and ultimately frustrates the achievement of American foreign policy goals?

What can be done to improve not only America's image in the world but also its actual exercise of power and influence in pursuit of American interests and ideals? I have noted that part of the problem is a series of daunting dilemmas that would challenge even the wisest foreign policy leadership. What adds to the problem is the absence of any overall "game plan" for trying to cope with these dilemmas. Such an overarching plan may or may not be possible, but it is worth considering. The fact is that the United States is having to function in a strange new international environment that is far more complex and messy in many respects than was the Cold War system, yet thus far has not developed anything approaching a coherent set of objectives and strategies akin to the containment doctrine that guided American policy during the Cold War.

In Chapter 1, the elements of complexity in the post–Cold War system were identified as a growing diffusion and ambiguity of power (with hegemons frustrated by ostensibly much weaker foes and threatened more by failed states than by rival great powers), a growing fluidity of alignments (with "the west versus the rest" axis of conflict accompanied by west-west, north-south, south-south, and assorted other axes of conflicts), a growing agenda of issues (with economic, environmental and other concerns competing for attention with traditional military-security concerns), and a growing number of actors (with not only the proliferation of states but also nonstate actors competing in shaping events on the world stage). Recalling the musings of Václav Havel, the world seems an increasingly schizophrenic place, characterized by the long war and the long peace, the forces of disintegration alongside integration (what Benjamin Barber has called "jihad versus McWorld"[12]), and other anomalies. In Chapter 2, we noted that foreign policy is not just the product of reactions to one's external environment but also one's internal environment, and that public opinion and other domestic factors (e.g., a burgeoning federal budget deficit tied to spiraling social security and health care costs) may well constrain the decision calculus of American foreign policymakers in the future. In Chapter 3, a history lesson was offered indicating that previous leaders at the helm of the American ship of state were also faced with often difficult contradictions, choices, constraints, and challenges—dilemmas—sometimes responding well and other times less so. Chapters 4 and 5 attempted to frame some of the key puzzles today's leadership must try to resolve.

It was noted earlier, also, that foreign policy often seems to consist of crisis management much more than long-term planning. Although there is more to foreign policy than putting out one fire after another, it is nevertheless true that when a country is preoccupied with a major foreign policy crisis, as with the United States in Iraq, it can be difficult to focus on much else. Other concerns, such as global warming or various "global governance" projects, tend to be put on the backburner or addressed only halfheartedly. Some concerns may indeed have to await the end of the Iraq War, but one would hope that Washington could begin looking well beyond that timetable, since problems are only going to pile up if unattended.

It would seem reasonable that any vision of the United States' role in a post–Cold War world might start with a commitment to a new multilateralism that would attempt to reconcile the competing views of neoconservatives, liberal internationalists, and realists. Perhaps there are other schools of thought as well that deserve to be included in a national dialogue. Although everybody today would seem to be a multilateralist of some sort—even the neocons have relied on coalitions of the willing while realists acknowledge the need not to offend potential allies—the devil is in the details. The sheriff of the posse image remains a useful metaphor, although there can be a fine line between, on the one hand, being accepted as the sheriff (the leader) and, on the other hand, being seen as a bully or even an outlaw. The United States needs to walk this line carefully. The United States also needs to find the right balance between, on the one hand, seeking to retain as much decision-making autonomy as possible, preserving its sovereignty in trying to maximize American national security and well-being, and, on the other hand, seeking to promote a pooling of sovereignty with other states in support of international security and well-being, especially in those issue-areas where American interests require collaboration in developing global institutions and regimes. The lessons of the Interwar Period remind us that a hegemon, or some functional equivalent, is needed to maintain order and that in the absence of such an actor or mechanism, should the United States forego its responsibility to help provide global leadership, disorder is the likely result.

Though always envied, and therefore only grudgingly liked by many countries over the past half-century, the United States nevertheless for many years was widely admired and respected for the values it seemed to project, not only democracy and economic vitality but also a commitment to global institution-building and multilateralism. Washington led the way after World War II in fostering global institution-building, partly through sheer dominance and partly through the art of compromise in various negotiations on everything from air transport to public health to trade regimes and through the judicious blend of carrots and sticks, in recognition that some concessions had to be made in pursuit of American national interests. U.S. policymakers grasped that the United States, in providing the lion's share of collective goods that Americans benefited from, sometimes had to tolerate free riders. A return to such thinking could help enhance American "soft power" today.[13]

Perhaps the best of all worlds would be the revival of a "concert of great powers" approach to world order, as Kupchan, Haass, and some others have suggested. First, there would be the need to overcome disagreements between the United States and the likes of Russia, China, and France.[14] Second, there is the need to open up the "concert" enough, in terms of insuring diverse regional and cultural representation, that at least it could stand a chance of being perceived by the international system as a whole as a relatively legitimate body. Neither of these moves would be easy. Forging cooperation among the current Perm Five itself, much less an expanded UN Security Council, poses huge challenges. Still, it might be doable. Although power has become more diffused, there still remains a considerable concentration of power sufficient to move the system; led by the United States, less than twelve states account for the great bulk of the planet's military and economic resources.[15] What has been lost in power concentration in the end of the superpower era has been offset by the reduced rigidity and polarization of alignments and reduced thinkability of great-power war. It helps that, despite all the criticism it gets, the United States is generally not viewed as a predator hegemon. Furthermore, a concert of great powers hopefully could co-opt other, middle powers to support its leadership. If a critical mass of states, accounting for much of the world's hard and soft power—the industrialized democracies led by the United States, the European Union, and Japan, joined by Russia, India, and China, each with growing economies in need of a stable world order—can somehow join forces, a new world order could be attainable.[16] Utopian as this may sound, it is no more so than thinking that the United States ship of state can continue on its present course without suffering further wreckage.

SHOULD WE BE OPTIMISTIC OR PESSIMISTIC ABOUT THE FUTURE?

It is said that a pessimist is an optimist with experience. That seems unduly cynical. True, another 9/11, or something still worse, could befall the United States homeland. However, great perils today are matched by great possibilities. Charles Dickens's much-repeated 1859 saying that it was the best of times and the worst of times fits the current era as well as any, exemplified by the fact that life expectancy in most countries extends beyond anything imaginable in Dickens's day, even as the entire human species now can be extinguished in a manner of hours and maybe minutes. Among prognosticators, one can find optimistic as well as pessimistic readings of the human condition, generally, and the American condition, in particular.

The optimists since the end of the Cold War have included the likes of Charles Maynes, who has decried "the new pessimism"[17]; Julian Simon, who before his death in 1998, posited "no limit in sight," environmental or otherwise, for America and the rest of the planet[18]; Max Singer and Aaron Wildavsky, whose *The Real World Order* envisioned, a la Dickens's *Tale of Two Cities*, the current "zone of peace" inhabited by the United States and other Northern Hemisphere states (the former Yugoslavia aside) eventually extending into and replacing the current "zone of turmoil" inhabited by much of the South[19]; Alan Goodman, whose *A Brief History of the Future* heralded the twenty-first century as an era that "will encompass the longest period of peace, democracy, and economic development in history"[20]; John Mueller, who contends that we are witnessing "the obsolescence of major war" and that terrorist threats are "overblown"[21]; and, of course, Francis Fukuyama, who by 1989 had already proclaimed that "the end of history" had occurred with the final triumph of western liberal democracy and free-market capitalism over all other competitors.[22]

The ranks of the pessimists have included John Mearsheimer, who, a year after Fukuyama's pronouncement, was already lamenting "why we will soon miss the Cold War"[23]; Samuel Huntington, who hypothesized about the "clash of civilizations" pitting "the West versus the rest" as the successor to the East-West ideological axis of conflict[24]; Robert Kaplan, who has written of "the coming anarchy" and the "shattering of the dreams of the post–Cold War" era, stemming from ecological and other catastrophes, citing contemporary Rwanda as a metaphor for how both the South and the North will evolve[25]; Paul Kennedy, who, at times writing in a doomsdayish tone reserved usually for biologists, finds us wholly unprepared for the twenty-first century[26]; and Robert Heilbroner, who finds "the human prospect" rather dim, given what he sees as a persistent "what has posterity ever done for me?" attitude held by publics everywhere.[27]

Henry Kissinger, whose central challenge for the United States was cited earlier, poses a further challenge that he calls "America's assignment": "Opportunity for world order presents itself to each generation disguised as a set of problems. The dilemma of our age was perhaps best summed up by the philosopher Immanuel Kant over two hundred years ago. In his essay 'Perpetual Peace,' he wrote that the world was destined for perpetual peace. It would come about either by human foresight or by a series of catastrophes that leave no other choice."[28] It may seem odd for Kissinger, whose name is closely associated with the realist school of international relations, to be invoking Kant, who is considered one of the founders of the idealist school; but such labels are becoming almost as blurred as borders these days.

Many different **alternative world order models** have been suggested by various analysts who have speculated about how global governance might evolve in the twenty-first century.[29] To the extent we might be witnessing the beginning of the end of the nation-state as the primary form of human political organization on the planet, then what might replace it? If integrative, centripetal, "McWorld" trends were to be carried to their ultimate conclusion, we could get **world government**, either in the form of a single supreme, unitary authority presiding directly over some ten billion human beings or a somewhat less ambitious but still radical federation or confederation of states. A bit more likely might be a **regionalism** scenario, that is, instead of two hundred or so nation-states, we might see a system composed of five or so regional units, along the lines of the European Union, which some see as an emergent United States of Europe. If the disintegrative, centrifugal, "jihad" forces were to dominate, we could see the exact opposite, a kind of **polis** model akin to the Greek city-state system, where the world would be organized in thousands of smaller communities modeled after many of today's ministates. Or, if the current mix of McWorld *and* jihad trends were to become accentuated, with transnational forces (cyberspace, multinational corporations, and other boundary-busting phenomena) and subnational forces (separatist movements and calls for local autonomy) increasingly competing with each other above and below the nation-state (at times feeding each other), we could end up with what some observers have called **the new feudalism**, that is, an even more complex system of overlapping hierarchies of authority and multiple loyalties.[30]

Joseph Nye suggests that talk of a new feudalism may not be far-fetched:

Traffic on the Internet has been doubling every hundred days for the past few years. In 1993, there were about fifty web sites in the world; by the end of the decade, that number had surpassed five million. . . . In terms of 1990 dollars, the cost of a three-minute transatlantic phone call has fallen from $250 in 1930 to considerably less than $1 at the end of the century. In 1980, a gigabyte of storage occupied a room's worth of space; now it can fit on a credit-card-sized device in your pocket. . . . At the turn of the twenty-first century, there were 610 billion e-mail messages and 2.1 billion static pages on the World Wide Web, with the number of pages growing at a rate of 100 percent annually. . . . This . . . third industrial revolution is changing the nature of governments and sovereignty.

Nye goes on to explain:

What this means is that foreign policy will not be the sole province of governments. Both individuals and private organizations, here and abroad, will be empowered to play direct roles in world politics. . . . [We could see] a new cyberfeudalism, with overlapping communities and jurisdictions, laying claims to multiple layers of citizens' identities.[31]

Gar Alperovitz envisions a "decentralization of power" that "could easily shake up America's fundamental political structure" and have far-reaching implications for

American foreign policy. Pointing to the recent "accord between California and Britain on global warming," where the state of California (the eighth largest economy in the world), impatient with Washington's inaction on climate change, decided to pursue its own environmental policy in concert with another country, Alperowitz sees this as the tip of the iceberg in a rising new sectionalism within the United States. On this subject, he quotes none other than George Kennan, the father of containment, who long before the Iraq War "worried that what he called our 'monster country' would, through the 'hubris of inordinate size,' inevitably become a menace, intervening all too often in other nations' affairs" and who contemplated "regional devolution" as a possible solution.[32] It might be noted that, already, virtually each state in the union has its very own overseas trade offices in the European Union and elsewhere and that they are likely promoting Missouri's or other local interests more so than U.S. national interests.[33]

Some of these alternative world order models are more possible than others; few, if any, would necessarily be an improvement on the current state system. Although in the long run any one of the above models may eventually become the dominant mode of human political organization, it is probable that for the foreseeable future we are stuck, for better or worse, with the world order structure we now have. The contemporary post–Cold War international system will likely continue in its basic characteristics for quite some time, that is, a world whose dominant feature remains the competition between the governments of sovereign nation-states, albeit a game played in an increasingly complicated fashion, contested by a wider circle of participants, aligned in more fluid coalitions, squabbling over a wider set of issues. As Kissinger indicates, America needs to figure out how to play this game in a manner that produces enough win-win outcomes to satisfy both American national interests as well as larger global interests. If the United States fails to take up this challenge, it is possible the next "catastrophe" could be the last one, and the room for "choice" might be nonexistent. To quote Richard Lamm, "It has historically been one thing to die for your country. It is a different thing [in the event of a major war in the nuclear age] to die *with* your country."[34]

CONCLUSION:
TOWARD A MORE ASTUTE FOREIGN POLICY

Dickens also wrote that it "was the age of wisdom and the age of foolishness." Neither the United States nor the world can afford for Washington to behave foolishly. As Kofi Annan said shortly before leaving the UN Secretary-General's office in 2006, "More than ever, Americans, like the rest of humanity, need a functioning global system. Experience has shown, time and again, that the system works poorly when the United States remains aloof but it functions much better when there is farsighted U.S. leadership. That gives American leaders of today and tomorrow a great responsibility."[35] One hopes U.S. foreign policymakers decide to take actions that are legal and moral; above all, one hopes they are wise.

Annan added, "The American people must see that they live up to their responsibility."[36] Not only practitioners but also citizens will need to be astute in evaluating foreign policy decisions, since, in a democracy such as the United States, citizens ultimately are asked to pass judgment on the decision makers themselves. In order to perform sound evaluative analysis, one must be able to perform sound empirical analysis, that is, try to understand the dynamics of world politics and the forces affecting other countries' behavior as well as one's own behavior. In short, we all need to become better students of foreign policy.

For Americans, this is a special challenge. Stephen Walt notes that "Americans remain remarkably ignorant of the world they believe it is their obligation and destiny to run, and the topic of foreign affairs captures public attention only when major mistakes have already been made. If the United States wants to make its privileged position acceptable to others, then the American body politic must acquire a more serious and disciplined attitude toward the conduct of foreign policy."[37] The insular, parochial disposition of the American public is evidenced by the fact that, in any given year, five of the lowest selling newsstand issues of America's leading weekly news magazines (*Time, Newsweek,* and *U.S. News and World Report*) have cover stories featuring foreign affairs.[38] If the average person's appetite for news coverage of world events in popular periodicals is limited, the demand for lengthier, more substantive treatments of world events is even more limited. A culture that already prefers sound bites to dense text seems to have an especially short attention span the further away the story is from the United States. Somehow, Americans are going to have to find a way to become more informed and more analytical about the outside world.

This book has attempted to offer a fairly concise overview of American foreign policy. There is much more that can be said. The purpose here has not been to provide the reader with answers regarding what direction U.S. foreign policy ought to take, but to help crystallize the questions and stimulate further inquiry, leaving it to the student of foreign policy to struggle with the complex dilemmas that American decision makers themselves are having to confront.

At the end of his travels, as told by Swift, Gulliver returned home a misanthrope, feeling dejected about the future of humanity. One can only wish that, as the current generation of American leaders and citizens, along with the leaders and publics in other countries, engage in their own journey of discovery—in search of what Barry Buzan once called "a more mature anarchy"[39]—they will end up in a happier condition.

DISCUSSION QUESTIONS

1. How can the United States become more "multilateralist"—more sensitive to and accommodating of the concerns of others, both friends and foes—and at the same time preserve American sovereignty and protect American national interests, including America's security and well-being?

2. Are you optimistic or pessimistic about the future? Explain your answer.
3. When the United States approaches its tricentennial celebration later in the twenty-first century, what will the world look like in its essential features? What "alternative world order models" are (1) likely and (2) desirable?
4. Americans often are criticized for being more parochial in their knowledge and understanding of world politics than people in other countries. Do you think this is a fair indictment? How informed are *you* about U.S. foreign policy and world affairs?

NOTES

Chapter 1

1. Richard N. Haass, "What to Do with American Primacy," *Foreign Affairs* 78 (September/October 1999): 37.

2. Richard N. Haass, *The Opportunity* (New York: PublicAffairs, 2005). For the gorilla comparison, also see Fareed Zakaria, book jacket testimonial for Michael Mandelbaum, *The Case for Goliath: How America Acts As the World's Government in the 21st Century* (New York: PublicAffairs, 2005).

3. This definition is derived from Robert Dahl, "The Concept of Power," *Behavioral Science* 2 (July 1957): 202–203.

4. The first headline was from David S. Broder, "For Bush, a World of Worry," *Washington Post*, July 13, 2006. The second headline was on the cover of *Newsweek*, June 11, 2007.

5. Based on an interview reported in Stephen M. Walt, *Taming American Power: The Global Response to U.S. Primacy* (New York: W. W. Norton, 2005), 109.

6. Charles Kupchan, *The End of the American Era* (New York: Random House, 2003), 12.

7. Harold J. Laski, "America–1947," *The Nation*, 165 (December 1947): 641.

8. "The End of the American Century," *Harvard International Review* (Winter 1997/1998): 44.

9. George F. Kennan, *American Diplomacy 1900–1950* (New York: Mentor, 1951), foreword.

10. "I still believe he [President Lyndon Johnson] found it viscerally inconceivable that what Walt Rostow [Johnson's chief national security advisor] kept telling him was 'the greatest power in the world' could not dispose of a collection of night-riders in black pajamas." Quoted from Arthur Schlesinger, Jr., "The Quagmire Papers," *New York Review of Books* (December 16, 1971): 41.

11. Stanley Hoffmann, *Gulliver's Troubles, Or the Setting of American Foreign Policy* (New York: McGraw-Hill, 1968), 9–10. More recently, Hoffmann has written *Gulliver Unbound: America's Imperial Temptation and the War in Iraq* (New York: Rowman and Littlefield, 2004).

12. Walt, *op.cit.*, 65.

13. See the polling data in Andrew Kohut and Bruce Stokes, *America Against the World* (New York: Times Books, 2006), and David Rieff, "America the Untethered," *New York Times Sunday Magazine*, July 2, 2006, 11–12.

14. Fareed Zakaria, in "Why We Don't Get No Respect," *Newsweek*, July 10, 2006, 49, notes that "a poll published in the Financial Times [of London] on the eve of [President Bush's visit to Europe] . . . showed that across the continent, the United States was considered a greater threat to world peace than Iran or North Korea." The mayor of London, Ken Livingstone,

recently called George W. Bush "the greatest threat to life on this planet that we've most probably ever seen." Cited in Walt, *op.cit.*, 69.

15. Fareed Zakaria, "Beyond Bush," *Newsweek*, June 11, 2007, 25.

16. Mandelbaum, *op.cit.*, xv.

17. Joseph S. Nye, Jr., *The Paradox of American Power* (New York: Oxford University Press, 2002), 9.

18. C. William Maynes, "America Without the Cold War," *Foreign Policy* 78 (Spring 1990): 5; cited in Richard N. Haass, *The Reluctant Sheriff: The United States After the Cold War* (New York: Council on Foreign Relations, 1997), 3.

19. Henry A. Kissinger, "Clinton in the World," *Newsweek*, February 1, 1993, 45.

20. Charles Krauthammer, "The Unipolar Moment," *Foreign Affairs*, 70 (1991): 23–33; also see Kupchan, *op.cit.*, 28, and the epigram by Brooks and Wohlforth at the beginning of Chapter 1, taken from Stephen G. Brooks and William Wohlforth, "American Primacy in Perspective," *Foreign Affairs* 81 (July/August 2002): 20–25. For another view, see William R. Thompson, "Systemic Leadership, Evolutionary Processes, and International Relations Theory: The Unipolarity Question," *International Studies Review* 8 (2006): 1–22.

21. Quoted in Charles Krauthammer, "An American Foreign Policy for a Unipolar World," speech given to the American Enterprise Institute, February 10, 2004.

22. Stephen M. Walt, "American Primacy: Its Prospects and Pitfalls," *Naval War College Review* (Spring 2002): 1. In *Taming American Power*, 11, Walt says that "describing the United States as the mightiest state since Rome has become a cliché, but like most clichés, it also captures an essential feature of reality."

23. Timothy Garten Ash, "The Peril of Too Much Power," *New York Times*, April 9, 2002.

24. Josef Joffe, "Bismarck's Lessons for Bush," *New York Times*, May 29, 2002.

25. Walt, *Taming American Power*, 31.

26. Ibid., 38; statistics on U.S. power can be found on pp. 31–39. Also, see Nye, *op.cit.*, 35–40; Haass, *The Opportunity*, 7–9; and Niall Ferguson, *Colossus* (New York: Penguin, 2004), 16–19.

27. Walt, *Taming American Power*, 38. Walt quotes Josef Joffe as noting that "wealthy Romans used to send their children to Greek universities; today's Greeks, that is, the Europeans, send their kids to Roman, that is, American universities." However, Thomas Friedman, in *The World Is Flat* (New York: Farrar, Straus and Giroux, 2005), notes a possible decline in foreign students attending U.S. universities in the post–9/11 era, due to security-related immigration restrictions and other factors.

28. On potential rivals and an emergent multipolarity, see, for example, Kupchan, *op.cit.*, 28–29. Kupchan is especially high on the European Union. Ferguson, *op.cit.* also discusses possible "counterweights" but dismisses most of them as not likely to challenge American power. See also, Nye, *op.cit.*, 18–33.

29. The quote is from Henry Kissinger's memoirs; cited in *New York Times*, October 17, 2003. See Raymond Vernon, ed., *The Oil Crisis* (New York: W. W. Norton, 1976).

30. Ferguson, *op.cit.*, 288.

31. The unit veto system, in which each state had nuclear weapons, was one of the models described by Morton Kaplan in *System and Process in International Politics* (New York: John Wiley, 1957).

32. Walt, *Taming American Power*, 133.

33. On asymmetrical warfare, see *ibid.*, 133–135; and Donald M. Snow, *National Security for a New Era* (New York: Pearson, 2004), Chapter 9.

34. The term is Thomas Friedman's, in *The Lexus and the Olive Tree* (New York: Farrar, Straus and Giroux, 1999), 13.

35. Ferguson, *op.cit.*, 295.

36. Nye, *op.cit.*, 40. Also see Note 74.

37. John J. Mearsheimer, "Why We Will Soon Miss the Cold War," *The Atlantic Monthly* (August 1990): 35.

38. Abba Eban, "The UN Idea Revisited," *Foreign Affairs* 74 (September/October 1995): 50.

39. The term "bimultipolarity" was coined by Richard N. Rosecrance, "Bipolarity, Multi-polarity, and the Future," *Journal of Conflict Resolution* 10 (September 1966): 314–327.

40. Nicholas Kristof, "China Sees 'Market-Leninism' as Way to Future," *New York Times*, September 6, 1993.

41. John J. Mearsheimer, *The Tragedy of Great Power Politics* (New York: W. W. Norton, 2001). Also, see Kupchan, *op.cit.*, xvii and 29.

42. Nye, *op.cit.*, 18 and 25; ibid., 21, cites Robert Kagan as arguing that China aims "in the near term to replace the United States as the dominant power in East Asia and in the long term to challenge America's position as the dominant power in the world."

43. The quotes by the EU Commission president and Putin are cited in Walt, *Taming American Power*, 111.

44. Henry A. Kissinger, *The Troubled Partnership* (New York: McGraw-Hill, 1965).

45. Thomas Friedman, "Our War with France," *New York Times*, September 18, 2003.

46. Cited in Nye, *op.cit.*, 33. Ferguson, *op.cit.*, 236–237, notes that assumptions about "the fundamental unity of 'Western civilization' look increasingly questionable in view of Europe's precipitously declining religiosity" compared with the high percentage of regular church-goers in America. Also see Haass, *The Opportunity*, 145; and Robert Kagan, *Of Paradise and Power: America and Europe in the New World Order* (New York: Vintage Books, 2004).

47. Dominique Moisi, cited in Haass, *The Opportunity*, 145.

48. www.news.com.au/story. Accessed on September 17, 2006.

49. Kupchan, *op.cit.*, 51, citing Paul Kennedy.

50. John G. Stoessinger, *The Might of Nations*, 7th ed. (New York: Random House, 1982), 5.

51. Samuel P. Huntington, "The Clash of Civilizations," *Foreign Affairs* 72 (Summer 1993): 22–49.

52. Francis Fukuyama, "The End of History?," *The National Interest* 16 (Summer 1989): 3–16.

53. Fareed Zakaria cautions that, just as the United States at times during the Cold War mistakenly viewed the entire Communist world, including the Soviet Union and China, as a single-minded monolith, today Washington has to be careful not to treat all "Islamofascists" as "the enemy" since some leaders may be more amenable than others to deal-making with the United States. See "Mao and Stalin, Osama and Saddam," *Newsweek*, September 18, 2006.

54. Earl C. Ravenal, "The Regionalization of Power: General Unalignment in the Future International System," paper presented at the annual meeting of the International Studies Association, Washington, DC, April 14, 1990.

55. Michael Mandelbaum, "David's Friend Goliath," *Foreign Policy* (January/February 2006): 33.

56. Walt, *Taming American Power*, 125. Walt argues that, nonetheless, the functional equivalent of balance-of-power politics is occurring through "soft balancing" and other mechanisms.

57. Haass, *The Opportunity*, 6.

58. Mandelbaum, *The Case for Goliath*. Also see Ferguson, *op.cit.*

59. Stanley Hoffmann, "Choices," *Foreign Policy* (Fall 1973): 5.

60. The quote is from Daniel Bell in Fall 1990 issue of *Dissent*, cited in Samuel P. Huntington, "Why International Primacy Matters," *International Security* 17 (Spring 1993): 81.

61. On the "long peace," see John Lewis Gaddis, "Great Illusions, the Long Peace and the Future of the International System," in Charles W. Kegley, Jr., ed., *The Long Postwar Peace* (New York: HarperCollins, 1991), 25–55. Also, see Mark W. Zacher, "The Decaying Pillars of the Westphalian Temple: Implications for Global Order and Governance," in James N. Rosenau and Ernst-Otto Czempiel, eds., *Governance without Government* (Cambridge: Cambridge University Press, 1992); and John Mueller, *Retreat from Doomsday: The Obsolescence of Major War* (New York: Basic Books, 1989).

62. See *The Defense Monitor* XXVII, no. 1 (1998): 1; *The Defense Monitor* XXXII, no. 1 (2003): 1 and 3; and Michael Renner, "Violent Conflicts Continue to Decline," in Worldwatch Institute, *Vital Signs 2003* (New York: W. W. Norton, 2003), 74–75.

63. Jack S. Levy, "War and Peace," in Walter Carlsnaes et al., eds., *Handbook of International Relations* (London: Sage, 2002), 351. On the overall decline in the incidence of violence, see Gregg Easterbrook, "Explaining 15 Years of Diminishing Violence: The End of War?," The New Republic Online, May 24, 2005; and "Global Violence Has Decreased, UN Says," http://www.washingtonpost.com, October 18, 2005.

64. See Mary Kaldor, *New and Old Wars: Organized Violence in the Global Era* (Cambridge: Polity, 2001); and Meredith Sarkees et al., "Inter-State, Intra-State, and Extra-State Wars: A Comprehensive Look at Their Distribution Over Time, 1816–1997," *International Studies Quarterly* 47 (March 2003): 49–70.

65. On the historical roots of nonstate actors, see James A. Field, "Transnationalism and the New Tribe" and other articles in a special issue of *International Organization* entitled "Transnational Relations and World Politics," 25 (Summer 1971).

66. On subnational actors, see, for example, John Barkdull, "Globalization and Texas," paper presented at annual meeting of the International Studies Association, Minneapolis, March 20, 1998; and "California Takes on Global Warming," http://cnn.com, August 31, 2006.

67. Depending on the criteria used, the number of IGOs may exceed one thousand, and the number of NGOs may exceed 25,000. See Harold K. Jacobson et al., "National Entanglements in International Governmental Organizations," *American Political Science Review* 80 (March 1986): 141–159; and the Commission on Global Governance, *Our Global Neighborhood* (Oxford: Oxford University Press, 1995), 32.

68. On the growing importance of NGOs, see Jessica Matthews, "Power Shift," *Foreign Affairs* (January/February 1997): 50–66.

69. Gordon Smith and Moises Naim, *Altered States: Globalization, Sovereignty, and Governance* (Ottawa: International Development Research Centre, 2000), 10; cited in Nye, *op.cit.*, 74.

70. For example, see Joseph A. Camilleri and Jim Falk, *The End of Sovereignty?* (London: Edward Elgar, 1992).

71. See Benjamin Barber, *Jihad vs. McWorld* (New York: Times Books, 1995). Henry Kissinger, in "After Lebanon," *Washington Post*, September 13, 2006, called attention to the threat posed by "substates" operating within states, as in the case of Hezbollah having control over large parts of Lebanon.

72. Susan Strange, "The Defective State," *Daedalus* 124 (Spring 1994): 56–57.

73. Cautionary warnings about writing off the nation-state can be found in Paul Kennedy, "The Future of the Nation-State," Chapter 7 in *Preparing for the Twenty-First Century* (New York: Vintage, 1993); and Stephen Krasner, "Sovereignty," *Foreign Policy* (January/February 2001).

74. Haass, *The Reluctant Sheriff*, 6. Also, see Joseph S. Nye, "U.S. Security Policy: Challenges for the 21st Century," *Agenda* 3 (July 1998): 20: "While the United States cannot be a lone global policeman . . . it can at times serve as 'sheriff of the posse' that leads shifting coalitions of friends and allies to address shared security concerns."

Chapter 2

1. Deborah J. Gerner, "Foreign Policy Analysis: Exhilarating Eclecticism, Intriguing Enigmas," *International Studies Notes* (Winter 1992): 4.

2. Frederic S. Pearson and J. Martin Rochester, *International Relations: The Global Condition in the 21st Century*, 4th ed. (New York: McGraw-Hill, 1998), 686.

3. Bruce Russett, Harvey Starr, and David Kinsella, *World Politics: Menu for Choice*, 7th ed. (Belmont, Calif.: Wadsworth, 2004), 521.

4. Joshua Goldstein, *International Relations*, 5th ed. (New York: Longman, 2004), 155.

5. *St. Louis Post-Dispatch*, June 14, 1981, 1.

6. *Time*, January 1, 1990, 20.

7. *Harpers* 288 (January 1994): 57–64.

8. Henry A. Kissinger, "Bureaucracy and Policymaking: The Effects of Insiders and Outsiders on the Policy Process," in Morton H. Halperin and Arnold Kanter, eds., *Readings in American Foreign Policy: A Bureaucratic Perspective* (Boston: Little, Brown, 1973), 85. The essay originally appeared in a 1968 volume shortly before Kissinger became the chief foreign policy advisor to Richard Nixon.

9. Roger Hilsman, *To Move a Nation* (Garden City, NY: Doubleday, 1967), 5.

10. Margaret Hermann and Charles F. Hermann, "Who Makes Foreign Policy Decisions and How: An Empirical Inquiry," *International Studies Quarterly* 33 (December 1989): 361–387.

11. K. J. Holsti, *International Politics: A Framework for Analysis*, 7th ed. (Englewood Cliffs, NJ: Prentice-Hall, 1995), 267, based on testimony from U.S. State department officials. Similar estimates are reported in Lincoln P. Bloomfield, *The Foreign Policy Process: A Modern Primer* (Englewood Cliffs, NJ: Prentice-Hall, 1982), 143.

12. Michael Brecher and Jonathan Wilkenfeld, "Crises in World Politics," *World Politics* 34 (April 1982): 381. Also, see Brecher et al., *Crises in the Twentieth Century*, two vols. (Oxford: Pergamon, 1988); and Charles F. Hermann, "International Crisis as a Situational Variable," in James N. Rosenau, ed., *International Politics and Foreign Policy*, rev. ed. (New York: Free Press, 1969), 409–421.

13. Gerner, *op.cit.*, 4.

14. Arnold Wolfers, *Discord and Collaboration* (Baltimore: Johns Hopkins University Press, 1962), 37.

15. G. John Ikenberry, ed., *American Foreign Policy: Theoretical Essays*, 5th ed. (New York: Longman, 2005), 1.

16. Winston Churchill, radio broadcast, London, October 1, 1939.

17. Don Munton and David Welch, *The Cuban Missile Crisis: A Concise History* (New York: Oxford University Press, 2007), 1.

18. Graham T. Allison, "Conceptual Models and the Cuban Missile Crisis," *American Political Science Review* 63 (September 1969): 689. For Allison's fuller treatment, see his *Essence of Decision: Explaining the Cuban Missile Crisis* (Boston: Little, Brown, 1971); and a second edition coauthored with Philip Zelikow in 1999.

19. Allison, *Essence of Decision*, 131.

20. The "billiard ball" analogy was first suggested by Arnold Wolfers in Wolfers, *op.cit.*, 19.

21. David A. Lake, in *Entangling Relations: American Foreign Policy in Its Century* (Princeton: Princeton University Press, 1999), 265, points out that three leading theoretical approaches today in the international relations discipline—neorealism, neoliberal institutionalism, and constructivism—are "each premised on [states as] unitary actors." Both neorealists and neoliberals posit that states are driven by material self-interest, although neoliberals see more potential for interstate cooperation (based on mutual interests) than do neorealists. Constructivists stress the importance of ideational more than material factors, arguing that interests are not a given and that changing norms (e.g., in support of humanitarian intervention) can lead states to redefine their national interests in a somewhat more altruistic fashion.

22. Allison, *Essence of Decision*, 4–5. Herbert S. Dinerstein attempts to examine the Cuban missile crisis from the Soviet point of view in *The Making of A Missile Crisis* (Baltimore: Johns Hopkins University Press, 1976).

23. Morton H. Halperin, *Bureaucratic Politics and Foreign Policy* (Washington, DC: Brookings Institution, 1974), ix.

24. Kenneth N. Waltz, *Man, the State, and War* (New York: Columbia University Press, 1959). Waltz focused especially on the system level in his subsequent work, *Theory of International Politics* (Reading, Mass.: Addison-Wesley, 1979). Also see J. David Singer, "The Level-of-Analysis Problem in International Relations," in Klaus Knorr and Sidney Verba, eds., *The International System: Theoretical Essays* (Princeton: Princeton University Press, 1961), 77–92.

25. Ikenberry, *op.cit.*, 3.

26. Henry A. Kissinger, "Domestic Structure and Foreign Policy," *Daedalus* 95 (1966): 503–529. Bruce Bueno de Mesquita, in *Principles of International Politics: People's Power, Preferences, and Perceptions*, 2nd ed. (Washington, DC: Congressional Quarterly Press, 2003), argues that the focus of foreign policy analysis should be less on *national* interest than on understanding the *self*-interest of leaders, including the felt concern of leaders in democratic states to achieve reelection.

27. Henry A. Kissinger, "America at the Apex," *The National Interest* (Summer 2001): 15.

28. Stanley Hoffmann, *Gulliver Unbound: America's Imperial Temptation and the War in Iraq* (New York: Rowman and Littlefield, 2004), 12. On the role of public opinion and the extent to which "presidents incorporate the preferences of the public into their foreign policy decisions," see T. Knecht and M. S. Weatherford, "Public Opinion and Foreign Policy: The Stages of Presidential Decision Making," *International Studies Quarterly* 50 (September 2006): 705–727.

29. On the link between domestic political instability and war, see Jack Levy, "The Diversionary Theory of War: A Critique," in Manus L. Midlarsky, ed., *Handbook of War Studies* (Boston: Unwin Hyman, 1989), 259–288.

30. On bureaucratic politics and the Cuban missile crisis, see Timothy J. McKeown, "Plans and Routines: Bureaucratic Bargaining and the Cuban Missile Crisis," *Journal of Politics* 63 (2001): 1163–1191. On bureaucratic politics in general and American foreign policy, see Ikenberry, *op.cit.*, Part Six, "Bureaucratic Politics and Organizational Culture."

31. Deborah Shapley, "Technological Creep and the Arms Race: ICBM Problem A Sleeper," *Science* 201 (September 22, 1978): 105. On the reasons behind U.S. weapons procurement policies during the Cold War, see James Kurth, "Why We Buy the Weapons We Do," *Foreign Policy* 11 (Summer 1973): 33–56; and Matthew A. Evangelista, "Why the Soviets Buy the Weapons They Do," *World Politics* 36 (July 1984): 597–618.

32. "U.S. Accuses Soviets of Developing 4 New Long-Range Missiles," *St. Louis Post-Dispatch*, October 18, 1990.

33. Transcript of joint press conference, October 21, 2001, on the White House Web site at http://www.whitehouse.gov.

34. Statement by Theodore Sorenson; cited in Allison, *Essence of Decision*, 57.

35. A pioneering study that focused attention on the individual decision makers inside the foreign policy process was Richard C. Snyder, H. W. Bruck, and Burton Sapin, *Foreign Policy Decision-Making: An Approach to the Study of International Politics* (New York: The Free Press, 1962). Other studies examining psychological variables include Irving Janis, *Groupthink*, 2nd ed. (Boston: Houghton Mifflin, 1982); Robert Jervis, *Perception and Misperception in International Politics* (Princeton: Princeton University Press, 1976); and David G. Winter, "Personality and Political Behavior," in D. O. Sears et al., eds., *Oxford Handbook of Political Psychology* (Oxford: Oxford University Press, 2003).

36. Munton and Welch, *op.cit.*, 4. On cognitive factors in general and American foreign policy, see Ikenberry, *op.cit.*, Part Seven, "Perceptions, Personality, and Social Psychology."

37. Ronald Steele, interview with Robert Kennedy, *New York Review of Books*, March 13, 1963, 22.

38. Richard Reeves, "Kennedy's Private Ills," *New York Times*, December 21, 2002. Also, see Robert Dallek, *An Unfinished Life: John F. Kennedy 1917–1963* (New York: Penguin, 2004).

39. On "biopolitics," see Gordon Hilton et al., *Leaders Under Stress: A Psychophysiological Analysis of International Crises* (Durham: Duke University Press, 1985); and Thomas Wiegele, *Biopolitics* (Boulder: Westview, 1979).

40. For example, see Steve A. Yetiv, *Explaining Foreign Policy: U.S. Decision-Making and the Persian Gulf War* (Baltimore: Johns Hopkins University Press, 2004), an examination of the First Gulf War in 1991, which takes an "integrated" approach in looking at the following perspectives: the rational actor model, cognitive factors, domestic politics, groupthink, and the government politics model. One scholar reduces all this to just two sets of factors, what he calls *Realpolitik* and *Innenpolitik*. Walter Carlsnaes, "Foreign Policy," in Carlsnaes et al., eds., *Handbook of International Relations* (Thousand Oaks, CA: Sage, 2002), 334.

41. James N. Rosenau, "Pre-Theories and Theories of Foreign Policy," in R. Barry Farrell, ed., *Approaches to Comparative and International Politics* (Evanston: Northwestern University Press, 1966), 27–92. Deborah Gerner referred to these in her statement I cited earlier; see Note 13.

42. Janis, *op.cit.*, 14.

43. Rosenau, *op.cit.*, 45–46.

44. Allison, *Essence of Decision*, 195–196.

45. Janis, *op.cit.*, Chapter 2.

46. Good treatments of morality and foreign policy can be found in Raymond Wolfers's essay "Statesmanship and Moral Choice" and in his *Discord and Collaboration, op.cit.*; Stanley Hoffmann, *Duties Beyond Borders* (Syracuse: Syracuse University Press, 1981); and Rachael M. McCleary, ed., *Ethics and International Affairs* (Boulder: Westview, 1991).

47. This view was expressed by Hurst Hannum of Tufts University at a talk at the University of Missouri-St. Louis on February 6, 2003.

48. See Martha Finnemore, "Constructing Norms of Humanitarian Intervention," in Peter J. Katzenstein, ed., *The Culture of National Security: Norms and Identity in World Politics* (New York: Columbia University Press, 1996), 153–185; and James Lee Ray, "The Abolition of Slavery and the End of International War," *International Organization* 43 (Summer 1989): 405–439. Although some scholars argue that slavery and colonialism ended because the costs of engaging in such activities eventually outweighed the benefits for the perpetrators, the explanation would seem to understate the importance of the evolution of new value systems.

49. Janis, *op.cit.*, 157. Robert Kennedy was further quoted as saying "my brother is not going to be the Tojo of the 1960s," referring to the Japanese commander who ordered the Pearl Harbor attacks; cited in Ronald Steel, "The Kennedys and the Missile Crisis," in Halperin and Kanter, *op.cit.*, 205.

50. On how international law affects foreign policy behavior, see J. Martin Rochester, *Between Peril and Promise: The Politics of International Law* (Washington, DC: Congressional Quarterly Press, 2006).

51. Contemporary offshoots of these schools are called neorealists and neoliberals. The debate is discussed in Charles W. Kegley, Jr., *Controversies in International Relations Theory: Realism and the Neoliberal Challenge* (New York: St. Martins Press, 1995); and David A. Baldwin, ed., *Neorealism and Neoliberalism: The Contemporary Debate* (New York: Columbia University Press, 1993).

52. Alexander DeConde, *American Diplomatic History in Transformation* (Washington, DC: American Historical Association, 1976), 10.

53. See George F. Kennan, *American Diplomacy 1900–1950* (New York: Mentor, 1951).

54. See Joseph S. Nye, Jr., *The Paradox of American Power* (New York: Oxford University Press, 2002).

55. John Mearsheimer, "The False Promise of International Institutions," *International Security* (Winter 1994): 5–49.

56. Robert Osgood, *Ideals and Self-Interest in America's Foreign Policy* (Chicago: University of Chicago Press, 1953), 449.

57. Ralph K. White, *Nobody Wanted War* (Garden City, NY: Anchor Books, 1968).

58. David Kinsella, *Regime Change* (Belmont, CA: Wadsworth, 2004), 1. Kinsella updated his study of the Iraq War in a second edition written in 2007. On "the road to war," see also Todd S. Purdum, *A Time of Our Choosing: America's War in Iraq* (New York: Times Books, 2004).

59. Kinsella, *op.cit.*, 1.

60. Ibid., 10–11.

61. Reported by Evan Thomas in "The 12-Year Itch," *Newsweek*, March 31, 2003.

62. *Meet the Press* telecast of August 27, 2000.

63. Michael Elliott and James Carney, "First Stop, Iraq," *Time*, March 31, 2003.

64. Ibid.

65. According to Glenn Kessler, "U.S. Decision on Iraq Has Puzzling Past," *Washington Post*, January 12, 2003, six days after the attack on the World Trade Center, a document marked "Top Secret" was signed by President Bush that "outlined the plan for going to war in Afghanistan as part of a global campaign against terrorism" and that also, "almost as a footnote," "directed the Pentagon to begin planning military options for an invasion of Iraq."

66. Elliott and Carney, *op.cit.*

67. See Graham Allison, *Nuclear Terrorism* (New York: Times Books, 2004), 1.

68. Elliott and Carney, *op.cit.*

69. Mohammed Nuruzzaman, "Beyond the Realist Theories: 'Neoconservative Realism' and the American Invasion of Iraq," *International Studies Perspectives* 7 (August 2006): 240. The author challenges the conventional "realist," national interest-based explanation.

70. Hoffmann, *op.cit.*, 48.

71. George W. Bush, speech in Cincinnati, Ohio, delivered on October 7, 2002.

72. Cited in Kinsella, *op.cit.*, 14.

73. Interview with Wolf Blitzer on CNN on September 8, 2002.

74. Michael Mandelbaum, *The Case for Goliath* (New York: PublicAffairs, 2005), 98–99.

75. "Operation Iraqi Freedom – By the Numbers," US CENTAF Assessment and Analysis Division, U.S. Department of Defense, April 30, 2003.

76. John Mearsheimer and Stephen Walt, "The Israel Lobby," *London Review of Books* 28 (March 23, 2006). On the role of domestic politics generally in U.S. foreign policy, see Walt's *Taming American Power* (New York: W. W. Norton, 2005), 194–205.

77. Hoffmann, *op.cit.*, 33.

78. Ibid., 65.

79. Kinsella, *op.cit.*, 12. Kinsella points out (p. 13) that "in fact, public opinion polls conducted in February and March 2003 showed that 50 to 60 percent of the American public believed that Saddam Hussein was personally involved in orchestrating the September 11 attacks."

80. Stephen Dyson, "Personality and Foreign Policy: Tony Blair's Iraq Decisions," *Foreign Policy Analysis* 2 (2006): 290.

81. Hoffmann, *op.cit.*, 55.

82. Thomas, *op.cit.*

83. The reference to a "war council" appeared in a headline in the *New York Times*, September 23, 2001, which read "Forging a War Council Out of a Disparate Bush Team."

84. Evan Thomas reports that, in addition to the Hanson book, Cheney was also reading books about anthrax and the plague following 9/11. See Thomas, *op.cit.* Thomas reports that on *Meet the Press* in March 2003, Cheney "actually embraced, as he put it, 'the notion that the president is a cowboy.' Cheney said: 'I don't think that's necessarily a bad idea.'"

85. Elliott and Carney, *op.cit.*

86. Thomas, *op.cit.*

87. Ibid.

88. Elliott and Carney, *op.cit.*

89. Comment by my political science colleague Joyce Mushaben, at a meeting of the Political Science Academy at the University of Missouri-St. Louis, on November 20, 2001.

90. For discussion of the hypothesis, see the debate between Francis Fukuyama and Mary Caprioto in John T. Rourke, *Taking Sides: Clashing Views in World Politics*, 11th ed. (New York: McGraw-Hill, 2004), 232–251. Also see V. Spike Peterson and Anne Sisson Runyan, *Global Gender Issues*, 2nd ed. (Boulder: Westview, 1999).

91. Dyson, *op.cit.*, 289.

92. Phillip Stephens, *Tony Blair: The Making of a World Leader* (New York: Viking Books, 2004), 234.

93. Mark Schafer and Stephen G. Walker, "Democratic Leaders and the Democratic Peace: The Operational Codes of Tony Blair and Bill Clinton," *International Studies Quarterly* 50 (September 2006): 573.

94. Based on an exchange I had with A. J. R. Groom of the University of Kent on September 28, 2001.

95. Niall Ferguson, *Colossus* (New York: Penguin, 2004), 161.

96. Given on the floor of the British House of Commons on March 18, 2003. Ibid., 160.

97. Janis, *op.cit.* Janis notes that groupthink operated in the Bay of Pigs decision but not nearly as much in the Cuban missile crisis, even though the members of ExCom in 1962 were largely the same as had met to plan the Bay of Pigs invasion in 1961; Janis indicates that the group members had learned some lessons from their previous experience, such as encouraging President Kennedy to allow the group to meet at times without him being present, so as to minimize the pressure to defer to the group leader.

98. Cited in *Newsweek*, July 19, 2004, 38. Also, see National Public Radio, "Report Faults Intelligence for WMD 'Groupthink,'" July 9, 2004.

99. http://www.sfgate.com/cgi-bin/article.cgi?file=/c/a/2004. One CIA official accused the Bush administration of "cherry-picking" the intelligence to highlight those data that might justify an invasion. See "Ex-CIA Official Faults Use of Data on Iraq," *Washington Post*, February 10, 2006.

100. Kinsella, *op.cit.*, 18.

101. Thomas, *op.cit.*

102. Ferguson, *op.cit.*, 164.

103. There is some scattered evidence that during the 1930s Japan may have used chemical weapons in Manchuria and Italy may have used them in Ethiopia, but other than these and a few other isolated cases, there is general agreement that lethal chemical weapons were not used on any large scale after World War I, including during World War II.

104. Kinsella, *op.cit.*, 4. Kinsella notes that Halabja at the time was controlled by Iranian forces, at war with Iraq. Also see "Prosecutors Detail Atrocities in Hussein's Trial, *New York Times*, August 22, 2006.

105. David J. Scheffer, "Use of Force After the Cold War," in Louis Henkin et al., *Right v. Might* (New York: Council on Foreign Relations Press, 1991), 141–143.

106. Walt, *op.cit.*, 168.

107. "How Precise Is Our Bombing?," editorial, *New York Times*, March 31, 2003. Also, on the "selective and restrained" nature of the aerial targeting, see Kinsella, *op.cit.*, 23; also Colin H. Kahl, "How We Fight," *Foreign Affairs* 85 (November/December 2006): 83–101.

108. Richard N. Haass, *The Opportunity* (New York: Public Affairs, 2005), 185. Also see Adam Roberts, "The Use of Force," in David M. Malone, ed., *The UN Security Council* (Boulder: Lynne Rienner, 2004), 140.

109. Remarks opening the 54th General Assembly, cited in Judith Miller, "Sovereignty Isn't So Sacred Anymore," *New York Times*, April 18, 1999.

110. Scheffer, *op.cit.*, 144. On the failure of state practice to support the right of humanitarian intervention, see Michael J. Glennon, *Limits of Law, Prerogatives of Power* (New York: Palgrave, 2001).

111. Ferguson, *op.cit.*, 154.

112. "UN Chief Ignites Firestorm by Calling Iraq War 'Illegal'," *New York Times*, September 17, 2004. For Bush's legal defense of the war, see his UN speech reported in the *New York Times*, September 22, 2004. Also, on whether the invasion could be considered a "just war" under international law, see Kinsella, *op.cit.*, pp. 26–35 and Hoffmann, *Gulliver Unbound*, 68–73.

113. See "Cost of Iraq War $291 Billion So Far," *Los Angeles Times*, July 14, 2006; also see *Wall Street Journal*, November 25, 2006, A-7.

114. Cited in Ferguson, *op.cit.*, 155. Pollack has since had second thoughts about the war.

115. Among the leading realist scholars who signed the ad were Kenneth Waltz of the University of California, John Mearsheimer of the University of Chicago, and Stephen Walt of Harvard.

116. These included Joseph Nye, dean of the John F. Kennedy School of Government at Harvard, and Michael Ignatieff, director of the Carr Center for Human Rights at Harvard. See "Intellectual Left's Doves Take on Role of Hawks," *New York Times*, March 14, 2003; and Ignatieff, "The Burden," *New York Times Magazine*, January 5, 2003. They also had some second thoughts later; see Ignatieff, "The Year of Living Dangerously," *New York Times*, March 14, 2004. Also, see Robert Kaplan, "Haunted by Hussein, Humbled by Events," *Los Angeles Times*, April 17, 2006.

117. Ferguson, *op.cit.*, 164.

118. In Bob Woodward's *The Plan of Attack* (New York: Simon and Schuster, 2004), George Tenet, when pressed about the latest intelligence on whether Saddam had WMDs, was reported to have told President Bush, "Don't worry, it's a slam-dunk."

119. The quote is from Jon Wolfsthal, cited in "Experts: Iraq has Tons of Chemical Weapons," CNN, accessed at http://wwwarchives.cnn.com/2002/WORLD/meast/09/02/iraq.

120. The characterization of Saddam's "full disclosure" report belongs to Marvin Zonis of the University of Chicago. The evidence for WMDs is discussed in Kinsella, *op.cit.*, 13–15.

121. The "laughable contradiction" quote is from Charles Hill, cited at http://www.powerlineblog.com/archives/007246.

122. See Jeffrey Pickering and Mark Peceny, "Forging Democracy at Gunpoint," *International Studies Quarterly* 50 (September 2006): 539–559.

123. Hoffmann, *Gulliver Unbound*, 101. One set of options that has been suggested is to break up Iraq into several countries or make it into a loose confederation of several autonomous regions, organized around Kurdish, Shiite, and Sunni communities. See, for example, Joseph Biden and Leslie Gelb, "Unity Through Autonomy in Iraq," *New York Times*, May 1, 2006.

124. "Go Big, Go Long, or Go Home: Few Easy Options for Iraq," accessed on November 20, 2006, at http://www.cnn.com/2006/POLITICS/11/20/us.iraq.ap Also see special issue of "Iraq: What Next?," *The New Republic* (November 27 and December 4, 2006).

125. *The Iraq Study Group Report* (New York: Vintage Books, 2006).

Chapter 3

1. See Note 8 in Chapter 2.

2. Thomas A. Bailey, *A Diplomatic History of the American People*, 7th ed. (New York: Appleton-Century-Crofts, 1964), 1.

3. Ibid.

4. Stephen E. Ambrose, *Rise to Globalism*, 2nd ed. (New York: Penguin Books, 1980).

5. The phrase is taken from an exchange between Bozo and Hoffmann in Stanley Hoffmann, *Gulliver Unbound: America's Imperial Temptation and the War in Iraq* (New York: Rowman and Littlefield, 2004), 19.

6. James Schlesinger, quoted in Joseph S. Nye, Jr., *The Paradox of American Power* (New York: Oxford University Press, 2002), 112.

7. Nye, *op.cit.*, 112.

8. Robert Osgood, *Ideals and Self-Interest in America's Foreign Relations* (Chicago: University of Chicago Press, 1953), 1.

9. Hoffmann, *op.cit.*, 19–21.

10. Osgood, *op.cit.*, 17–18.

11. Lawrence J. Korb, *A New National Security Strategy* (New York: Council on Foreign Relations, 2003), 13.

12. Quoted in Daniel Smith, ed., *Major Problems in American Diplomatic History: Documents and Readings*, vol. I (Boston: D.C. Heath, 1964), 104.

13. Quoted in David A. Lake, *Entangling Relations* (Princeton: Princeton University Press, 1999), 3.

14. Quoted in Bailey, *op.cit.*, 84.

15. Albert H. Bowman, "Jefferson, Hamilton, and American Foreign Policy," in Smith, *op.cit.*, 57, citing the work of Hans Morgenthau. Smith argues that Jefferson was no more an idealist than Hamilton was a realist, that each blended elements of both.

16. Bailey, *op.cit.*, 85.

17. Smith, *op.cit.*, 102–103.

18. Lake, *op.cit.*, 78, cites Walter McDougall's statement that "American isolationism is a myth. The word—which did not come into common usage until the 1890s, when propagandists for empire flung it at their Mugwump critics—should be struck from America's vocabulary." Also see Robert Kagan, *Dangerous Nation* (New York: Knopf, 2006); and Smith, *op.cit.*, 101.

19. Smith, *op.cit.*, 104.

20. Jules Jusseraud, quoted in the early 1900s; cited in Stephen M. Walt, *Taming American Power* (New York: W. W. Norton, 2005), 39.

21. The reference to "liquid assets" is found in Bailey, *op.cit.*, 4. The Hoover quote is taken from Lake, *op. cit.*, 101.

22. Bailey, *op.cit.*, 71.

23. Smith, *op. cit.*, 117. For the role played by domestic partisan politics in influencing U.S. foreign policy from the beginning, see Alexander DeConde, *American Diplomatic History in Transformation* (Washington, D.C.: American Historical Association, 1976).

24. Bailey, *op.cit.*, 5.

25. The phrase is from *ibid.*, 34. Many of the Founding Fathers did, in fact, refer to America as an "empire" in the making. See Niall Ferguson, *Colossus* (New York: Penguin Books, 2004), 34.

26. The "empire of liberty" phrase appeared in Jefferson's correspondence with George Rogers Clark, December 25, 1780; cited in Ferguson, *op.cit.*, 2. The "Colossus" phrase was mentioned by Jefferson in 1816; cited in *ibid.*, epigram at start of book.

27. Bailey, *op.cit.*, 104. Bailey notes that, by this time, Jefferson saw France as a bigger threat than Britain.

28. Ibid., 184.

29. Adams uttered the "monsters" remark in 1821, prior to assuming the presidency; see Paul Starobin, "The Realists," *National Journal*, September 16, 2006, 27. The "destined by God" remark was made in 1817; see Robert Kagan, "Against the Myth of American Innocence: Cowboy Nation," *The New Republic*, October 23, 2006, 20.

30. Senator Dickinson of New York, cited in Bailey, *op.cit.*, 263.

31. Osgood, *op.cit.*, 32.

32. Bailey, *op.cit.*, 421.

33. Ibid., 435.

34. Ibid., 451.

35. Ibid., 471.

36. Quoted in F. R. Dulles, *America in the Pacific* (Boston: Houghton Mifflin, 1932), 227–228.

37. Osgood, *op.cit.*, Chapter II.

38. Ibid., 34–35.

39. Ibid., 40.

40. Ibid., 45.

41. Ibid., 45–47.

42. Bailey, *op.cit.*, 484.

43. Ibid., 301 and 310.

44. Lake, *op.cit.*, 96. Ferguson, *op.cit.*, 42, notes the comparison with Sweden.

45. See Smith, *op.cit.*, 347 and 350–351; and Bailey, *op.cit.*, 504–505. Henry Kissinger stresses Roosevelt's realist inclinations, noting that "no other president defined America's world role so completely in terms of national interest, or identified the national interest so comprehensively with the balance of power." Henry A. Kissinger, *Diplomacy* (New York: Simon and Schuster, 1994), 39.

46. From a 1913 speech, cited in Bailey, *op.cit.*, 544.

47. Ibid., 556.

48. Walter LaFeber, *The American Age: United States Foreign Policy at Home and Abroad*, 2nd ed. (New York: W. W. Norton, 1994).

49. Bailey, *op.cit.*, 554.

50. Attributed to the journalist George Harvey, cited in ibid., 556.

51. Ferguson, *op.cit.*, 54.

52. On misperceptions and World War I, see Ralph K. White, *Nobody Wanted War* (Garden City, NY: Doubleday, 1968); and Ole R. Holsti et al., "Perception and Action in the 1914 Crisis," in J. David Singer, ed., *Quantitative International Politics: Insights and Evidence* (New York: Free Press, 1968), 123–158. On the beginnings of World War I, see Barbara Tuchman, *The Guns of August* (New York: Macmillan, 1988); and Paul Schroeder, "World War I as Galloping Gertie," *Journal of Modern History* 44 (September 1972): 319–345.

53. Bailey, *op.cit.*, 596.

54. Lake, *op.cit.*, 83.

55. Osgood, *op.cit.*, Chapter XII.

56. Abba Eban, "The United Nations Idea Revisited," *Foreign Affairs* 74 (September/October 1995): 42. Eban cites one writer's description of Wilson as "living on terms of such intimacy with his conscience that any little disagreement between them could always be arranged."

57. Osgood, *op.cit.*, 191.

58. Ibid., 172.

59. Ibid.

60. From Sigmund Freud and William C. Bullitt, *Thomas Woodrow Wilson: A Psychological Study* (London: Weidenfeld and Nicolson, 1967), cited in Raymond Hopkins and Richard W. Mansbach, *Structure and Process in International Politics* (New York: Harper and Row, 1973), 210.

61. Bailey, *op.cit.*, 616.

62. *Boston Herald*, July 8, 1919.

63. Bailey, *op.cit.*, p. 624. Other analyses of the determinants of U.S. failure to join the League are found in Lake, *op.cit.*, 92–121; and Kupchan, *op.cit.*, 185–187.

64. See Note 35 in Chapter 1.

65. Charles Kindleberger, "Hierarchy Versus Inertial Cooperation," *International Organization* 40 (Autumn 1986): 841.

66. Thomas A. Bailey, "America's Emergence as a World Power: The Myth and the Verity," *Pacific Historical Review* 30 (February 1961): 15; also see Lake, *op.cit.*, 102.

67. Osgood, *op.cit.*, 364.

68. Lake, *op.cit.*, 121.

69. Osgood, *op.cit.*, 349.

70. Paul Kennedy, *The Parliament of Man* (New York: Random House, 2006), 19.

71. Osgood, *op.cit.*, 365.

72. Ibid., 409.

73. Irving L. Janis, *Groupthink*, 2nd ed. (Boston: Houghton Mifflin, 1982), Chapter 4.

74. Osgood, *op.cit.*, 410–411.

75. Wartime discussions about the United Nations and the diplomatic intrigue surrounding the drafting and signing of the United Nations Charter are described in Stephen C. Schlesinger, *Act of Creation: The Founding of the United Nations* (Boulder: Westview, 2003).

76. Cited in Moshe Sachs, ed., *The United Nations* (New York: John Wiley, 1977), 7.

77. *U.S. Department of State Bulletin* 12 (April 29, 1945): 789.

78. See Schlesinger, *op.cit.*, 5–6; and Kennedy, *op.cit.*, xi–xii.

79. Quoted in ibid., 287.

80. The quote is from Senator Tom Connally. Ibid., 171.

81. John G. Ruggie, "Multilateralism: The Anatomy of an Institution," *International Organization* 46 (Summer 1992): 584.

82. See Judith Goldstein and Robert Keohane, "Ideas and Foreign Policy: An Analytical Framework," in Goldstein and Keohane, eds., *Ideas and Foreign Policy* (Ithaca: Cornell University Press, 1993). Kupchan, *op.cit.*, 194–195, adds that it was regional realignment in American domestic politics that helped support the move toward liberal internationalism, in particular a coalition between Northeast interests wanting access to global markets and Southern interests benefiting from growing defense industries.

83. See Mandelbaum, *op.cit.*, 18–20. It should be noted that the United States refused to endorse the creation of the International Trade Organization in 1947 because, unlike GATT, its decision-making procedures were viewed as potentially threatening U.S. sovereignty. On the U.S. willingness to accept some loss of autonomy in return for greater international "order," see Mark W. Zacher and Brent A. Sutton, *Governing Global Networks* (Cambridge: Cambridge University Press, 1996).

84. Bailey, *op.cit.*, 893 and 895.

85. Stephen E. Ambrose, *Rise to Globalism*, 4th revised ed. (New York: Penguin, 1985), xiii.

86. Ferguson, *op.cit.*, 86. The "empire by invitation" phrase is credited to Geir Lundestad, "Empire By Invitation? The United States and Western Europe 1945–1952," *Journal of Peace Research* 23 (1986): 263–277.

87. See Geir Lundestad, *The American "Empire" and Other Studies of U.S. Foreign Policy in a Comparative Perspective* (New York: Oxford University Press, 1990), 65; and Charles W. Kegley, Jr. and Gregory A. Raymond, *After Iraq: The Imperiled American Imperium* (New York: Oxford University Press, 2007), 117–118.

88. Charles Kupchan, *The End of the American Era* (New York: Random House, 2003), 38.

89. George F. Kennan, *American Diplomacy 1900–1950* (New York: Mentor, 1951), 99 and 104.

90. Kupchan, *op.cit.*, 39–40.

91. This is the line attributed to General Omar Bradley.

92. Lake, *op.cit.*, 150–151. Lake himself argues it was a bit more complicated than bipolarity alone determining the competition.

93. Ibid., 194.

94. Delivered January 20, 1961.

95. Taken from the documentary film, *I. F. Stone's Weekly*, directed by Jerry Bruch.

96. On the military-industrial complex, see Richard J. Barnet, *Roots of War* (Baltimore: Penguin, 1972). Radical left critiques include William Appleton Williams, *The Roots of the Modern American Empire* (New York: Vintage Books, 1969); and Harry Magdoff, *The Age of Imperialism* (New York: Monthly Review Press, 1969). On personal issues, see Paul Kattenburg, *The Vietnam Trauma in American Foreign Policy, 1945–1975* (New Brunswick, NJ: Transaction Books, 1980).

97. Although the U.S. Constitution states that only Congress may declare war, presidents have seen fit to involve the country in hostilities on numerous occasions without such a declaration. In fact, more than two hundred times in American history, an American president has sent troops into harm's way, with only five formal declarations of war being issued by Congress. The War Powers Act was an effort to address the fact that formal declarations of war were no longer being issued worldwide by any countries. The statute permits the president to send troops into a war zone on his own initiative, under three limited conditions, and even then the president must come to Congress within sixty days following the start of hostilities to obtain explicit approval to continue the action.

98. The remarks were made by Charles Lichtenstein in 1983, after growing frustrations with Soviet behavior and the failure of the United States to win UN support for American policies.

99. The "amiable dunce" line belonged to former Johnson administration official Clark Clifford, while the "attention span" quip belonged to *New York Times* columnist Anthony Lewis. See Peter Schweizer, *Reagan's War* (New York: Random House, 2003), 1.

100. George H. W. Bush, State of the Union Address, January 29, 1991. Also, see the Summer 1991 issue of *Foreign Policy*.

101. George H. W. Bush, speech at West Point, January 5, 1993.

102. *New York Times*, March 8, 1992. Also, see Walt, *op.cit.*, 42–43; and Mohammed Nuruzzaman, "Beyond the Realist Theories: 'Neoconservative Realism' and the American Invasion of Iraq," *International Studies Perspectives* 7 (August 2006): 250.

103. Cited in Walt, *op.cit.*, 43.

104. Ibid., 30–31.

105. Ibid., 58.

106. The term was coined by Madeleine Albright, who succeeded Warren Christopher as Secretary of State in the Clinton administration. See Albright's *Madam Secretary: A Memoir* (New York: Miramax Books, 2003). She referred to herself as a "pragmatic idealist."

107. Kupchan, *op.cit.*, 14–15 and 216, makes the point that Clinton was not as multilateralist in deed as in rhetoric.

108. Kagan, "The Myth of American Innocence: Cowboy Nation," 21. In *Dangerous Nation*, *op.cit.*, Kagan tries to show how U.S. foreign policy behavior in the second Bush administration was in many respects simply an extension of long-term historical behavior on the part of America.

109. See Anthony Lake, "From Containment to Enlargement," address to SAIS, Washington, DC, September 21, 1993, published in *U.S. Department of State Dispatch* 4, no. 39 (September 27, 1993): 658–664; and William Safire, "The En-En Document," *New York Times*, August 25, 1994.

110. Warren Christopher, "The Strategic Priorities of American Foreign Policy," statement before the Senate Foreign Relations Committee on November 4, 1993, published in *U.S. Department of State Dispatch* 4, no. 47 (November 22, 1993): 797–802.

111. Interview of President Clinton by Wolf Blitzer, CNN *Late Edition*, June 20, 1999.

112. Mandelbaum, *op.cit.*, 65–67.

113. Ferguson, *op.cit.*, 139.

114. Peter Viggo Jakobsen, "National Interest, Humanitarianism, or CNN: What Triggers UN Peace Enforcement After the Cold War?," *Journal of Peace Research* 33, no. 2 (1996): 205–215; and Eytan Gilboa, "Global Television News and Foreign Policy: Debating the CNN Effect," *International Studies Perspectives* 6 (2005): 325–341.

115. Remarks of J. Brian Atwood, director of the Agency for International Development (AID) under Clinton, published in "Suddenly, Chaos," *Washington Post*, July 31, 1994.

116. Presidential debate, October 11, 2000.

117. Kupchan, *op.cit.*, 15. Also, see James Traub, "W's World," *New York Times Magazine*, January 14, 2001.

118. Evan Thomas, "The 12-Year Itch," *Newsweek*, March 31, 2003.

119. Andrew Sullivan, former editor of *The New Republic*, cited in Kupchan, *op.cit.*, xvi.

120. Ibid., 220. The "à la carte multilateralism" phrase is attributed to Richard Haass when he was director of the State Department Policy Planning Staff.

121. While addressing a gathering in South Dakota in November 2002, Bush said "it is important to have people in the Senate who are clear-eyed realists." Cited in Nuruzzaman, *op.cit.*, 248.

122. Ibid., 249.

123. Charles Krauthammer, "Democratic Realism: An American Foreign Policy for a Unipolar World," speech to the American Enterprise Institute, February 12, 2004.

124. Max Boot, "What the Heck Is a 'Neo Con'?" *Wall Street Journal Online*, December 30, 2002.

125. Cited in Bob Woodward, *Bush at War* (New York: Simon and Schuster, 2002), 131.

126. President George W. Bush, Inaugural Address, January 20, 2005.

127. *National Security Strategy of the United States*, September 17, 2002. The "axis of evil" phrase was contained in the president's State of the Union Address, January 29, 2002.

128. Hoffmann, *op.cit.*, 22–23, says that the Bush policy "is no longer the assertion of a doctrine of national interest pure and simple; it is something profoundly new which takes us very far away from the Wilsonian syndrome." He argues that, while "there is indeed in a sense a Reaganesque origin to the present policy," Reagan "never treated allies the way the current administration does."

129. November 11, 2006; accessed at http://news.bbc.co.uk/2/hi/americas/6137278.stm. The shift could be seen even before the election; see "Bush's Shift: Being Patient with Foes," *New York Times*, July 11, 2006.

130. Charles Krauthammer, "Liberal Democrats' Perverse Foreign Policy," *Washington Post*, July 11, 2003.

Chapter 4

1. Richard N. Haass, *The Opportunity* (New York: Public Affairs, 2005), 25.

2. Ibid., 25–26. John Ikenberry has said that a single grand strategy may not be appropriate in the post–Cold War era since instead of one big threat, there will be a "diffuse, shifting, and uncertain array of security challenges." Cited in David Brooks, "A New Global Blueprint," *New York Times*, June 19, 2007.

3. Richard N. Haass, "Is There A Doctrine in the House?," *New York Times*, November 8, 2005.

4. Joseph S. Nye, Jr., *The Paradox of American Power* (New York: Oxford University Press, 2002), 154. Nye dismisses isolationism as a serious option and discusses "the battle between unilateralists and multilateralists."

5. See Note 19 in Chapter 1. Also see Henry A. Kissinger, *Diplomacy* (New York: Touchstone Books, 1995); and his *Does America Need a Foreign Policy?* (New York: Simon and Schuster, 2001).

6. Niall Ferguson, *Colossus* (New York: Penguin Press, 2004), 132.

7. Robert Osgood, *Ideals and Self-Interest in America's Foreign Relations* (Chicago: University of Chicago Press, 1953), 14.

8. See Note 74 in Chapter 1. See Richard N. Haass, *The Reluctant Sheriff* (New York: Council on Foreign Relations, 1997); and Joseph S. Nye, "Conflicts After the Cold War," *Washington Quarterly* (Winter 1996), 2.

9. Remarks at Ohio State University, February 18, 1998.

10. Robert Kagan, *Of Paradise and Power* (New York: Vintage Books, 2004), 36 and 95.

11. Cited in Ferguson, *op.cit.*, 58.

12. Henry Kissinger was reputed to have said about Iran and Iraq that it was "a pity they both can't lose." Cited in ibid., 118.

13. See Harold K. Jacobson et al., "National Entanglements in International Governmental Organizations," *American Political Science Review* 80 (March 1986): 157–158; and Richard Gardner, "The Case for Practical Internationalism," *Foreign Affairs* 66 (Spring 1988): 827–845.

14. President Truman's address to the UN Conference on International Organization, *U.S. Department of State Bulletin* 13 (July 1, 1945): 4.

15. Geraldine Brooks, "It's UN Protocol: No Chair, No Office for Tajikistan's Man," *Wall Street Journal*, September 20, 1993.

16. On these issues, see Miles Kahler, "Multilateralism with Small and Large Numbers," in John G. Ruggie (ed.), *Multilateralism Matters* (New York: Columbia University Press, 1993), 681–708.

17. In the United States' case, it is actually somewhat more complicated than this, since, although most major international treaties require approval of two-thirds of the U.S. Senate, the American constitutional system allows for the president to enter into "executive agreements" requiring only his signature and "congressional-executive agreements" requiring a simple majority vote of each house of Congress. See David J. Bederman, *International Law Frameworks* (New York: Foundation Press, 2001), 166–169.

18. On the growing politicization of U.S. foreign policy, see Steven W. Hook, *U.S. Foreign Policy: The Paradox of World Power* (Washington, D.C.: Congressional Quarterly Press, 2005).

19. Robert D. Putnam, "Diplomacy and Domestic Politics: The Logic of Two-Level Games," *International Organization*, 42 (Summer 1988): 434.

20. Robert S. Strauss, "Foreword," in Joan E. Twiggs, *The Tokyo Round of Multilateral Trade Negotiations: A Case Study in Building Domestic Support for Diplomacy* (Washington, DC: Georgetown Institute for the Study of Diplomacy, 1987): cited in Putnam, *op.cit.*, 433.

21. Maria Cowles, *The Politics of Big Business in the European Community*, Ph.D. dissertation, The American University, 1994. On two-level and three-level games played at the UN Law of the Sea Conference that produced the 1982 Law of the Sea Treaty, see J. Martin Rochester, *Between Two Epochs* (Upper Saddle River, NJ: Prentice-Hall, 2002), 105–107.

22. Clyde Prestowitz, *Rogue Nation* (New York: Basic Books, 2003).

23. Churchill's remarks were made at a White House luncheon on June 26, 1954; reported in the *New York Times*, June 27, 1954. Borah's remarks were cited in Charles Krauthammer, "Democrats Will Lose in Long Run," *St. Louis Post-Dispatch*, August 13, 2006.

24. "Tentative Nuclear Deal Struck With North Korea," *Washington Post*, February 13, 2007. The agreement was unclear as to whether North Korea was merely suspending operations, partially dismantling its program, or terminating its program altogether.

25. For example, see Noah Chomsky, *Hegemony Or Survival: America's Quest for Global Dominance* (New York: Metropolitan Books, 2006); and V. Spike Peterson and Anne Sisson Runyan, *Global Gender Issues*, 2nd ed. (Boulder: Westview Press, 1999).

26. Neocon views could be found frequently expressed in the journal *The National Interest*.

27. Speech from the Oval Office, September 11, 2006.

28. Charles Krauthammer, "The New Unilateralism," *Washington Post*, June 8, 2001.

29. Joseph S. Nye, Jr., "U.S. Power and Strategy After Iraq," *Foreign Affairs* 82 (July/August, 2003): 61.

30. See Note 129 in Chapter 3.

31. See "The Last Man Standing," *Newsweek*, December 4, 2006, 39.

32. See Francis Fukuyama. *America at the Crossroads* (New Haven: Yale University Press, 2006); and Paul Berman, "Neo No More," *New York Times*, March 26, 2006. By 2005, Fukuyama had ended his association with the neocon-oriented journal *The National Interest* and founded a new journal called *The American Interest*.

33. Michael Mandelbaum, *The Case for Goliath: How America Acts As the World's Government in the 21st Century* (New York: PublicAffairs, 2005), 1.

34. See Note 25; also, see Noah Chomsky's "The American Empire Project," accessed at http://www.americanempireproject.com/chomsky.

35. See Note 10.

36. Robert Kagan, "Against the Myth of American Innocence: Cowboy Nation," *The New Republic* (October 23, 2006): 20–22.

37. Ibid., 23. As for the Iraq War, his recipe is "send more troops." See Robert Kagan, "Send More Troops," *The New Republic* (November 27 and December 4, 2006): 12–13. This contrasts with Michael Walzer's prescription in the same magazine, "Talk, Talk, Talk," 23.

38. Written in an article in the *New York World* in 1926; cited in Ferguson, *op.cit.*, 62.

39. Charles Krauthammer, "Democratic Realism: An American Foreign Policy for a Unipolar World," speech given to the American Enterprise Institute, February 10, 2004.

40. Statement made at the World Economic Forum in Davos, Switzerland, January 2003, in response to a question from the former Archbishop of Canterbury as to whether the United States had engaged in aggression in Afghanistan and elsewhere. For similar quotes by American officials over the years, both in Democratic and Republican administrations, see Ferguson, *op.cit.*, 6–7.

41. Michael Ignatieff, "American Empire: The Burden," *New York Times Magazine*, January 5, 2003, 22.

42. On the trend away from territorial annexation through the use of armed force, see Mark W. Zacher, "The Territorial Integrity Norm: International Boundaries and the Use of Armed Force," *International Organization* 55 (Spring 2001): 215–250. Zacher notes that the last successful use of armed force for purposes of territorial annexation was Morocco's seizure of the Spanish Sahara in 1976. Other countries may have tried to seize territory through force but have not succeeded in obtaining international acceptance.

43. Ferguson, *op.cit.*

44. See Note 35 in Chapter 1 and Notes 64 and 65 in Chapter 3. Also, see Charles Kindleberger, *The World in Depression, 1929–1939* (Berkeley: University of California Press, 1973); and Robert Gilpin, *War and Change in World Politics* (New York: Cambridge University Press, 1981).

45. Niall Ferguson, "A World without Power," *Foreign Policy* (July/August 2004): 32 and 34. Also, see Max Boot, "The Case for an American Empire," *Weekly Standard*, October 15, 2001.

46. Here Ferguson is quoting Sebastian Mallaby in "Reluctant Imperialist," *Foreign Affairs* 81 (March/April 2002): 6.

47. Ferguson, *Colossus*, 24.

48. Ibid., 2.

49. Ibid., 2.

50. Ibid., 86.

51. Ibid., 28–29.

52. Ibid., 204.

53. Based on a CNN poll taken in October 2006. "Poll: Support for Iraq War at All-Time Low," accessed on October 16, 2006, at http://www.cnn.com/2006/US/10/16/Iraq.poll/index.html.

54. Paul Starobin, "Beyond Hegemony," *National Journal*, December 1, 2006.

55. Ferguson, *Colossus*, 28.

56. Ibid., 268–280. Also, see "Don't Know Much About History," *New York Times* editorial, July 1, 2006; and Emmanuel Todd, *After the Empire: The Breakdown of the American Order* (New York: Columbia University Press, 2004).

57. Mandelbaum, *op.cit.*, 138.

58. Ferguson, *Colossus*, 295 and 297.

59. Ibid., 297.

60. Mandelbaum, *op.cit.*, 10.

61. Ibid., 161.

62. Ibid., 157.

63. Fouad Ajami, "Iraq and the Arabs' Future," *Foreign Affairs* 82 (January/February 2003): 18.

64. Mandelbaum, *op,cit.*, 223.

65. Ibid., 164.

66. Ibid., 30.

67. C. Fred Bergsten, "Interdependence and the Reform of International Institutions," *International Organization* 30 (Spring 1976): 364. On public goods and free riders in the area of trade, see Note 83 in Chapter 3.

68. Mandelbaum, *op.cit.*, xvi. Also, see Mandelbaum, 6–7. On a recent trip to China, I heard a Chinese professor say, when asked what Beijing was doing about North Korean nuclear proliferation, that "this is an American problem mainly because you are the superpower who is supposed to provide public goods, and China is a free rider."

69. Ibid., 194.

70. Ibid., 7 and 39–40.

71. Ibid., xvii.

72. Robert Samuelson, "Farewell to Pax Americana," *Washington Post*, December 14, 2006.

73. Mandelbaum, *op.cit.*, 10–11.

74. Ibid., 10.

75. Ibid., 184–185.

76. Ibid., 218.

77. Ibid., 226.

78. An exemplar of this school is G. John Ikenberry and Anne-Marie Slaughter, *Forging a World of Liberty Under Law* (Princeton: Princeton Project on National Security, 2006).

79. Madeleine Albright, "United Nations: Think Again," *Foreign Policy* (September/October 2003): 24.

80. Strobe Talbott, "The Birth of the Global Nation," *Time*, July 20, 1992. When Clinton was elected president in November of 1992, he named Talbott assistant secretary of state for global affairs, a new position in the State Department.

81. Starobin, *op.cit.*

82. Zbigniew Brzezinski, *The Choice: Global Domination or Global Leadership* (New York: Basic Books, 2004).

83. The Tarnoff Doctrine was unveiled on May 25, 1993. The remarks are those of Secretary of State Warren Christopher, seeking to respond to criticism of what seemed to be the adminis-

tration's deference to the United Nations; cited in Charles W. Kegley, Jr. and Eugene R. Wittkopf, *American Foreign Policy: Pattern and Process*, 5th ed. (New York: St. Martins Press, 1996), 80.

84. Stanley Hoffmann, *Gulliver Unbound: America's Imperial Temptation and the War in Iraq* (New York: Rowman and Littlefield, 2004), 143.

85. See Note 116 in Chapter 2.

86. On FDR's idealism, see Richard Gardner, "Franklin Roosevelt and World Order: The World We Sought and the World We Have," remarks at the Conference on "The Legacy of FDR," Turin, Italy, September 17, 1996.

87. Robert Keohane, in *After Hegemony: Cooperation and Discord in the World Political Economy* (Princeton: Princeton University Press, 1984), argues that a liberal international economic order based on free trade can get along fine without a hegemon providing public goods, as long as states recognize their mutual interests in developing and observing international regimes in economic and other areas.

88. On "shooting pool" while "pooling sovereignty," see Rochester, *op.cit.*, 98.

89. "A Critique of the Bush Administration's National Security Strategy," *Policy Analysis Brief* (Muscatine, Iowa: Stanley Foundation, June 2006), 1 and 5. Also, see Korb, "Speech Three: A Cooperative World Order," in *A New National Security Strategy in an Age of Terrorists, Tyrants, and Weapons of Mass Destruction* (New York: Council on Foreign Relations, 2003), 77–96.

90. Peter Katel, "Ending Poverty," *Global Issues* (Washington, DC: CQ Press, 2006), 116.

91. Nye, "U.S. Power and Strategy After Iraq," 68–69.

92. Ibid., 71–72.

93. Thomas Friedman, "The Bus Is Waiting," *New York Times*, October 11, 2006. On China as a "free rider," see Note 68.

94. Nye, *The Paradox of American Power*, 154.

95. Ibid., 158.

96. Ibid., 137.

97. Ibid., 159–163.

98. Ibid., 104–105.

99. Ibid., 167.

100. Ibid., 165.

101. Ibid., 169. Nye is quoting here Coral Bell, "American Ascendancy—and the Pretense of Concert," *The National Interest* (Fall 1990): 60.

102. Ibid., 170. He is citing U.S. Department of State, Opinion Analysis, "Sizable Majority of U.S. Public Supports Active, Cooperative Involvement Abroad," Washington, D.C., October 29, 1999. Also, see Note 54. U.S. public opinion polls over the years persistently have shown generalized support for American membership in and financial contributions to the United Nations.

103. Haass, *The Reluctant Sheriff*, 8, 80, 93, 103, and 139.

104. Ibid., 91–92.

105. Ibid., 97.

106. Haass, *The Opportunity*, 24.

107. Ibid., 197–199.

108. Stanley Hoffmann, *Primacy or World Order* (New York: McGraw-Hill, 1978), 193.

109. Haass, *The Opportunity*, 16–17.

110. Ibid., 117–118.

111. Ibid., 5, 16–18. In *The Reluctant Sheriff*, Haass was much less supportive of a concert of great powers approach.

112. Ibid., 26–27.

113. Ibid., 175.

114. Ibid., 178–180.

115. Charles Kupchan, *The End of the American Era* (New York: Random House, 2003), 33 and 230.

116. Ibid., 295.

117. Ibid., 296–297.

118. Ibid., 301.

119. Cited in Gardner, *op.cit.*

120. See Kenneth Oye, ed., *Cooperation Under Anarchy* (Princeton: Princeton University Press, 1986); and Joseph Grieco, "Anarchy and the Limits of Cooperation: A Realist Critique of the Newest Liberal Institutionalism," *International Organization* 42 (Summer 1988): 486–507.

121. See Note 55 in Chapter 2.

122. See Notes 115 and 116 in Chapter 2.

123. See Note 129 in Chapter 2. Also, "Bush Is Turning to the 'Realists,'" *St. Louis Post-Dispatch*, November 26, 2006.

124. Although, as George W. Bush's secretary of state, Colin Powell himself had been one of the chief proponents of the 2003 invasion of Iraq, and had seemingly ignored his own strictures in this case, most observers assumed that Powell was nonetheless one of the leading voices of caution in the administration and was ambivalent about the decision to intervene.

125. See John J. Mearsheimer, "Why We Will Soon Miss the Cold War," *The Atlantic Monthly* (August 1990): 35–50; and *The Tragedy of Great Power Politics* (New York: W. W. Norton, 2001).

126. David A. Lake, *Entangling Relations* (Princeton: Princeton University Press, 1999), 261.

127. Mandelbaum, *op.cit.*, 208. Also, see Ferguson, *Colossus*, Chapter 7. Kupchan, *op.cit.*, 119 and 132, is much more impressed with Europe's potential to rival the United States.

128. Cited in ibid., 209.

129. See Anatol Lieven and John Hulsman, *Ethical Realism: A Vision for America's Role in the World* (New York: Pantheon, 2006).

130. Neoisolationist thinking is represented by Eugene Gholz, Daryl G. Press, and Harvey M. Sapolsky, "Come Home, America: The Strategy of Restraint in the Face of Temptation," *International Security* 21 (1997): 5–48.

131. Paul Starobin, "The Realists," *National Journal*, September 16, 2006, 24. The author of this article is generally supportive of realist thinking.

132. These are the words of Stephen Walt, quoted in ibid., p. 28.

133. Quoted in ibid.

134. Mearsheimer, quoted in ibid., 29.

135. Ibid.

136. Henry A. Kissinger, "After Lebanon," *Washington Post*, September 13, 2006.

137. Stephen M. Walt, *Taming American Power: The Global Response to American Primacy* (New York: W. W. Norton, 2005), 12.

138. Ibid., 121–132.

139. Ibid., 128.

140. Ibid., 130.

141. Ibid., 12. On "offshore balancing," see 222–223.

142. Ibid., 26.

143. Ibid., 223.

144. Ibid., 23.

145. Ibid., 221–222.

146. Jean-Marie Colombani, "We Are All Americans," *Le Monde*, September 12, 2001.

147. See Note 56 in Chapter 2.

148. Walt, *op.cit.*, 100.

149. Ibid., 52–53.

150. Ibid., 222.

151. Ibid., 233.

152. See Josef Joffe, "A World Without Israel," *Foreign Policy* (January/February 2005): 37.

153. Walt, *op.cit.*, 244.

154. On the "non-aggression pact," see ibid., 240. On permitting Iran to obtain nuclear weapons, this view was expressed by Professor Walt in a public lecture given at the University of Missouri-St. Louis on September 1, 2004. When asked what he meant by "vigilant containment," he responded that it meant the United States could not and should not stop countries like Iran from acquiring nuclear weapons, but should do everything possible to manage proliferation carefully. On the realist view of the acceptability of nuclear proliferation, also see Mearsheimer, "Why We Will Soon Miss the Cold War."

155. Mandelbaum, *op.cit.*, 41.

156. Walt, *op,cit.*, 247.

157. Daniel Drezner, "The Grandest Strategy of Them All," *Washington Post*, December 17, 2006.

Chapter 5

1. See Notes 32, 33, 63, and 64 in Chapter 1.

2. Stephen M. Walt, *Taming American Power* (New York: W. W. Norton, 2005), 134.

3. For references to "the long war," see *Washington Post*, February 3, 2006, reporting on Donald Rumsfeld's speech to the National Press Club.

4. Christopher J. Fettweis, "A Revolution in International Relations Theory: Or, What If Mueller Is Right?" *International Studies Review* 8 (December 2006): 677.

5. http://www.defenselink.mil/qdr/, accessed on January 8, 2007.

6. Charles W. Kegley, Jr., and Gregory A. Raymond, *After Iraq: The Imperiled American Imperium* (New York: Oxford University Press, 2007), 59.

7. From the Pentagon's 2005 *National Defense Strategy*, cited in Walt, *op.cit.*, 133.

8. In 2006, President Bush acknowledged for the first time that the U.S. Central Intelligence Agency was operating secret prisons overseas, partly to deny alleged terrorists the legal protections that criminal defendants typically are entitled to under U.S. law. See Deb Riechmann, "Bush Calls CIA Prisons 'Vital' Tool"; accessed on September 7, 2006 at http://customwire.ap.org.

9. Quoted in "Unrepentant Neocon," *Wall Street Journal*, August 12, 2006.

10. Quoted in Kate Zernike, "Rebuff for Bush on Terror Trials in a Senate Test," *New York Times*, September 15, 2006.

11. Richard N. Haass, *The Opportunity* (New York: PublicAffairs, 2005), 53–54.

12. This was the same speech, in June 2002, in which President Bush announced the Bush Doctrine; cited in Ivo H. Daalder and James M. Lindsay, *America Unbound: The Bush Revolution in Foreign Policy* (Washington, DC: Brookings Institution, 2003), 90.

13. See Notes 135 and 136 in Chapter 4.

14. Based on a study by Alex Schmid, cited in Anthony Clark Arend and Robert J. Beck, *International Law and the Use of Force* (New York: Routledge, 1993), 140.

15. Cited in ibid.

16. *Patterns of Global Terrorism 2001* (Washington, DC: U.S. Department of State, 2002), xvi. This discussion draws on J. Martin Rochester, *Between Peril and Promise: The Politics of International Law* (Washington, D.C.: Congressional Quarterly Press, 2006), Chapter 5.

17. On the changing nature of the terrorism threat, see Walter Laqueur, "Postmodern Terrorism," *Foreign Affairs* (September/October 1996): 24–36; and Bruce Hoffman, *Inside Terrorism* (New York: Columbia University Press, 1998).

18. On state sponsorship of terrorism during the Cold War, see Claire Sterling, *The Terror Network* (New York: Holt, Rinehart and Winston, 1981). On the somewhat novel problem of "substates," that is, of terrorist groups becoming part of state legislatures and cabinets, see Henry A. Kissinger, "After Lebanon," *Washington Post*, September 13, 2006.

19. *A More Secure World: Our Shared Responsibility*, Report of the Secretary-General's High-Level Panel on Threats, Challenges, and Change (New York: United Nations, 2004).

20. The 1977 Geneva Protocols, one (Protocol I) dealing with international armed conflict and the other (Protocol II) with non-international armed conflict, attempted to go beyond the 1949 Geneva Conventions and fill in gaps in international humanitarian law but have been largely unsuccessful. See Boleslaw A. Boczek, *International Law: A Dictionary* (Lanham, MD: Scarecrow Press, 2005), 459.

21. *National Strategy for Combating Terrorism* (Washington, DC: February 2003), 12.

22. Although many analysts see another 9/11–type attack as almost inevitable, two writings that are somewhat optimistic that the United States may be able to avoid such a catastrophic attack are John Mueller, "Is There Still a Terrorist Threat?," *Foreign Affairs* (September/October 2006): 2–8; and James Fallows, "Declaring Victory," *The Atlantic* (September 2006): 60–73.

23. On definitional problems surrounding "aggression," see Boczek, *op.cit.*, 391. On "self-defense," see ibid., 411–413. On the uneven record of the United Nations in outlawing aggression, and the particular failure of collective security, see Arend and Beck, *op.cit.*; John F. Murphy, "Force and Arms," in Christopher C. Joyner, ed., *The United Nations and International Law* (Cambridge: Cambridge University Press, 1997), 97–130; and Michael J. Glennon, *Limits of Law, Prerogatives of Power* (New York: Palgrave, 2001).

24. See Arend and Beck, *op.cit.*, Chapter 9.

25. See Note 112 in Chapter 2.

26. Roosevelt fireside chat on September 11, 1941; found in *The Public Papers and Addresses of Franklin D. Roosevelt, 1941* (New York: Harper, 1950), 390.

27. Hugo Grotius, *The Law of War and Peace*, Chapter 22, trans. by R. Kelsey et al. (1925).

28. On the *Caroline* incident and anticipatory self-defense, see Arend and Beck, *op.cit.*, Chapter 5; Arend, "International Law and the Preemptive Use of Military Force," *Washington Quarterly* (Spring 2003): 89–103; and Rochester, *op.cit.*, 96–99.

29. Presidential debate on October 13, 2004. Haass, *op.cit.*, 177, also questions how realistic it is to expect any country to entrust its national security to the UN Security Council. A somewhat different view is expressed in Walt, *op.cit.*, 226, where the author suggests that "the United States can reduce the fear created by its superior power by giving other states a voice in the circumstances in which it will use force" through a "de facto 'buddy system' to regulate the large-scale use of its military power—whether by NATO, the UN Security Council, or other international institutions."

30. Thomas C. Schelling, "Thinking About Nuclear Terrorism," *International Security* 6 (Spring 1982): 76. This discussion draws on Rochester, *op.cit.*, 102–105.

31. Accessed at http://www.acda.gov/factshee/conwpn/small.htm, on November 24, 1999.

32. See Note 103 in Chapter 2.

33. Robert J. Mathews and Timothy L. H. McCormack, "Entry into Force of the Chemical Weapons Convention," *Security Dialogue* 26, no.1 (1995): 93.

34. Data are from "The Chemical Weapons Ban: Facts and Figures," accessed at http://www.opcw.org/factsandfigures/index.html, on January 12, 2007.

35. See "Briefing on Biological Weapons," provided by the Arms Control Association, accessed at http://www.armscontrol.org/factsheets/bwissuebrief.asp, on January 12, 2007; and "US Biodefense Programs," provided by the Federation of American Scientists, accessed at http://www.fas.org/bwc/usbiodefense.htm, on January 18, 2007.

36. As with chemical weapons, there are sketchy reports of biological weapons having been used on rare occasions, such as Soviet germ warfare in Afghanistan in the 1980s, but these, too, are not fully documented. See John Barry, "Planning a Plague?," *Newsweek*, February 1, 1993, 40–41.

37. Remark by President Clinton in his address to the UN General Assembly on September 22, 1997.

38. See U.S. Arms Control and Disarmament Agency discussion at http://www.acda.gov/ctbtpage/quotes.htm, accessed November 24, 1999.

39. See Carnegie Endowment for International Peace, "Nuclear Weapons Status 2005," accessed at http://www.carnegieendowment.org/images/npp/nuke.jpg, January 12, 2007.

40. See "UN Agrees Sanctions for North Korea," *The Sunday Times* (UK). October 15, 2006; and "U.S. Pushes for More N. Korean Sanctions," http://washpost.com, January 11, 2007. On the February 2007 agreement, see Note 24 in Chapter 4.

41. "Sanctions on Iran Approved by UN," *Washington Post*, December 14, 2006; and "UN Draft Resolution on Iran Loosens Travel Ban and Time Limits," *New York Times*, December 21, 2006.

42. On North Korea, in particular, see Haass, *op.cit.*, 90.

43. See ibid., 98; and Graham Allison, in comments made in a presentation at the University of Missouri-St. Louis, April 7, 2005.

44. See Haass, *op.cit.*, 102–103.

45. Ibid., 82. Also, see the "three no's" policy proposed by Graham Allison in *Nuclear Terrorism* (New York: Times Books, 2004), 141, where he urges "no loose nukes" (securing the nuclear weapons facilities in the former Soviet Union that are now vulnerable to theft and sabotage due to poor surveillance), "no new nascent nukes" (closing the loophole in the NPT that allows member states to start up the nuclear fuel cycle), and "no new nuclear weapons states" (preventing the addition of new members to the nuclear club).

46. See Haass, *op.cit.*, 84–88; and Walt, *op.cit.*, 239–240.

47. Hedley Bull, *The Anarchical Society* (New York: Columbia University Press, 1977), 8.

48. Stephen D. Krasner has pointed out the distinctions between the theory and practice of sovereignty in *Sovereignty: Organized Hypocrisy* (Princeton: Princeton University Press, 1999).

49. See Bull, *op.cit.*

50. See Note 70 in Chapter 1.

51. On human rights, see Rochester, *op.cit.*, Chapter 4; and Jack Donnelly, *International Human Rights*, 3rd ed. (Boulder: Westview Press, 2007).

52. David J. Bederman, *International Law Frameworks* (New York: Foundation Press, 1999), 95.

53. Anne-Marie Slaughter, "Leading Through Law," *The Wilson Quarterly* (Autumn 2003): 38.

54. See Note 109 in Chapter 2.

55. Cited in Donald Puchala et al., *United Nations Politics* (New York: Pearson, 2007), 69.

56. Slaughter, *op.cit.*, 38.

57. See Note 110 in Chapter 2.

58. Martha Finnemore, "Constructing Norms of Humanitarian Intervention," in Peter J. Katzenstein, ed., *The Culture of National Security: Norms and Identity in World Politics* (New York: Columbia University Press, 1996), 170.

59. William R. Slomanson, *Fundamental Perspectives on International Law*, 3rd ed. (Belmont, CA: Wadsworth, 2000), 463.

60. Remarks made by Algerian President Abdelaziz Bouteflika, chair of the Organization of African Unity, quoted in Barbara Crosette, "UN Chief Wants Faster Action to Halt Civil Wars and Killings," *New York Times*, September 21, 1999.

61. Cited in Glennon, *op.cit.*, 158. Glennon (159–160) provides quoted statements representing the official positions of many different states objecting especially to interventions unauthorized by the UN. Also, see Boczek, *op.cit.*, 404–406; and Puchala, *op.cit.*, 69–73.

62. http://www.freedomhouse.org/uploads/pdf/Charts2006.pdf, accessed on January 19, 2007.

63. On how humanitarian concerns *plus* national interest concerns are a sounder basis for intervention than merely humanitarian concerns alone, see Charles Krauthammer, "Liberal Democrats' Perverse Foreign Policy," *Washington Post*, July 11, 2003.

64. See David J. Scheffer, "Use of Force After the Cold War," in Louis Henkin et al., *Right v. Might* (New York: Council on Foreign Relations, 1991).

65. Printed in *Al-Shaab*, an Egyptian opposition newspaper, cited in Puchala et al., *op.cit.*, 70.

66. Comments made by a Latin American UN diplomat in 2003, based on an interview reported in ibid., 71.

67. Peter Rodman, *Uneasy Giant: The Challenges to American Predominance* (Washington, DC: The Nixon Center, 2000), 44.

68. One attempt to provide guidelines is found in Joseph S. Nye, *The Paradox of American Power* (New York: Oxford University Press, 2002), 150–152.

69. For other views on whether intervention should be held hostage to a Security Council vote, see Haass, *op.cit.*, 172–177; and Hoffmann, *Gulliver Unbound*, 120–121.

70. On the Rwanda episode, see Niall Ferguson, *Colossus* (New York: Penguin, 2004), 148.

71. Quoted in Michael Mandelbaum, *The Case for Goliath* (New York: PublicAffairs, 2005), 74. Mandelbaum discusses "state-building" on 73–81.

72. Boutros Boutros-Ghali, *An Agenda for Peace*, UN Doc. A/47/277 and S/24111, 1992.

73. Quoted in Puchala et al., *op.cit.*, 140–141.

74. One empirical analysis finds that multilateral interventions under UN auspices may succeed more than unilateral interventions, as "it appears that the likelihood that a state will democratize increases both during a UN military intervention and in the first few years after the Blue Helmets arrive." See Jeffrey Pickering and Mark Peceny, "Forging Democracy at Gunpoint," *International Studies Quarterly* 50 (September 2006): 555.

75. Puchala et al., *op.cit.*, 150.

76. The International Criminal Court (ICC) is a separate institution from the International Court of Justice (ICJ). The latter was created in 1945 as part of the United Nations system, to deal with a wide range of international legal issues but not to address human rights-related violations. My discussion of the ICC in this section draws on Rochester, *op.cit.*, 72–73.

77. "Pinochet Is Ruled Unfit to Be Tried and May Be Freed," *New York Times*, January 12, 2000. Pinochet returned to Chile and died in 2006.

78. A 1993 Belgian law had authorized "Belgian judges to hear war crimes and genocide cases regardless of where they occurred or who committed them." However, in 2002, the International Court of Justice ruled that, based on the laws governing diplomatic immunity, Belgium could not try former and current world leaders for such actions. Belgium had instituted criminal proceedings against Fidel Castro of Cuba and Ariel Sharon of Israel among others. See "UN Court Rules Belgium Can't Hold War Crimes Trials," *Baltimore Sun*, February 15, 2002.

79. See Bruce Broomhall, *International Criminal Justice and the International Criminal Court* (New York: Oxford University Press, 2003).

80. Michael Ignatieff, "Human Rights: The Midlife Crisis," *New York Review of Books*, May 20, 1999, 61. See Prestowitz cited in Note 22 in Chapter 4.

81. Cited in "U.S. Bans Child Soldiers," CBS News, accessed on September 19, 2004 at http://www.cbsnews.com/stories/2002/12/24/national.

82. See "U.S. Has Lost Credibility on Rights, Group Asserts," *Washington Post Foreign Service*, January 12, 2007.

83. On the pros and cons of the U.S. joining the ICC, see John Washburn, "Tyrants Beware: The International Criminal Court Is Born," *The Interdependent* (Summer 1998), 5–7; and Ruth Wedgwood, "An International Criminal Court Is Still a Bad Idea," *Wall Street Journal*, April 15, 2002. Also, see the statements by the Lawyers Committee for Human Rights and by John Bolton (former U.S. Assistant Secretary of State) before the hearings of the International Relations Committee of the U.S. House of Representatives on July 25, 2000 (Washington, DC: U.S. Government Printing Office, 2000).

Chapter 6

1. Speech in Philadelphia on July 4, 1994; reported in *Newsweek*, July 18, 1994, 66. The reference to a "declaration of interdependence" is *Newsweek*'s characterization of the speech. At the outset of Chapter 6, I borrow wording from my *Between Two Epochs: What's Ahead for America, the World, and Global Politics in the Twenty-First Century* (Upper Saddle River, NJ: Prentice-Hall, 2002), 255–256.

2. Quoted in Stanley Karnow, *Vietnam: A History* (London: Penguin, 1994), 14; found in Niall Ferguson, *Colossus* (New York: Penguin, 2004), 65–66.

3. See Note 6 in Chapter 1.

4. Donald J. Puchala et al., *United Nations Politics* (Upper Saddle River, NJ: Prentice-Hall, 2007), 94.

5. See Robert Kagan, *Of Paradise and Power* (New York: Knopf, 2003), 43.

6. Comment by former State Department advisor Charles Maechling, Jr., quoted in Thomas W. Lippman, *Madeleine Albright and the New American Diplomacy* (Boulder: Westview, 2000), 165.

7. Nigel Morris, "Livingstone Says Bush Is Greatest Threat to Life on Planet," *Financial Times* (of London), November 18, 2003.

8. "World View of US Role Goes from Bad to Worse," based on a survey taken in January 2007; accessed on February 1, 2007, at http://www.worldpublicopinion.org. In five of the twenty-five countries, a majority felt the United States was playing, on balance, a positive role, with the highest approval ratings found in Nigeria (72 percent) and the Philippines (72 percent). The most negative countries were Germany (74 percent) and Indonesia (71 percent). *Newsweek*, June 11, 2007, 25, reported that "in a new global survey, most nations polled believed that China would act more responsibly than the United States."

9. Stephen M. Walt, *Taming American Power* (New York: W. W. Norton, 2005), 63–64.

10. Ibid., 79.

11. The first phrase is from Max Boot, "Power: Resentment Comes With the Territory," *Washington Post*, March 3, 2003; the second is from Robert Kagan and William Kristol, "The Present Danger," *The National Interest* 59 (Spring 2000): 67.

12. See Note 71 in Chapter 1.

13. On the need for hegemons to blend carrots and sticks, soft and hard power, see G. John Ikenberry and Charles A. Kupchan, "Socialization and Hegemonic Power," *International Organization* 44 (Summer 1990): 284.

14. By 2007, Russia appeared to be increasingly growing apart from the United States and engaging in hostile rhetoric, with President Vladimir Putin accusing Washington of trying to dominate the world as "one master, one sovereign" that had "overstepped its national borders, and in every area." Although some observers worried about the specter of a Cold War revival, most saw this as a fairly normal attempt by Russia to recapture some of its lost superpower status. See Steven Lee Myers, "No Cold War, Perhaps, But Surely A Lukewarm Peace," *New York Times*, February 18, 2007.

15. See data in Rochester, *op.cit.*, 20.

16. On the challenges of getting the Perm Five to work together, and to get the UN membership at large to follow the lead of the Security Council, see Puchala et al., *op.cit.*, 56–57.

17. Charles Maynes, "The New Pessimism," *Foreign Policy* (Fall 1995): 33–49.

18. Julian Simon, *The Ultimate Resource* (Princeton: Princeton University Press, 1982).

19. Max Singer and Aaron Wildavsky, *The Real World Order*, revised ed. (Chatham, N.J.: Chatham House, 1996).

20. Allan E. Goodman, *A Brief History of the Future* (Boulder: Westview Press, 1993).

21. John Mueller, *Retreat from Doomsday: The Obsolescence of Major War* (New York: Basic Books, 1989); and *Overblown: How Politicians and the Terrorism Industry Inflate National Security Threats and Why We Believe Them* (New York: Free Press, 2006). Also, see James Lee Ray, "The Abolition of Slavery and the End of International War," *International Organization* 43 (Summer 1989): 406–439, which suggested we might be on the brink of the end of international war altogether.

22. Francis Fukyama, "The End of History?," *The National Interest* 16 (Summer 1989): 3–16.

23. John J. Mearsheimer, "Why We Will Soon Miss the Cold War," *The Atlantic Monthly* (August 1990): 35–50; and "Back to the Future: Instability in Europe After the Cold War," *International Security* 15 (Summer 1990): 5–56. Also see his *The Tragedy of Great Power Politics* (New York: W. W. Norton, 2001).

24. Samuel P. Huntington, "The Clash of Civilizations," *Foreign Affairs* 72 (Summer 1993): 22–49; and *The Clash of Civilizations and the Remaking of World Order* (New York: Simon and Schuster, 1996).

25. Robert D. Kaplan, *The Coming Anarchy: Shattering the Dreams of the Post Cold War* (New York: Random House, 2000).

26. Paul Kennedy, *Preparing for the Twenty-First Century* (New York: Random House, 1993).

27. Robert Heilbroner, *An Inquiry into the Human Prospect*, 2nd ed. (New York: W. W. Norton, 1991). Heilbroner's first edition, written in 1975, had painted a grim portrait of the future. The second edition, which took as its subtitle "Looked At Again for the 1990s," was no more hopeful than the earlier work.

28. Henry A. Kissinger, "America's Assignment," *Newsweek*, November 8, 2004, 38.

29. "Alternative world order models" were first discussed by Saul Mendlovitz and other scholars involved in the World Order Models Project of the 1970s.

30. For a discussion of all these alternative world order models, see Rochester, *op.cit.*, 238–245.

31. Joseph S. Nye, Jr., *The Paradox of American Power* (New York: Oxford University Press, 2002), 42–43 and 53–54. On "the new feudalism" or "new medievalism," also see James A. Nathan, "The New Feudalism," *Foreign Policy* 42 (Spring 1981): 156–166; and Susan Strange, "The Defective State," *Daedalus* 124 (Spring 1995): 55–74.

32. Gar Alperovitz, "California Split," *New York Times*, February 10, 2007. There remain legal restrictions contained in the U.S. Constitution that limit to some extent the autonomous involvement of subnational jurisdictions in foreign relations. Also see Kenichi Ohmae, "The Rise of the Region-State," *Foreign Affairs* 72 (Spring 1993): 78–87; and John Newhouse, "Europe's Rising Regionalism," *Foreign Affairs* 76 (January/February 1997): 67–84. Charles Kupchan, too, even though he adopts a state-centric perspective that urges better statesmanship in the form of a concert of great powers approach to world order, speculates about the reemergence of American sectionalism and the long-term possibility of a back-to-the-future "rebirth of history" resembling the feudal era, sparked by "the arrival of the digital era." See Charles Kupchan, *The End of the American Era* (New York: Random House, 2003), 327–332.

33. See, for example, "Missouri Will Open Trade Office in China," *St. Louis Post-Dispatch*, September 11, 2004. On the proliferation of trade missions, see Earl Fry, *The Expanding Role of State and Local Governments in U.S. Foreign Affairs* (New York: Council on Foreign Relations Press, 1998). Even American cities are now competing with each other in establishing overseas trade ties. See Heidi Hobbs, *City Hall Goes Abroad: The Foreign Policy of Local Governments* (Beverly Hills, CA: Sage, 1994).

34. Cited in the *Christian Science Monitor*, April 24, 1985, 5.

35. Kofi Annan, "What I've Learned," accessed at http://washpost.com/wp-dyn/content/article/2006 on December 11, 2006.

36. Ibid.

37. Walt, *op.cit.*, 245.

38. Reported by James Fallows, former editor of *U.S. News and World Report*. Public igno-rance of political issues is not limited to foreign policy, as discussed in Michael X. Delli Carpini and Scott Keeter, *What Americans Know About Politics and Why It Matters* (New Haven: Yale University Press, 1996); also see Thomas E. Patterson, *The Vanishing Voter* (New York: Knopf, 2002).

39. Barry Buzan, *People, States, and Fear* (Chapel Hill: University of North Carolina Press, 1983), 97.

Suggested Reading

Current Events and Issues

Journals that cover current events and issues relevant to American foreign policy are:
Foreign Affairs
Foreign Policy
International Security
The National Interest
The American Interest

Useful Web sites containing sources of news coverage include:
New York Times: www.nytimes.com
Washington Post: www.washingtonpost.com
Cable News Network: www.cnn.com
The Economist: www.economist.com
UNWire: www.unwire.org (a free email news service that posts announcements of global developments in the fields of energy, health, economics, environmental, and other policy issue-areas)
Foreign Affairs Online: http://www.people.virginia.edu/~rjb3v/rjb.html (a site that provides comprehensive access to many useful sources of information about world affairs, including the CIA World Factbook, the United Nations homepage, the body of treaties to which the United States is a party, and other information relevant to foreign policy)

General Textbooks and Collections of Readings on American Foreign Policy

Carter, Ralph. *Contemporary Cases in U.S. Foreign Policy* (Washington, DC: Congressional Quarterly Press, 2002).

Jentelson, Bruce W. *American Foreign Policy: The Dynamics of Choice in the 21st Century*, 3rd ed. (New York: W. W. Norton, 2007).

Nathan, James, and James Oliver. *Foreign Policy Making and the American Political System*, 3rd ed. (Baltimore: Johns Hopkins University Press, 1994).

Wittkopf, Eugene R., Christopher Jones, and Charles W. Kegley, Jr. *American Foreign Policy: Pattern and Process*, 7th ed. (Belmont, Calif.: Thomson Wadsworth, 2007).

Theories About Foreign Policy Making: Determinants and Patterns

Allison, Graham and Philip Zelikow. *Essence of Decision: Explaining the Cuban Missile Crisis,* 2nd ed. (New York: Longman, 1999).

Carlsnaes, Walter. "Foreign Policy," in Walter Carlsnaes et al., eds., *Handbook of International Relations* (Thousand Oaks, Calif.: Sage, 2002), 331–349.

George, Alexander L. *On Foreign Policy* (Boulder: Paradigm Publishers, 2006).

Hagan, Joe D., and Margaret G. Hermann. *Leaders, Groups, Coalitions: Understanding the People and Processes in Foreign Policymaking* (Boston: Blackwell, 2001).

Halperin, Morton, and Priscilla Clapp, with Arnold Kanter. *Bureaucratic Politics and Foreign Policy,* 2nd ed. (Washington, DC: Brookings Institution Press, 2006).

Hermann, Margaret G., ed. *Comparative Foreign Policy Analysis: Theories and Methods* (Upper Saddle River, N.J.: Prentice-Hall, 2007).

Hudson, Valerie. "Foreign Policy Analysis Yesterday, Today, and Tomorrow," *Mershon International Studies Review* 39 (October 1995): 209–238.

Ikenberry, G. John, ed. *American Foreign Policy: Theoretical Essays,* 5th ed. (New York: Longman, 2005).

Janis, Irving J. *Groupthink,* 2nd ed. (Boston: Houghton Mifflin, 1982).

Putnam, Robert D. "Diplomacy and Domestic Politics: The Logic of Two-Level Games," *International Organization* 42 (Summer 1988): 427–460.

Rosenau, James N. "Pre-Theories and Theories of Foreign Policy," in R. Barry Farrell, ed. *Approaches to Comparative and International Politics* (Evanston, Ill.: Northwestern University Press, 1966).

Snyder, Richard C., H. W. Bruck, Burton Sapin, and Valerie M. Hudson. *Foreign Policy Decision Making (Revisited)* (London: Palgrave, 2003).

Welch, David A. *Painful Choices: A Theory of Foreign Policy Change* (Princeton, N.J.: Princeton University Press, 2005).

Yetiv, Steve. *Explaining Foreign Policy: U.S. Decision-making and the Persian Gulf War* (Baltimore: The Johns Hopkins University Press, 2004).

History of U.S. Foreign Policy

Ambrose, Stephen A. and Douglas G. Brinkley, *Rise to Globalism,* 8th rev. ed. (New York: Penguin, 1997).

Bailey, Thomas A. *A Diplomatic History of the American People,* 7th ed. (New York: Appleton-Century-Crofts, 1964).

Chace, James, and Caleb Carr. *America Invulnerable: The Quest for Absolute Security from 1812 to Star Wars* (New York: Summit Books, 1988).

Graebner, Norman, ed. *Ideas and Diplomacy: Readings in the Intellectual Tradition of American Foreign Policy* (New York: Oxford University Press, 1964).

Hoffmann, Stanley. *Gulliver's Troubles, Or the Setting of American Foreign Policy* (New York: McGraw-Hill, 1968).

Kagan, Robert. *Dangerous Nation* (New York: Knopf, 2006).

Kennan, George F. *American Diplomacy,* expanded edition (Chicago: University of Chicago Press, 1984).

Lake, David A. *Entangling Relations: American Foreign Policy in Its Century* (Princeton, N.J.: Princeton University Press, 1999).

McDougall, Walter. *Promised Land, Crusader State* (Boston: Houghton Mifflin, 1997).

Mead, Walter Russell. *Special Providence: American Foreign Policy and How It Changed the World* (New York: Knopf, 2001).

Nathan, James and James Oliver. *U.S. Foreign Policy and World Order*, 4th ed. (New York: Longman, 1989).

Osgood, Robert E. *Ideals and Self-Interest in America's Foreign Relations* (Chicago: University of Chicago Press, 1964).

Williams, William Appleman. *The Roots of the Modern American Empire* (New York: Vintage Books, 1969).

Yergin, Daniel. *Shattered Peace: The Origins of the Cold War and the National Security State* (Boston: Houghton Mifflin, 1978).

Contemporary US Foreign Policy Debates

Brezinski, Zbigniew. *Second Chance: Three Presidents and the Crisis of American Superpower* (New York: Basic Books, 2007).

Etzioni, Amitai. *Security First: For a Muscular, Moral Foreign Policy.* (New Haven: Yale University Press, 2007).

Ferguson, Niall. *Colossus* (New York: Penguin, 2004).

Friedman, Thomas. *The World Is Flat* (New York: Farrar, Straus and Giroux, 2005).

Fukuyama, Francis. *America at the Crossroads: Democracy, Power, and the Neoconservative Legacy* (New Haven: Yale University Press, 2006).

Gaddis, John Lewis. "A Grand Strategy," *Foreign Policy* 133 (November/December 2002): 55–56.

Haass, Richard N. *The Reluctant Sheriff: The United States After the Cold War* (New York: Council on Foreign Relations, 1997).

———. *The Opportunity* (New York: PublicAffairs, 2005).

Halper, Stefan and Jonathan Clarke. *The Silence of the Rational Center: Why American Foreign Policy Is Failing.* (New York: Basic Books, 2007).

Johnson, Chalmers. *Nemesis: The Last Days of the American Republic.* (New York: Metropolitan Books, 2007).

Kagan, Robert. *Of Paradise and Power: America and Europe in the New World Order* (New York: Vintage, 2004).

Kegley, Charles W., Jr., and Gregory A. Raymond. *After Iraq: The Imperiled American Imperium* (New York: Oxford University Press, 2007).

Kissinger, Henry A. "America's Assignment." *Newsweek*, November 8, 2004, 35.

Kohut, Andrew, and Bruce Stokes. *America Against the World* (New York: Times Books, 2006).

Korb, Lawrence J. *A New National Security Strategy in An Age of Terrorists, Tyrants, and Weapons of Mass Destruction* (New York: Council on Foreign Relations, 2003).

Kupchan, Charles A. *The End of the American Era* (New York: Random House, 2003).

Mandelbaum, Michael. *The Case for Goliath: How America Acts As the World's Government in the 21st Century* (New York: PublicAffairs, 2005).

Nye, Joseph S., Jr. *The Paradox of American Power* (New York: Oxford University Press, 2002).

———. *Soft Power: The Means to Success in World Politics* (New York: PublicAffairs, 2004).

Shapiro, Ian. *Containment: Rebuilding a Strategy Against Global Terror.* (Princeton: Princeton University Press, 2007).

Snow, Donald M. *National Security for a New Era* (New York: Pearson, 2004).

Walt, Stephen. M. *Taming American Power: The Global Response to U.S. Primacy* (New York: W. W. Norton, 2005).

Index